GRACE
IN EXPERIENCE
AND THEOLOGY

GRACE
IN EXPERIENCE
AND THEOLOGY

Harold H. Ditmanson

AUGSBURG PUBLISHING HOUSE
Minneapolis, Minnesota

GRACE IN EXPERIENCE AND THEOLOGY

Copyright © 1977 Augsburg Publishing House

Library of Congress Catalog Card No. 77-72447

International Standard Book No. 0-8066-1587-7

Scripture quotations unless otherwise noted are from the Revised Standard Version of the Bible, copyright 1946, 1952, and 1971 by the Division of Christian Education of the National Council of Churches.

MANUFACTURED IN THE UNITED STATES OF AMERICA

Contents

Preface

This study of grace was drafted in response to an invitation from the Men of First Lutheran Church in Minot, North Dakota to deliver the T. F. Gullixson Memorial Lectures in November, 1973. The invitation stipulated that the lectures be published. But lectures are lectures and a book is or ought to be a book. I have, therefore, recast the manuscript for those who read rather than listen. This is a difficult thing to do. If lectures are left in their spoken form, much that is of importance or interest must be omitted. But if they are revised extensively with an eye to eliminating the faults of research and expression that students and reviewers are sure to find, they come to bear little resemblance to the original production. On balance, however, it has seemed best to extend and support the line of thought presented in the lectures.

It is impossible to track down and acknowledge, except through footnotes, my debt to those who have contributed to my thought. But among former teachers, special thanks are due to Joseph Sittler and George Aus. Although not one of my teachers, Clemens M. Granskou, president emeritus of St. Olaf College, has been over the years a constant source of encouragement and an exemplar of grace both in theology and action. My wife deserves thanks for her patience in waiting for the manuscript and her diligence in typing it. Finally I must express my deep appreciation to the Men of First Lutheran Church in Minot for honoring me with the invitation to give the T. F. Gullixson Memorial Lectures. It is a pleasure to recall the gracious hospitality and thoughtful attention given by Pastor and Mrs. Wade E. Davick during my stay.

H. H. D.

Introduction:

A Personal Perspective

Karl Barth, probably the most famous Protestant theologian of the twentieth century, died in 1968. As a teacher of several generations of theological students and as the author of a whole shelf of books, including one of the most massive works ever written about the Christian faith, Barth made an enduring contribution to the life of the church. In the weeks and months following his death, many articles, books, and symposia attempted to assess his importance. One of his former students reported on a seminar Barth had conducted at Basel. A member of the class had prepared a paper on a christological issue suggested by Barth's major work, the *Church Dogmatics*. Another student made a critical response, arguing that the speaker had misunderstood Barth's method. A vigorous and complex debate continued for an hour. Throughout the hour, Barth peered over his spectacles, puffed his big pipe, sipped his wine, and spoke not one word. As the debate moved into a second hour, it suddenly occurred to one of the students that an important resource person was present, who might possibly be able to settle the dispute about Barth's method. So the question was addressed to Barth. After a full minute of heavy silence, the professor raised his head, looked out over the table, and said: "If I understand what I am trying to do in the *Church Dogmatics,* it is to listen to what Scripture is saying and tell you what I hear."

On a quite different scale, this is what I want to do in this study of "Grace in Experience and Theology." For many years I have listened to Scripture, to the Christian tradition, to the testimony of fellow-Lutherans, and to the chorus of ecumenical voices. If I were to tell about what I have heard, only one term will suffice—*grace*. I heard it first from those who taught me my earliest lessons in trust, hope, and love. The disposition to affirm life rather than to regard it with fear or contempt was reinforced by a succession of ministers, teachers, and friends who gave grace convincing utterance and embodiment.

I remember very clearly a day in my first year of theological study when a professor of church history remarked that St. Paul never could get over the fact that God loved him and had redeemed him in Christ, and that his sense of almost breathless wonder came out very strongly in the great words he wrote to the Galatians: "It is no longer I who live, but Christ who lives in me; and the life I now live in the flesh I live by faith in the Son of God, who loved me and gave himself for me" (2:20).

For some reason, the idea that one could see behind the missionary and the theologian a Paul who lived in a state of constant religious surprise, came to me as a kind of surprise. I looked more carefully in the New Testament for signs of the fundamental experience which was at the center of Paul's personal religion. The placement and repetition of certain phrases made it clear that Paul was indeed *surprised by grace*. He begins and closes his letters by saying, "grace and peace," and at strategic points in his testimonies he speaks of "the grace of God," "the God of all grace," "the grace of the Lord Jesus Christ," and "the spirit of grace." For Paul a man's religious experience was his experience of the grace of God. For Paul, as for others before him and after him who entered into Christianity as the Faith or the Truth or the Way opened up by Jesus the Lord, the essence of the redeeming transaction was seen to be man's faith answering to God's grace.

The Christian religion has come to be a complex historical institution which embraces a diversity of theological, liturgical, and moral components. Christian people reflect this diversity in the manner in which they focus their interests and energies on different aspects of the church's life. Neither in theology nor in practical Christian living would every Christian fix in a deliberate way upon "grace" as the summarizing Christian word. The immediate and effective center of attention could be Jesus, faith, the Word of God, the church, justification, holy living, the gifts of the Spirit, the Bible, worship, Christian responsibility for social reform, and so on. Each of these themes can serve as a satisfactory focus for mental and moral attention, although some are more valuable than others in their power to maintain and express the classic identity and mission of the church.

But many of us will be able to agree that "grace" is and ought to be the central, dominant, and illuminating Christian word. Martin Luther echoed Paul when he wrote: "These two words, grace and peace, do contain in them the whole sum of Christianity." The benefits of highlighting grace as the heart of Christian experience and theology will be touched upon in the course of our study. But, at the outset it can be said that there can never be too many studies of grace if in fact grace is at the center of Christian experience and, indeed, sums it up in a single word.

Since grace is so central, it is clear that Christianity is injured if the idea of grace is weakened, displaced, or misused. We know that words are subject to the fortunes of history. They can gain and lose in value. Their original meanings can be obscured and their full range of possibilities can go unexploited. The word "grace" has had a turbulent history. Although it is superbly fitted to unify and to illumine the widest range of theological and moral concerns, conflicting interpretations of the concept of grace have been the causes of division between Christian people. It is when grace is an under-utilized resource that tensions in Christian thought and practice grow into dichotomies and even divisions.

If the idea of grace has been under-used or mis-used, there is good reason to restate its original significance and to illustrate its coordinating power. The restatement of traditional beliefs is actually a necessary and normal operation. Since the day of Pentecost and the occasion of Paul's sermon on Mars' hill, the missionary church has tried continually to put its preaching of the faith once delivered to Galilean fishermen into words that would come home to Greeks and barbarians, to scholars and simple folk. So the problem of communication is not a new one. But it presses upon us today because nothing is stable in our world and the church always finds itself in a new situation. The explosion of knowledge about the world and history, the expansion of horizons, the revolution in social and political patterns, and drastic changes in theological insight and in ecclesiastical relationships have all conspired to cause many to cease listening to the church, others to wonder if what they are listening to is important, and still others whose business it is to preach and teach to consider the advisability of rethinking and restating the church's message.

Even if the problem of communication were not acute, the very nature of Christian theology would necessitate the continual restatement of great Christian words and meanings. For theology is not a final and completed system. It took shape slowly and painfully in response to the necessity of answering questions, of conforming the answers to expanding knowledge, and of adapting the answers to the thinking of new ages. Protestant Christians reject the view that the church in any particular age understood the apostolic message so fully and clearly that its doctrine is *necessarily* the correct and final interpretation of Scripture.

It is quite clear from a study of the history of the church and its theology, that behind every idea of God which takes shape in a given generation, there begins to form another idea which commends itself as more true in the new situation into which the Lord has led his church. This happens because our theological words and images are subject to distortion, and because God is a personal reality who reveals himself in fresh encounters with his children in the ever-changing circumstances of life.

Thus, our ideas about God may be sufficiently true and adequately expressed in a particular situation to give us the conviction that we are in communion with him. And events may show that God honors our faith. But it is vital that we should not assume from this that the formulation we have achieved is definitive, and needs no further critical reexamination. It is quite certain that our formulation contained within itself elements of error which at the time it was devised may not have been sufficient to lead us astray but which become increasingly evident as we move into a new situation. Then our words and ideas, no longer corresponding to the realities of men's relation with God, become barriers to our communion with God. There are certain images which are fundamental and permanent, and which any generation must appreciate before moving on to formulations of its own. But the critical work of theology must go on continually.

On the more positive side, God is personal and free and does not say exactly the same thing to all his children all the time. There is yet more truth and light to break forth from the word of God. This means that God must be waited upon in prayer, meditation, and hard thought until new light comes. When it does, the church will find herself thrust into new situations, where she can no longer proceed on the basis of precedent, and where she can do no other than commit herself in faith to her Lord. This exposes the church to the danger of being led astray, but this risk must be accepted as a normal state of affairs.

The attempt to say over again what is meant by grace is a difficult project. Grace is so central in our faith that any effort to explain its meaning makes it almost necessary to give an account, at least in outline, of the entire Christian religion. For the doctrines of Christianity do not, or should not, exist as a set of unrelated propositions. They are closely interrelated and give witness to a single reality, namely, the gracious activity of God. This single reality provides the unifying principle through which all Christian doctrines are interconnected. If a serious effort were made to refocus on grace as the central thrust of the Gospel, then the single doctrines which acquired meaning from their relationship to any previous focus would have to be reinterpreted in the light of the new focus so that they could bear a unified and effective witness to the gracious action of God. It is not surprising that grace, because of its central position, should be in an unusual sense a coordinating doctrine, linking together all the basic truths of Christianity. An interpretation of grace makes heavy demands upon us not only because the doctrine is profound and comprehensive, but also because it is forbidding in its possession of a technical terminology and confusing in the variety of formulations which have been given to it.

It is a curious thing that such a pivotal Christian word should have received so little attention in recent years. Grace has, of course, been treated with respect in commentaries, in biblical and theological dictionaries, and in studies of the sacraments. But doctrinal interpretations of grace are rare. We have a handful of standard books on the history and significance of the concept, and we will refer to these in the course of our study. These books have great value, although they tend to be modest in size and few have been written within the past twenty-five years. Some recent attempts to up-date the discussion of grace are of great interest: *The Concept of Grace* (1959) by Philip Watson, *Nature and Grace* (1963) by Karl Rahner, *The Scope of Grace* (1964) edited by Philip Hefner, *The New Life of Grace* (1971) by Peter Fransen, S. J., *Essays on Nature and Grace* (1972) by Joseph Sittler, *Grace and the Common Life* (1971) and *Faith and Virtue* (1973) by David Bailey Harned, and *Living by Grace* (1975) by William Hordern. The theme of grace has been given substantial attention in the several volumes of Jaroslav Pelikan's history of doctrine, *The Christian Tradition* (1971). These authors are unique in their determination to take grace not as a synonym for something else or as part of a system, but as the distinctive trademark of the gospel and of Christian theology. Yet the interpretations of grace mentioned above stand almost alone in the stream of theological busy-work.

It is said that "fools rush in where angels fear to tread." That may be so, but more blame may rest with the angels than with the fools, who at least have the excuse that the way is open and there is plenty of room. So the effort to put grace at the center of the theological stage is called for. The present study is not put forward as an adequate answer to that need. It is not a theological treatise but is at most a preliminary report on what I have heard about both the presence and the absence of grace as I have listened to many Christian voices. In an era when much of the most interesting theological work is addressed to the problem of speaking intelligibly and persuasively about God to the secular world it is perhaps justifiable that an occasional "tract for the times" should be addressed mainly to those interested lay people and busy pastors who live and work at the points of intersection between the church and God and the church and the world.

The topic of grace has, of course, endless ramifications and in putting forth this study I cannot but feel how inadequate it is to the greatness of its theme. The book does, however, have a plan, even though a limited one. It is my aim to focus on the power of the concept of grace to reconcile discordant, divisive, isolated themes. I wish to show the common thread which makes Christianity a single, adequate, and—despite its massive coherence—even a simple way of being related to God. How can grace be both simple and complicated? It must be an axiom of Christian theology that God's way of acting remains self-consistent. God's action is one and undivided in its fullness. But within the world of human experience, God's one action is seen in multiform aspects, much as the rich white light of the sun is broken up by a prism and spread out in a colorful spectrum. The optical analogy must not suggest that the diversity under which God's single gracious action is seen is due only to an inevitable and semi-mechanical filtering process. Our limited vision is caused not only by our finitude but also by the aggressive presence of evil in the world. God's grace brings reconciliation on the existential level by overcoming alienation, by the incorporation of parts into a whole. John Oman's classic work, *Grace and Personality* (1919), sets forth the claim that grace, understood not as the force of omnipotence but as personal influence, achieves a "harmony of opposites." Grace as love overcomes contradictions in living. Should not the doctrine of grace enable it to serve as the solvent of theological disagreements and even ecclesiastical divisions? It would be too much to hope for such a happy outcome. But some steps may be taken toward theological clarity and personal integration by an effort to reconceive grace.

In taking another look at grace it is important to draw some rather large maps rather than to specialize in details. More than two decades ago, Herbert Farmer insisted that if the truth of the Christian message is to come home to a person, it must be set in a context that is both wide and deep. He wrote: "If by 'God' we mean that final reality of righteousness and love from which all things, including ourselves, depend for their existence, their nature, their coherence, their unfolding history, and final outcome, then the whole meaning of our existence is at stake in him, and nothing less than the whole breadth of our experience could be the appropriate and sufficient context for thinking about him."[1]

The same need for large theological maps was expressed by Claude Welch when he wrote that the essential context for theology must be "the whole history of Christian thought" and "the entire Christian community, . . . continental as well as Anglo-Saxon, Catholic as well as Protestant, Eastern as well as Western."[2] It is my belief as well that the theologian should draw upon the whole company of Christian thinkers of the past and upon the many perspectives that are to be found within the ecumenical church. It is true that a theologian has a denominational tradition to which he is responsible. But within recent years it has become ever more clear that the subject matter of theology overflows any one tradition and escapes being fully comprehended by any one generation. It is not surprising, therefore, that there should have been differences of emphasis and interpretation within the Christian community. Gordon Kaufman argues that "one group grasps more firmly than another the meaning of one side of the Christian faith; accordingly it emphasizes the doctrines which most clearly express the crucial importance of this insight. . . . Although these differences in perspective and mode of life have often led to regrettable consequences, they should not be regarded as wholly unfortunate. For the denominations are living witnesses to the importance of the insight into Christian faith which each knows. . . . Such divisions . . . may well be the essential sociological expression of the necessity to correct the one-sidedness of every interpretation and every tradition, so that the fullness of the whole Christian faith is not lost."[3]

Such a point of view should not be unacceptable to a Lutheran. Nearly all Lutherans would want to say that they see Lutheranism as an interpretation of Christianity, as one tradition of churchmanship alongside others. As Lutheranism marked itself off from the Roman and non-Roman churches of the day, it seemed a curious combination of radicalism and conservatism. The principle of firmness at the center and flexibility on the periphery made it almost inevitable that this effect should be created. The center was defined as the experience of the gracious forgiveness of sins by faith in the atoning work of Christ as revealed in Scripture. All other matters were regarded as instrumental to the experience of "justification by faith alone." The confessions of the Lutheran church were meant to be biblical in content and catholic in attitude. Their distinguishing feature does not lie in a claim to possess a set of special "Lutheran" doctrines or peculiar Christian truths. It lies rather in a determination to penetrate to the center of biblical truth and to proclaim that which makes a church into the church of Christ. Thus, neither ecclesiastical separation nor theological parochialism has a right to exist in the Lutheran communion. Lutherans should not be interested in any "Lutheran" doctrines that are not simply "Christian" doctrines. Lutherans have never claimed to be the only true church or to have a monopoly of Christian truth. Whether or not the Lutheran church is a "better" church than others, only God knows. What more could Lutherans want than to be members of the one body of Christ? If this is true, then it follows that the whole history of Christian thought and the whole spread of contemporary theological perspectives must supply the context for an effort to take a new look at the doctrine of grace. It may be added that clarity more often comes from seeing things in broad perspective. The interests of clarity are, of course, served by detailed study. But the kind of clarity that makes for poise in times of crisis is the fruit of perspective.

What is said in these chapters will strike some readers as highly selective and lacking in balance. But I must go to where I believe the root of the matter lies. One must proceed to difficult tasks of this sort with the sense of confidence and freedom made possible by the insight that we are saved by grace through faith, not by doctrines. This is not to say that doctrinal clarity and purity are unimportant. But they do not exist for themselves. They have never had any other purpose than to set the church free to love more fully and to risk its life in service.

Part One

THE
SHAPE OF THE
DOCTRINE OF GRACE

1

Thinking about God: Experience and Theology

To think about grace is to think about God. And to *think* about God is no simple matter. Perhaps we can ease into the subject by noting that thinking about God does not take the form of sitting quietly, staring off into space, and seeking to encompass with one's mind the substance and scope of ultimate reality and then arranging all one's thoughts into a logical system. The church's doctrines or affirmations about God were never shaped in that manner. Doctrines did not grow out of the ingenious speculations of individuals, nor were they invented by a bishop, a pope, or a council of venerable old men sitting around a table and agreeing to set forth a new proposition for belief.

Theology as a crystallization of experience

In its beginnings Christian doctrine developed out of a direct, living experience. In his little book on the early creeds, Alan Richardson insists that "all Christian doctrine arises from Christian experience. The first formulations of doctrine were merely an attempt to tell others about this experience, so that they too might understand and share it." [1] What the early Christians thought they were doing is well summed up in these words: "That which we have seen and heard we proclaim also to you, so that you may have fellowship with us; and our fellowship is with the Father and with his Son Jesus Christ" (1 John 1:3).

Doctrines were not attempts to foist speculative theories on people, but were efforts to record facts and to state what must be true about ultimate Reality in the light of what experience had said about that Reality. What actually happened on the stage of history was the data upon which theology worked. Its task was to give an intelligible account of the data afforded by Christian experience and to interpret its significance with whatever mental constructs were available.

The act of giving expression to those moments when God's presence and power were uniquely experienced can be seen in the literature of the Old Testament. The Hebrew belief in God was not based on rational proofs of theism but on perception of God's presence in actual and concrete events in the ordinary sphere of history. "The supreme event to which the people of Israel looked back as the foundation of their personal trust and confidence in God was the Exodus." [2] Tremendous events had occurred through which they had gained their liberty. The God of the exodus was not a philosopher's First Cause, but the Living God who intervened in history to rescue those whom he had chosen to be his servants (Deuteronomy 6:21-23). In the light of their conviction that their nation owed its existence as a people to God's actions in history, the Israelites found God's activity revealed in the whole course of their subsequent history. God was their savior and what he had done for them once, he could do again. It was by thinking out the implications of the experience of redemption that they came to believe that this God must be the Lord of all the peoples of the world and the creator of all things. From the focal moment when God's hand was upon them, they thought backwards, and forwards, and upwards, and outwards, and came to conclusions about the origin, the purpose, and the destiny of the world under God.

In the literature of the New Testament, the resurrection was the central and decisive event in which God had acted, just as the exodus was the focal point of experience and theology for the Hebrews. Early Christianity did not rest on logical deductions or on the memory of a martyred leader. It was the religion of a present experience and a future hope. It is a plain historical fact that the experience of the resurrection was the beginning of Christianity, and on it were founded the doctrines of the church (1 Corinthians 15:3-8, 14-17; 2 Corinthians 4:8-15).

Theology thus crystallizes out of experience. Both in biblical literature and in successive deposits of biblically inspired testimony to God, we find theological affirmations functioning as transcripts of experience.

Statements about the nature and will of God abound in the familiar "call stories" in the Old Testament. Abraham, Moses, Samuel, Isaiah, Jeremiah, Amos, Hosea, and others reported on the disclosure of God in the particular events of their lives. The New Testament has its "call stories" too. The conversation between Philip and the Ethiopian eunuch generated a disclosure of God's presence in Jesus as the Suffering Servant. The call to Peter on the lakeshore and the more dramatic experience of Paul on the road to Damascus resulted in Christian witness that was practical for one, elaborate for the other, and costly for both. It is only necessary to mention the names of Augustine, Luther, and Wesley to make the point that experience makes statements about itself, and Christian experience talks about what God has done in Jesus Christ.

The theological interpretation of experience recorded in the New Testament is one part only of the continuing experience of the Christian community which extends from Pentecost to the present day. Taking the apostolic interpretation as normative, later Christians reflected on their continuing experience of the grace of God in changing historical situations, and in doing so built up coherent intellectual presentations of the implications of their belief. The doctrinal interpretations of Christian experience were given classic expression in the early creeds of the church. Some creeds were intended to serve as brief summaries of Christian belief and were used in connection with baptism. Others were designed to provide authoritative statements of the church's doctrine and were used to refute heresies. But whether simple or elaborate, the creeds were essentially interpretations of experience. Credal phrases, embedded in the Scriptures, were regarded as fitting and reliable currency for Christian commitment.

This is obviously true of the earliest baptismal creeds, of which our Apostles' Creed is typical. But what about the Nicene Creed which includes phrases like "being of one substance with the Father"? Such phrases seem to have the ring of philosophical argument and learned detachment rather than living response to a Lord of grace. Yet such statements were not merely abstract expressions. The Nicene Creed arose from an attempt to bring order and consistency into Christian thinking, not least when an appeal to the Scriptures resulted in debate and division among believers who took their lead from apparently conflicting scriptural phrases. In order to deal with misunderstandings caused by biblical phrases taken in isolation, the early theologians sought to forge consistency-links which would underscore the central and controlling images and relate them to the whole range of biblical speech. For some of these links men needed to look outside Scripture and in this way the philosophical language of the day entered into the authoritative interpretation of Christian experience.

As we know, by the time of the Reformation the primitive theological paradise had proliferated into a veritable linguistic and conceptual jungle. Yet, even in the many confessions, catechisms, and articles of later centuries, the intention was to bear witness in specific historical situations to the vision of God's love and power in Christ. They have for their topic Christian commitment and their defence must be that they are currency for that same disclosure of God in Christ which the Bible and the creeds were meant to speak of.

The human experience of grace

Applied to our topic, this means that the idea of grace is not first of all a dogma of theology, but a datum of experience. The experience itself long antedated any doctrine of grace. But what *is* the experience which the concept of grace interprets? Familiar language is available to describe the Christian experience of grace on the most immediate and concrete level. "Since all have sinned and fall short of the glory of God, they are justified by his grace as a gift, through the redemption which is in Christ Jesus" (Romans 3:24). "For if many died through one man's trespass, much more have the grace of God and the free gift in the grace of that one man Jesus Christ abounded for many" (Romans 5:15). "For you know the grace of our Lord Jesus Christ, that though he was rich, yet for your sake he became poor so that by his poverty you might become rich" (2 Corinthians 8:9). "For by grace you have been saved through faith; and this is not your own doing, it is the gift of God" (Ephesians 2:8). "Through him we have obtained access to this grace in which we stand" (Romans 5:2). "Of this gospel I was made a minister according to the riches of God's grace" (Ephesians 3:7). "He said to me: 'My grace is sufficient for you'" (2 Corinthians 12:9). "Let us then with confidence draw near to the throne of grace, that we may find mercy and grace to help in time of need" (Hebrews 4:16).

From a small sampling of grace-passages, it is clear that the grace of God signifies the incredibly generous and utterly unexpected action he took in coming in Christ to this world of sinful men. The "grace of God" is a mode of speech which describes God himself, bestowing his healing and empowering presence on man. But beneath the characteristically Christian experience, we can see a deeper and generically human level of meaning. As men living a threatened existence within a mysterious world, we learn through grace that we are not alone nor need we rely only on our own small resources for life. "In spite of all the harshness and futility that surround us, there is at work on a still more fundamental level a love which seeks to enter and transform our lives and the lives of all men." [3]

Despite many ambiguous statements on the subject, Christian theology has never been prepared to exclude utterly the adherents of other religions from the saving grace of God. Paul denied exclusive knowledge of God for Christians when he said in his sermon at Lystra that God had not left himself without witness among all the nations (Acts 14:17). St. Augustine echoed the view of many earlier theologians when he referred on several occasions to "the one and true religion" which had always existed unchanged, though it had assumed a variety of symbols, rites, and forms, in accordance with the rhythm of ages and civilizations. Against the background of first-hand knowledge of Roman religion, Augustine affirmed that true religious content was to be found in its rituals and practices. [4]

For the most part, Augustine's openness to the presence of God outside the biblical community was affirmed in the traditional concepts of the "natural knowledge of God" or of "general revelation." It was held that genuine knowledge of God came through the reverent contemplation of nature, through response to the imperatives of conscience, through awareness of the holy, and through the sincere search for truth. [5] The idea of general revelation implied that a Christian could not say that in the non-Christian religions there is no apprehension of God's healing and saving power and no measure of trustful acceptance of it. Through the years this implication did not function as a major theme in Christian theology, but it was there to be reemphasized in our day.

Karl Rahner, one of the influential shapers of the theology of the Second Vatican Council, speaks for most Catholics and Protestants when he writes: "Belief in God through Jesus Christ does not take a purely negative attitude toward other religious traditions of mankind, even though its mission is to be a sign for the religions of the nations. It embraces those forms of faith which existed before and exist along with it as unconscious participations in the pardoning and divinizing grace of Christ." [6] In arguing that the order of grace is not confined to the visible church, but is present and operative throughout mankind, Rahner develops a concept of anonymous or implicit Christianity. "We Christians do not look on non-Christians as people who have mistaken error for truth because they are more stupid, more wicked and more unfortunate than we, but as people who in the depths of their being are already pardoned, or can be pardoned, by God's infinite grace in virtue of his universal salvific will and are on the road to perfection, as people who have simply not yet come to an explicit awareness of what they already are: men called by God." [7] Such anonymous Christianity is not confined to pagans who have never heard of the Gospel. It also includes those living in Christian countries who know about the Christian message but have not felt confronted with a personal obligation to believe.

The growth of the conviction that all men, insofar as they believe life has meaning at all, are aware in some way of God's grace is supported by much research. Christian historians invariably point out that in the first century a religious sense of grace was widely diffused, and that the primitive church found itself in a world in which, so far as interests in the gods went, the situation was favorable to the presentation of religion as grace. But the sense of grace is thought to have existed prior to the first century and beyond the Mediterranean world. H. R. Mackintosh wrote: "The Christian thought of grace is heralded in ethnic religions by the widespread feeling that the gods are kindred and friendly beings, guardians of morality, and, up to a certain point, able to help men. From the earliest times a corresponding confidence and trust . . . differentiate religion from magic or sorcery." [8] In his book *The Christian Doctrine of Grace*, H. D. Gray is much less cautious. After a survey of anthropological findings and of nine or ten major religions, he exclaims "grace is everywhere!" [9]

T. F. Torrance is more restrained in his survey of the usage of the word *charis* in classical and Hellenistic Greek. In its original sense, the word is applied to a wide range of pleasure-giving qualities such as charm, beauty, elegance, attractiveness, good-will, and favor. But the idea that *charis* is divine is never far away. As divine favor, *charis* is prayed for and sacrifices are offered to gain it. It comes to signify any beneficial supernatural influence and even the idea of divinity itself. [10]

We recall that when Paul visited Athens, he found an abundance of gods and observed about the Athenians that they were "very religious" (Acts 17:22). Greek religion was not all of one piece. The pantheon of popular deities is said to have had an impact on the faithful that "was something close to a reign of terror. The sky deities . . . were whimsical at best. . . . . The earth deities were as insatiable as the life-forces they controlled—and as irrational." [11] Yet, many investigators have found in primitive religion something deeper than fear—"something more like friendly intercourse and fellowship, love and trust in the gods." [12]

If the pagan pantheon presents us with ambiguity, the record is much clearer with respect to the poets, tragedians, and philosophical religions that developed after the cultural breakdown of fifth-century Greece. One finds in the tragedies the faith that all is in God's hands, that he looks with pity upon his suppliants, and that it is a good thing to rely on him in trouble. Outler affirms that the several systems of philosophical religion "had two common aims: (1) to ease man's terror of the divine by re-conceiving the cosmos in moral and rational terms and (2) to offer men ways of salvation that promised human dignity, freedom, and happiness. . . . In both Platonism and Stoicism there were multiple versions of a concept of divine foreknowledge and purpose based on the eternal pre-existence of the forms and forces that make the good life possible. . . . The summative Form of all the forms is the Good. This means that the value-tone of all real being is good and, therefore, that life is good as men participate in this ambient goodness." [13]

It seems undeniable that the sense of grace found in the Greek world had its analogues elsewhere. Lewis Farnell wrote: "It is a fact of great significance that the history of religions nowhere presents us with the phenomenon of a High God conceived as malevolent and definitely accepted by the worshipper as such." [14] It is safe to say that grace is attributed to the deity wherever it is thought possible for reconciliation to be effected by means of sacrifice, or through the intercession of qualified agents, or simply by leaving everything in divine hands. Christians who affirm that grace is the ultimate word to be spoken about the one God, should not find it difficult to believe that all men everywhere should sense the stirrings of grace as they reach out toward a supportive and positive reality beyond, yet within, the world of their experience.

As we have seen, theology—and not only *Christian* theology—crystallizes out of experience. Christian faith shares with other religions of "redemption" the sense that human life is lived within an infinite environment, a wider context of being which is active in giving the resources to meet the demands that existence lays upon us. The attitude toward this wider and supportive framework of reality is no mere belief but an existential attitude which includes acceptance and commitment. The attitude of the religious man can be called "faith." John Macquarrie says of faith that it "discovers a meaning for existence that is already given with existence." In the absence of faith, one would look for "no support from beyond man, who must rely on his own resources, and who must himself create for his life any meaning that it can have." [15]

But it is the testimony of the religions, philosophies, and arts of mankind that very few people rely entirely on their own resources to find meaning in life. Man may be understood as the "religious animal" in the sense that he is the one being in whom the question of the purpose of existence as such becomes explicit both as a question and as a supreme interest. In distinguishing between philosophy and religion, Langdon Gilkey asserts that the religious question takes the form: "Amidst all the helplessness, tragedy, frustration, and waywardness of life, is there One who has set us here, and so through whose power and purpose we can find a meaning to our personal and social existence?" [16] Only if we can grasp some assurance of life's ultimate coherence and purpose can we affirm the immediate meanings of our day-to-day life.

Different religions have different concepts of God. But there is also a generic idea of God, a concept of the reality that is the source, purpose, and fulfillment of existence. When we ask about the quality and meaning of life and of our own being, we cannot escape this concept. Alan Richardson offers a definition of religion from an anthropological or sociological standpoint: "It would be adequate to define religion as man's response to the exigency of the human condition, in which he is driven to seek security, status, and permanence by identifying himself with a reality greater, more worthy, and more durable than himself." [17]

Man's basic insecurity, his felt insufficiency, his awareness of encompassing mystery have provided the soil in which religion came to birth. The universality of religion indicates that man, without special revelation, has an inkling, however dim, that his life touches upon a mysterious, transcendent, and supportive reality. John Calvin had this in mind when he spoke of a *sensus divinitatis* which God had implanted in the human soul. Whatever else reality may ultimately be, it does include experiences of support, acceptance, meaning, and hope. Out of the consciousness of our mortality and weakness arises talk of eternity and transcendence. Rudolf Bultmann claims that knowledge about God is initially "a knowledge which man has about himself and his finitude, and God is reckoned to be the power which breaks through this finitude of man and thereby raises him up to his real stature." [18]

The man who suffers from his isolation, from the burden of being himself, and from the meaninglessness of life, reaches out beyond the limits of his own feeble efforts for support. When he finds the support he has sought, he suddenly sees himself as a man with a destiny. He can acknowledge with surprise that life has meaning. He can trust that he is alive by a principle over which he has no power but which brings forth new life. Gregory Baum affirms that Christian faith in God as Father delivers one from the confines of his own existence and moves him into the presence of "the One who approaches him in grace." Now it is understood that "the author of reality is on our side. The ground of being is not far away, hostile or indifferent to us: the deepest dimension of the total reality facing us is for us. There is no reason to be afraid of the world: there is no reason to fear the unknown tomorrow; for the ultimate root of all being protects and favors human life. Despite the suffering and evil in the world . . . we are summoned to believe that the ultimate principle of reality is love itself." [19]

We will see that Christianity changes the content and scope of the fundamental elements of human religiousness. It is unique in its picture of the way in which the object of faith comes to meet the quest for sense and support in this world. With a distinctive concept of "revelation" as the manner in which the gracious Presence touches and changes life, biblical faith brought a radically new approach to the interpretation of religious experience.

Yet, Christianity's special sense of grace was and is continuous with the general idea of grace and it could thus be commended as the completion or fulfillment of the most profound and legitimate longings of the human spirit. In the most general sense, the Christian testimony to the grace of God means that life is worth trusting despite the threat of chaos and inevitable death.

The centrality of trust in life and religion

It was Luther who gave classic expression to the centrality of trust in life and in religion. In explaining the meaning of the First Commandment, Luther wrote: "What is it to have a god? What is God? Answer: A god is that to which we look for all good and in which we find refuge in every time of need. To have a god is nothing else than to trust and believe him with our whole heart. . . . The trust and faith of the heart alone make both God and an idol. . . . For these two belong together, faith and God. That to which your heart clings and entrusts itself is really your God." [20]

Luther is surely saying that it is only when we actually *trust* that we have any apprehension of the truths of religion. Only in this trust, this actual experience of religion, can we even understand what the very word "God" means. An usually forceful expression of the same point appears in the writings of Schubert Ogden. In working with the question, Where in our lived experience does God become real? Ogden argues that man has an interior awareness of worth, value, meaning, and significance. Underlying all our experience is the "foundational certainty" that we are significant and worthwhile. This "primal faith" or basic confidence in the worth of life is constitutive of our very lives as human beings. It is "the common faith" of mankind. Ogden writes: "The various 'religions' or 'faiths' of mankind . . . are one and all expressions or re-presentations of a yet deeper faith that precedes them. Logically prior to every particular religious assertion is an original confidence in the meaning and worth of life, through which not simply all our religious answers, but even our religious questions first become possible or have any sense." [21]

Ogden goes beyond this "common faith" to affirm that the word "god" is the objective ground in reality itself of the basic confidence in the worth of life. "The word 'God' . . . provides the designation for whatever it is about this experienced whole that calls forth and justifies our original and inescapable trust. . . . To be free of fear by existing in this trust is one and the same thing with affirming the reality of God." [22]

The practical, personal, existential character of the apprehension of grace and of the very act of raising and answering the religious question about "God" is said by Langdon Gilkey to be at the heart of the idea of creation. "The question of the meaning and destiny of our present life can only be answered if we can have confidence in the fundamental goodness of life as promising fulfillment; and such confidence in the promise of life is possible only if we have some basis for trust in the source of all being. . . . To the anxious question: Why are we, and on what do we ultimately depend? the Christian faith gives the answer: we are creatures of God dependent utterly upon his sovereign power and love." [23]

It is important for the aspects of grace we wish to develop to note that we do not raise the question of the ground of being because we are Christians, but because we are human beings. Both the just and the unjust live by faith that something makes life worth living. This generic intimation of grace is implied in Luther's understanding of the meaning of the word "God." He thought that "God" means the best that one can know. "God" functions as a value-word. Indeed, it denotes a supreme value. A man's "God" is what he sets his heart on and trusts to. Trust, then, is one of the fundamental aspects of life for every human being, going far beyond the range of the Christian creeds. Every day men base their lives on particular circumstances, things, and people. Trust is impossible without some sense of the reliability of definite factors. Yet, trust carries us beyond these into what is indefinite. For in addition to discerned reliability, the objects of trust invariably have something about them that is not yet externally evident. The very act of trust implies that reality does not merely consist of what is tangibly present. It is always directed toward still invisible and not yet available reality. "That is why trust can also be disappointed, and why trust and faith are always accompanied and threatened by doubt. . . . Doubt is the shadow which everywhere follows faith and trust." [24]

Because trust contains both the definite and the indefinite, it has the character not only of a primordial awareness, but also of a conscious decision. The radically experiential nature of grace has been translated by H. Richard Niebuhr into the idiom of trust and distrust. "Faith is the attitude of the self in its existence toward all the other existences that surround it, as beings to be relied upon or to be suspected. . . . Faith as trust or distrust accompanies all our encounters with others and qualifies all our responses. . . . When we say that the power by which we are is God, we may express our interpretation in trust, for to say 'God' is to say 'good' in our common speech; the word, God, means the affirmer of our being, not its denier. . . . Our primordial interpretation of the radical action by which we are is made in faith as trust or distrust. Between these two there seems to be no middle term. The inscrutable power by which we are, is either for us or against us." [25] Christian theology declares that the inscrutable power which has launched us into existence is *for* us, not against us. In saying this, Christianity expresses faith in the trustworthiness of life.

Theology and the conceptualization of religious experience

If it is the case that theology crystallizes out of experience, then it follows that theology is what we *say* about faith as trust, dependence, courage, hope. Although "the heart makes theology," as Augustine put it, theology is essentially a rational enterprise. It involves the use of ideas, words, and concepts, ranging from the simple to the complex. But no matter how hard it tries, theology can never achieve either adequacy or accuracy with respect to its data, for it is dealing with deeply mysterious facts of experience.

Theology is, of course, an interplay of experience and interpretation. The early Christians insisted that the message they proclaimed had not been spun out of thin air. The faith of the church was based on the encounter of the disciples with Jesus, in which they experienced nothing less than the saving love of God drawing them to himself. Christian preaching has always been the telling of news, the bearing of witness to certain historical events. The New Testament and the early creeds refer to some tremendous experiences which compelled Christian people to testify to that which they had heard and seen and to interpret the meaning of these experiences.

Over the centuries theology has undergone significant changes in conception and methodology. The traditional theologies have focused on biblical or institutional authority, on reason, or on intuition. Recently, theologies of social progress, of hope, of liberation, and of revolution have appeared. Dissatisfied with what seem to be irrelevant or awkward superstructures of thought, many theologians of all schools are returning to the examination of experience as a datum for theology. They are not content to say: we are taught thus and thus. They want to insist that the roots of religion lie in experience. In this time of religious ferment, they argue, we must reassess our approach. We should begin in our understanding of any phenomenon with what is most accessible to us. Since man is the one in whom the religious concern becomes explicit, we should begin with his religious experience.

In the most elementary sense, experience is our awareness of being in relation to some reality other than our own. The experiencer is actively involved in the transaction, but he is also conscious of being acted on by something which does not depend on him for its existence. As John E. Smith puts it, "we *find* something already there, we *come up against* something, we confront persons, objects, events, and we do so with the sense that we *undergo* or receive whatever it is that we meet without any sense of being responsible for having produced it." [26]

Broadly understood, religious experience may be any experience which involves the sense that life is trustworthy and which one refers to the object of his ultimate commitment. The theistic religions regard the extra-human structure of reality which is encountered as the presence of God. In the Christian tradition, God is apprehended as the ultimate power and goodness who is supremely manifest in Jesus Christ. Some Christians have come close to saying that the religious experience constitutes "God" or the religious object. In contrast to this view, it is important to see that experience is the medium through which God is disclosed and the contents of the Christian faith are existentially appropriated.

But the understanding of experience requires interpretation. It is interpretation that makes experience intelligible. Since there is no experience of God that is not also the experience of something else at the same time, the rational process "reads" the signs thrown up by experience, discriminates among them, classifies them, and, with the help of characteristic ideas, identifies what is present in the experiences as a divine reality. It is not possible to build up belief, or to build up a system of theology, on religious experience alone. As in science, it is necessary to "leap beyond the evidence." It is necessary to have a theory in order to make sense of particular experiences. The requisite theory contains numerous symbols. The human experience precipitates the symbol. The symbol is not arbitrarily imposed on the experience, but is a part of the experience itself, declaring its fullness. "The thematization of an experience in symbolic form makes it capable of communication. It can be told to others, and if they live within the symbol and surrender to its vision they can participate in the experience which gave it birth. For a Christian the paradigmatic symbols are those of the New Testament which he attempts to live within and out of and so experience the world, men, and God in the Christian way." [27] The interpretation of experience through symbols is an attempt to hold on to it, to make it a part of memory and not let it drift into forgetfulness, to clarify and help to reproduce it.

Revelation is inseparable both from experience and its conceptualization. In the Christian view, revelation means that there are events or occasions when God is present in certain mediating elements. Those elements constitute signals which require interpretation. The events are adopted as signs and the biblical speakers and writers borrow human concepts, images and words to express their message. By pointing beyond themselves, the biblical images demand that there shall be doctrines. Prophets and apostles provide interpretation by recording events and supplying commentary. In Paul the tradition takes the form of explicitly theological reflection. He interprets the meaning of God's self-disclosure in Christ by the use of consistent concepts pointing in the direction of a theological system. The work of theological interpretation has continued from the Church Fathers to the present day.

In the broadest sense, the process of interpretation can be described as a movement from the primary awareness of an awesome yet reconciling mystery to the generation of felt analogies through which content is given to the apprehension by models borrowed from the widest range of human experience. It is characteristic of understanding that it starts from certain direct experiences and moves toward the discovery of intelligible meanings within these experiences. It is the role of reason not to create events or awareness but to remove the sense of the strange and the untrustworthy.

There is a flow of primary experience which precedes interpretation even though symbols and elemental forms of language are implicit in the awareness. But experience is raised to the reflective level when the mind of the interpreter stops the flow and seeks to articulate meanings which are present in the experience. The meanings are patterns of significance which are given at least some elementary organization by dominant interests. A meaning thus arises within a context of interest and it may need to be reinterpreted as the context is broadened, particularly through sharing the experience of others. To have knowledge is "to be aware of, to understand the experienced world so that one can act in such a fashion that envisaged consequences actually occur." [28]

What specific interest organizes and interprets experience from a religious or theological perspective? What is it in primary experience which gives rise to religious and theological questions, answers, symbols, interpretations? As we have seen, theologians who are re-examining experience in reaction against the imposition of external authority, tend to focus on the question of trust. Perry LeFevre argues that the ultimate root of the question about God is the ambiguity and the insecurity of the human situation. Each of us confronts his world with all its possibilities of gain and loss. Risk and anxiety attend every move. "The crucial question facing all men at all times . . . is the question of trust. What can a man finally trust? This is the existence question. It is the religious question which gives all man's life a religious dimension. . . . In the face of such risk and insecurity man puts his trust now here and now there. Again and again he has found his trust betrayed. . . . Is there anything, anyone finally trustworthy? To seek what is finally trustworthy is the quest for God." [29]

Gordon Kaufman, in asking What function does the word "God"

perform in religious and theological speech? contends that "such speech appears within the context of man's sense of limitation, finitude, guilt and sin, on the one hand, and his question about the meaning or value or significance of himself, his life, and his world, on the other. . . . The emphasis of biblical faith on salvation, deliverance, succor, abundant life, forgiveness, resurrection, atonement, eternal life, etc. all have this double reference, negatively to man's inadequacy and need, and positively to man's meaningful destiny and fulfillment."[30]

All this means that the fundamental religious problem and theological interest is the existential and practical issue of salvation, of communion with God, of the strength to live with a sense of meaning and fulfillment in the face of the ambiguities of life.

As the theological interpreter proceeds from human experiencing to a conceptualization of God, he gives attention to emerging patterns or meanings. We move from the known to the unknown. One becomes aware of new patterns through a prior understanding of more familiar patterns. To observe similarities, relationships, and equivalences is a kind of analogical reasoning in which meanings emerge through the use of models or metaphors.

We cannot penetrate the human mind's strange faculty for perceiving analogies. We speak vaguely of insight and intuition but do not fully understand the phenomenon. But it is certain that all projects of thought require the capability of leaping ahead of the evidence to categories of interpretation which are adequate, systematic, and susceptible to verification of some kind. It has become a truism to say that all language about God and his relation to the world must be in terms of analogy. Since the ultimate realities of which it speaks are quite out of the ordinary, religion can speak of them only by saying they are "like" elements within our usual experience in some respects and "unlike" them in others. We are dealing not with identities but with analogies. Thus theology must employ language which has only approximate appropriateness. Theology "has no way of capturing within the limits of precise and unambiguous language insights which are themselves non-literal. It captures what it can, but always with the awareness that more has escaped through the meshes of the net than has been confined by the net. . . . It must say more than literal language can convey. In short, it must employ language with metaphoric force."[31]

The poetic imagery of Scripture confronts us with a riot of metaphor. God is a king, a judge, a priest, a warlord, a farmer, a shepherd, a friend, a bridegroom and husband, a guide, a teacher, a physician. Jesus is a son, a word, a door, a vine, a lamb, a messiah, a cornerstone, a loaf of bread. Life with God is a city, a plant, a banquet, a household, warfare. The church is a body, an army, a holy nation, a lamp, yeast, salt. In explicating the death of Christ, George Caird writes: "The New Testament . . . does not attempt to give any reasoned theory of the atonement. Instead it gives us a series of pictures, which tell us in the language of the heart what the Cross meant to those who wrote. We were in debt, and Christ paid our debt for us; we were slaves and he gave his life for our ransom; we were condemned before the judgment seat of God, and he bore our penalty that we might go free; . . . we were children in disgrace, and he restored us to the family circle; we were prisoners shut up in the fortress of Satan, and he broke in to set us free. The terminology of the bank, the slave market, the law courts, the temple, the home, and the field of battle is pressed into service in an attempt to do justice to the fact of experience that sin is no longer a barrier between man and God."[32]

The power of such metaphors lies in the fact that more meaning can be suggested than is specifically defined. Theological interpretation does not operate without metaphor but it seeks to develop metaphors which will increase the level of understanding by their controlled connotations and systematic interconnections. It is the task of theology to formulate categories by which the experiences, pictures, and images emerging from particular events will be adequately understood. Such theological categories are not unlike the key concepts employed by other disciplines of thought as they interpret the data of biology, physics, psychology, sociology, political science, history, and so on.

Such root metaphors as organism, mechanism, personality, and freedom facilitate the communication of knowledge. Mechanical, organic, and personal models have been used by theology to conceptualize God and his relation to the world. But theology has a marked tendency to draw its metaphors from the realm of interpersonal relationships: redemption, adoption, forgiveness, reconciliation, revelation, grace, inspiration, judgment. These symbols or metaphors direct one's attention to certain experiences and illuminate the depth and implications of those experiences. The symbols of God the Creator, the Trinity, the will of God, justification by faith, union with God, and resurrection have enormous power to direct attention, to interpret and integrate experiences, to entice the reason and imagination, and to summon one to a life-style that is consistent with the interpretation. All metaphors and theological perspectives, however, seek to free from the tangled density of the human experiences of insecurity, anxiety, guilt, injustice, love, integrity, and healing, the truth that the fulfilling ultimacy that pulses through man is the grace of God.

There is a constant tension between the pictorial data set forth in the first-hand reports of grace and the innate tendencies of theology as a form of systematic thought. The images thrown up by the primary experience of grace always have a certain character of incompleteness and indefiniteness, while theological expression strives for complete and clear definitions. As we work for systematic theological understanding are we doing violence to the Bible which speaks in metaphors and parables and contains no theology in the systematic sense? There is no easy answer to that question. The church requires both testimony and theology. We will have to live with two rather different modes of thought—the pictorial and the abstract, the dramatic and the analytical—and seeks ways to cope with their incompatibility for the sake of a witness that is authentic, intelligible, and capable of communicating with the culture of our time.

The supernatural and the modern mind

The "culture of our time"! What is it? Is it a single thing? What does it rule in and what does it rule out? What kind of power does it have? Some see it as a friend, some as an enemy, and some may be indifferent to it. It is clear that the form which theology takes in its effort to interpret experience depends very much on one's perception of the character of the "modern mind." Every culture tends to be characterized by a dominant problem which is its own peculiar experience of the human situation. The Christian message becomes relevant to a particular age by being apprehended in terms which can be correlated effectively with this experience. Thus in the formation of his theology every theologian must make a decision about the age in which he lives.

The history of the church abounds with examples of such decisions. Paul and John republished the primitive Palestinian gospel in terms that would come home to a wider Greco-Roman world. Others expressed the essence of the gospel in the apocalyptic imagery of late Judaism. Many Church Fathers utilized the thought-forms of Platonic and Stoic philosophy in an attempt to correlate the apostolic witness with the typical existential problems of their times. The Gnostics accepted the astrological picture of the world as the framework of their theological interpretation. During the Middle Ages, the feudal system in combination with Platonic or Aristotelian categories guided the formulation of the Christian message. The Reformation, the Enlightenment, the Romantic movement, and the first and second world wars of our century, produced characteristic efforts to achieve reciprocity between faith and its changing cultural environment.

In our own day, Karl Barth decided that humanism dominated the "modern mind" and attempted to interpret the faith in such a way that it would be protected from cultural influence. Rudolf Bultmann, on the other hand, accepted the dominance of science and used existentialist themes to make theology relevant to culture. Dietrich Bonhoeffer responded to secularization, Paul van Buren to empiricism, Schubert Ogden and John Cobb to process philosophy, and Jürgen Moltmann to the note of futurity. Such decisions about one's age are marked by ambiguity. If one does not intersect with the modern mood, he risks being totally irrelevant in his theology. If he does intersect in a substantial way, he risks distorting the faith by this very commitment.

David Woodyard argues that ours is not one of those times when the present state of thought can be assessed with any precision. There is no theological position today for which one cannot find a counterpart. The pendulum is swinging to the right and to the left simultaneously. Neither the "modern mind" nor the church gives overwhelming support to any particular way of structuring theological interpretation.[33]

As classical Christian theology addressed itself to whatever mind was "modern" at any given time, it saw clearly that to talk about the grace of God was also to say something about the universe. The baffling incompleteness of our knowledge about the vastness and ultimate constitution of the environment in which we live must not rule out such audacious yet necessary statements. Nor can we be intimidated by the "modern mind" or by the inconclusiveness of contemporary theology.

When Paul talked about the resurrection he was surely sketching out at the same time a view of the cosmos. If it be true that Jesus rose from the dead, then the universe must be accounted for in such a way as will explain that phenomenon. Religious experience leads one to accept one general account of the world and man's place in it and to reject another. Paul saw the world from a religious rather than from a non-religious or anti-religious viewpoint, thus he talked of events in terms of God's activity and purpose.

Most general world views construe reality in terms of a model derived from one small part of it. This is certainly true of the theistic world view, which construes the world in terms of the action of an intelligent agent. To be a traditional Christian theist, whether sophisticated or un-sophisticated, is to see the events of which nature and history consist as being the result of the actions of an intelligent and benevolent agent. By "God" is meant that of whose actions the universe consists. If God did not exist and act, there would be no universe and no man. Thus, the God of traditional Christianity is inevitably supernatural.

Telling the story of the exodus, the resurrection, the incarnation, Pente-cost, or the call of Abraham or Paul, presupposes that God is of a certain character. It presupposes that God has complete control of the world and the course of events in it; that he exercises this control in a way which is purposeful; that men have a place in his designs; and that he communicates with them in ways which they can legitimately under-stand as commands and promises, and by which their lives can be guided. This cluster of presuppositions must have been in Paul's mind when he defended himself before King Agrippa, and asked the ques-tion: "Why is it considered incredible among you that God should raise dead men to life?" Acts 26:8 NEB).

Such reports of divine action do, however, seem incredible to the "modern mind." The case of King Agrippa's disbelief prompts one to respond to the claim that traditional theism is out-moded, by asking at what point in history it was truly *in*-moded, at least as it was pro-pounded by Paul, Origen, Augustine, Aquinas, Luther, and Barth. Be that as it may, we often hear that we have come to "the end of the Christian era," and that talk of the living God, the creator of the world, has become a hollow sound today. In a world determined by science and technology the term "God" is said to be totally irrelevant. No mas-sive effort is being made to prove that religion is false; it is regarded instead as outworn or dead. Religious faith is superfluous in a scientific age.

It is true that modern man has a high regard for science and con-stantly appeals to it. It can be doubted, however, whether very many are really acquainted with it. Scientists themselves complain about a lack of understanding on the part of the public. A negative attitude toward religion may not be particularly scientific, even when it appeals to sci-ence. Unbelief existed long before science came into its own. We recall the Athenians who laughed when Paul spoke of the resurrection of the dead. Similarly, in a scientific age there are many people who can be committed to strange and unsupportable beliefs in blood and state or in astrology. The average "modern mind" contains a bizarre mixture of scientific and non-scientific factors.

But it can be argued that it is not the details or method of science that account for the claim that the term "God" is irrelevant. It is rather the pervasive secular mentality of our time. The secular mood grows out of a vision of reality, which is caused in part by science, and which sees man as set within a universe with neither a transcendant source nor an ultimate order. Whether secularism is confident or despairing, it sees the universe as blind nature, indifferent and faceless, even though not directly hostile to human purposes. Within such a vision of reality, the meaning and value of man's life cannot come from outside himself, but must come from his own efforts. To the secular mind with its this-worldly, empirical mood, the idea of God as a cosmic source of meaning, value, and purpose is irrelevant. It is the theme of Bishop John A. T. Robinson's popular book, *Honest to God,* and of many responses to it, that the world has become too adult for belief in the conventional theology of the past.

It would be unwise to deny or ignore the impact of secular thought and life upon traditional religion. We are acutely aware of the confused ideas and declining loyalties of Christian people. It may be doubted, however, whether disbelief is caused by the clear intellectual superiority of a self-consistent scheme of "modern thought," whatever that might be. Yet, sensitivity to the mood of the time calls for changes in the traditional patterns of Christian teaching. Fortunately, since the disorderly hodge-podge of ideas exists in the secular mind as well as within the church, Christians can choose different ways of responding to the situation.

Some will feel that no matter how ingenious we may be in finding fresh ways to interpret Christian experience to a de-theologized age, the doctrine of grace will continue to demand the recognition of a distinction between the natural and the supernatural. Joseph Sittler has addressed the modern temper with great sympathy, insight, and imagination. Yet he poses the unavoidable question very bluntly: "Is it possible to reconceptualize, expand, experience, and bear witness to the grace of God within a world that is beheld and practically dealt with as a closed system?" He argues: "If men accept an understanding of the world as independent, there is no place for God's agency, and the notion of grace is not credible; if men so radically historicize their understanding of the world as to bring all dynamics of world-happening within the orbit of man's determination, there is no place for God's agency, and the notion of grace is not credible." [34]

Even those theologians who have diverged rather substantially from the classical Christian tradition in their efforts to speak to the "modern mind" recognize that the very mission of the church drives us to face the relation of the natural to the supernatural. From the earliest times the concept of the supernatural had been used by Christian theologians as an appropriate means of stating the core of the Gospel. The creeds, in affirming faith in the triune God, in his redemptive acts, and in his grace in the church, say that the supernatural creates nature for its own supernatural purpose. The term "supernatural" has a complex history and has often been used in misleading ways, but the idea itself is an inescapable requirement of the Christian faith. For the essential structure of that faith has a genuine two-sidedness about it.

Eugene R. Fairweather puts it this way: "The terms of the question can be diversely stated from different viewpoints, so that we may speak of the creaturely and the divine, the secular and the sacred, the historical and the eschatological, or the natural and the supernatural, but all these dualities point to the same primary truths. On the one hand, man's life is the product of creaturely processes and it has to be lived out in this world of space and time. On the other hand, the ultimate foundation and the final destiny of that same life lie in a supratemporal relation to the reality which transcends all creaturely existence." [35]

The theism of the Bible and of the Christian tradition have always used the term "God" to affirm that the reality of the world is not exhausted by the realities in the world. God is characterized by a radical otherness. The significance of God's presence and availability, his love and grace, is derived from his otherness and his absoluteness. If God were not "other," God would simply not be. And if God were not "other" on a scale that transcends the natural and the human, there could be no saving intervention from outside the context of human need. Since the presence of God is the immanence of his transcendence, it is necessary to use analogy in speaking of the relationship between nature and the supernatural. For analogy acknowledges duality. It talks about relationships, not identities. It takes into account both sides of the experience of the divine presence, with-ness and other-ness, likeness and difference, immanence and transcendence. Thus, analogy is faithful to the gospel of divine action.

Schubert Ogden, Leslie Dewart, and others, have objected to the traditional idea of the supernatural and have argued that the category must undergo radical reconstruction. If the supernatural is spelled out in terms of absolute and total transcendence, it is of course unacceptable because it would deny the reality of a mutual relationship between man and God, it would render speech about God and his grace utterly unintelligible, it would imply that God is untouched by the novelty, suffering, and growth that characterize human experience, and it would make God a mere spectator of the passing parade. But it is not necessary to conceive the supernatural in such a way that the totally transcendent deity is irrelevant to ongoing human experience. Some theologies have come close to doing this, but no theology has ever remoted God out of all relation to the religious concerns of ordinary people.

On the theological level, the doctrine of grace does require a universe that is open to God's action. The materialist of a generation or two ago was sure that reality could be defined as those phenomena perceptible by the senses. Any event that contradicted the "laws of nature" must be either fictitious or capable of being included within a reformulated law. Nature for him was an enclosed system of causes within which there was no place or need for God. Most theists responded to materialism by holding that there are two more or less independent realms of reality—the material and the trans-material. The trans-material can impinge upon the material in such a way as to interrupt or suspend its limited regularity. According to this model, God remains self-consistent while "suspending the laws of nature."

But contemporary science is not deterministic in the way Newtonian physics was. The cosmos is seen not as a static hierarchy but as an open, evolving, and emerging process of nature. There is no unchanging law of nature. Yet the physical world is not an amorphous flux but a procession with an order and direction. We now think of nature in dynamic terms. It is quite true that the "uncertainty theorems" of modern physics do not point to God's presence. But they do point to the incompleteness of our knowledge both of nature and of any ultimate ground of its phenomena. Albert Outler comments: "Christian monotheism does not propose to displace all other accounts of existence. . . . It holds that it is rationally conceivable . . . to think of *nature as given* . . . , as a configuration of finite processes, contingent and interdependent but

neither self-contained nor self-explanatory. It regards it as at least theoretically admissable to think of nature as a sort of 'parenthesis,' the full
meaning of which is supplied 'from beyond' without negating the significance of what lies 'inside.' " [36] Theology has pondered and partici-
pated in the lengthy debates about the closed-universe, open-universe
issue and has produced several accounts, traditional and revisionist, of
the existence and agency of God in whatever kind of universe we live in.

For the sake of pursuing our interest in the doctrine of grace, it is
helpful to note three points. First, the Christian experience of grace is
an encounter between men and a transcendent Other. All religion is at
bottom the conscious recognition that we do not live in a merely natural
and human situation. The Christian idea of man's nature and destiny
is frankly supernatural. It does not find meaning and purpose simply
within the process of nature or human nature. This world is part of
another infinitely richer, fuller world which in the Christian tradition
goes under the names of eternity, heaven, the kingdom of God. The
impinging of the eternal world on this one is the real meaning of "miracle" in the Christian vocabulary. Miracle and grace are inseparable in
that both declare and, if they are to be "accounted for," require the
reality, the freedom, and the love of God, the transcendent Other. For
in the experience of grace we are not experiencing *ourselves,* just as in
worship it is God, not our own consciousness, that is the object. We
experience *God,* not ourselves worshiping. The grace-encounter has a
disclosure character with subjective and objective constituents. The disclosure reveals what is other than ourselves while being at the same
time a situation in which we come to ourselves and realize a distinctive
subjectivity. The objectivity which grace-encounters disclose is not the
"objectivity" which belongs to fantasies or to physical objects and scientific causes. Nor is it simply the "objectivity" which belongs to other
people as members of a population. It is the objectivity—the felt presence—"of what declares itself to us" as infinitely holy and gracious.
The objectivity challenges and supports us in "a way that persons may
do." [37]

No matter how many concessions we make to the modern mind in
order to reduce the difficulties of belief, we are still confronted, if we
wish to interpret grace, with the necessity to choose between believing
in a "closed" or an "open" system—either a mechanical, Newtonian system in which nothing can happen without causes which (potentially)
are physically perceptible, or else a system which has a theistic openness,

one in which the regularity and interlocking order of the world are *included* within the "transcendent."

The second observation we must make has a fairly aggressive, if not reactionary, sound. Granted that the classical terms and thought forms of Christianity are often a scandal and offense to the modern world, as we have been told by Altizer, Hamilton, Van Buren, and St. Paul (1 Corinthians 1:23), it is still required of Christian witness that it speak of God and in so doing should draw a distinction between the natural and the supernatural.

It is not mere obscurantism to say this. Langdon Gilkey points out: "The most pressing contemporary theological problem . . . is: How can we speak meaningfully and relevantly of God in a secular and empirical age? What do God and his will *mean* in the space age, the age of computers and commuters, when the things and values of this life seem so overwhelmingly real and all else so very unreal? . . . How can we speak to this age of God? So ponder the theologians. But what does the minister *do*, except what the theologians are talking about?" [38]

Ministers and lay-people may carry on in this manner not simply out of habit nor with any interest in defying the "modern mind," but because they sense that the case for modern disbelief is still very much on trial. Until the dust settles on the argument, if it ever does, Christian people may freely question whether the alleged consensus about the closed universe is as critical, decisive, and humane as some believe it to be. Albert Outler comments: "There is a rueful irony in the fact that just as modern man's bid for autonomy is being allowed, a drastic disenchantment with the marvels of modernity begins to deepen and spread." [39]

When Joseph Sittler recommends that the dismissal of the God-question by some scientists and philosophers should in itself be dismissed by those "who retain a primal curiosity about total-meaning," [40] he might well be echoing a sentence written by John Baillie in his classic work, *Our Knowledge of God.* Baillie says: "Just as the intellectual affirmation of God's existence is not of itself sufficient to initiate the soul's communion with God, so the corresponding denial is not of itself sufficient to destroy that communion. After all the central thing in religion is not our hold on God but God's hold on us; not our choosing him but his choosing us; not that we should know him but that we should be known of him." [41] In saying this, Baillie is testifying unapologetically to the reality of grace. There is no reason why we should not carry on with the theological task with whatever competence and courage we are provided, in the confidence that the tradition offers "rich resources of wisdom about our existence and destiny in this modern world even for those who take some pride in being modern." [42]

The third observation we must make has the character of a proposal that is surely unoriginal and inadequate, but which may nonetheless be inevitable for us in our time. Theology and philosophy have been pre-occupied for some time with the problem of finding adequate languages to match the diverse realms of human experience. Although some efforts have been made to impose a single scientific or logical language on all fields of inquiry, it is generally agreed that no such form of explanation has unlimited applicability. We need various types of language to ex-press various areas of experience. Man has the unique ability to approach reality from different points of view. He must, therefore, use alternative modes of expression as he describes phenomena that can be sorted out roughly under the headings of science, art, philosophy, religion, and morality. Within each of these areas, but more particularly with refer-ence to interpretations that bear on the meaning and value of human experience in its total range, men have used languages that are personal and impersonal, historical and ontological, mythological and metaphysi-cal, metaphorical and literal, dramatic and analytical. It is a truism by now to say that the same event can be described in two different ways. Reality is so rich and human experience so complex that we must tell at least two "stories" if we are to avoid reducing our grasp of things to a false simplicity.

If Christians can escape intimidation by the "modern mind," there is good reason for us to continue to tell two "stories" about the world in which grace is experienced. The necessity and style of adjusting factual and impersonal language about the empirical world to metaphorical and personal language about the realm of meaning and value, have pre-occupied some of the most productive contemporary theologians—Karl Rahner, Langdon Gilkey, John Macquarrie, Gordon Kaufman, John Cobb, Jr., Joseph Sittler, Ian Ramsey, and others. But it is doubtful whether any discussion of the theme has surpassed in clarity and sim-plicity the treatment given twenty years ago by J. V. L. Casserley.

Condensed and paraphrased, Casserley's line of thought begins by dis-tinguishing between the analytical story characteristic of the secular mind and the dramatic story characteristic of the Christian mind. If you ask a secular thinker what he believes to be the truth about ultimate reality, he will reply in terms of a theory. He will speak of atoms, molecules, quanta, cells, the absolute, or what not. But always for him reality will be reduced to abstract, impersonal concepts which possess the properties they require to fit the argument, and no others. Behind the dramatic clash of personalities and purposes which we call life and history, the secular thinker sees only the impersonal, serene, and orderly workings of a nicely proportioned scientific, mathematical, or logical scheme.

If you ask a Christian thinker the same question, he will set forth an interpretation of life that is dramatic from top to bottom. However deeply he pushes into the stuff of reality, he continues to find evidence of personality, life, purpose, sacrifice, and love. Behind the personality of man he discerns the personality of God in whose image man is made; behind the drama of time, the drama of eternity. Asked to give an account of the nature of ultimate reality, the Christian will begin by telling a story which presupposes that the *really* ultimate reality consists not of the physicist's particles and waves but of a system or network of personal relationships. Biblical religion above all others has used personality and personal relations as the key to reality.

It must not be supposed that the dramatization of truth is restricted to the child-like primitive mind, whereas the more mature and civilized modern mind prefers to express beliefs only in terms of abstract conceptual theories. The fact is that primitive man had his theories, and modern man makes his "myths." Drama and theory are parallel and alternative means of expression. Most truths and beliefs can be stated either dramatically or theoretically, according to the purpose of the speaker.

Yet the difference between the "stories" is important. Theory always carries with it the suggestion that the reality is impersonal process. Drama, on the other hand, always implies that the reality is ultimately personal. Each story has its appropriate uses. We do not talk about astronomy in personal and dramatic terms (the pathetic fallacy), nor do we describe political struggles in impersonal terms (the apathetic fallacy). But when we want to talk about that which transcends both nature and human history, what language shall we use? Here one's basic convictions make all the difference. The religious man insists that the drama is prior to the process. A modern Christian, committed to the dramatic view of reality, can hold that it is quite credible to think of the chief character in the universe-drama initiating the natural process to serve as the setting of the human and historical drama, and that it is quite incredible to think that the immediate drama of our own existence is a misinterpretation of a more than usually complicated kind of impersonal process.[43]

St. Augustine says that one will either psychologize the cosmos or cosmologize the psyche, and of the two, he preferred the former. It is the personal model, suitably expressed and safeguarded, that makes it possible for us to talk about grace.

2

Grace in the

Christian Tradition

The role that grace has played in the Christian tradition can be described historically. To look at this doctrine as it has journeyed from remote origins to the present day, through many debates and uproars, is a normal and helpful procedure. It can be said in fact that we cannot fully understand and appreciate the theological interpretation of the experience of grace unless we see it in historical perspective. The story of the rise and fall and restoration of the doctrine of grace has often been told by scholars, although such studies have not commanded sufficient attention to produce the widespread benefits within the church that one would hope for.

If, for example, we were to rehearse this long and complicated story, we would start with the idea of grace in the Old Testament, move on to classical Greek, then to the Septuagint, and settle down in the New Testament. There we would trace the word *charis* and the reality it stands for through the Synoptic Gospels, the Acts of the Apostles, the letters of Paul, the Fourth Gospel, and so on. From the New Testament we would move into the early church, East and West, giving special attention to Tertullian, Pelagius, and Augustine. We would look at the elaborate formulations of grace developed during the Middle Ages, especially by Thomas Aquinas and Duns Scotus. We would move on to the Reformation and observe Luther's radical simplification of the traditional theology of grace, and we would associate Calvin with Luther. Arriving at the period of the modern church, we would note the clash between Roman Catholic and Protestant understandings of grace, the opposition between conservative and liberal Protestant theologies, the idea of grace in neo-orthodoxy, and conclude with some barely classifiable contemporary movements in Christian thought.

To pursue the idea of grace through its historical transformations would be an exciting and worthwhile agenda. But alongside the historical approach, there is another way of looking at grace that is equally useful. Grace in the Christian tradition can be examined topically, that is, in terms of its essence, its operation, its goal, its unity, and its scope. Under the heading of any of these topics, one could move freely through periods of time and schools of thought to sketch out the anatomy of grace. Both approaches are in fact important. In this chapter we will look at the central themes of grace against the background of a rather impressionistic sketch of its historical development.

The biblical presentation of grace

There is no one word for grace in the Old Testament as there is in the New Testament, nor is the doctrine fully developed there. But no language excels the Hebrew of the Old Testament in its power to speak profoundly and tenderly of the free and unlimited love of God. The Old Testament speaks of God as gracious towards helpless humanity and often at the same time declares that he is merciful—he is full of compassion, slow to anger, plenteous in mercy, and he will abundantly pardon. But the dominant thought throughout is the amazing choice of Israel by God. God's love for Israel was not merited by any excellence whether of character or achievement on the part of Israel. It is an election of grace and the grace displays itself in the great saving acts of deliverance from Egypt and restoration from Babylonian captivity. It was an undeserved, unsolicited love. Hosea movingly expresses the holy, patient, constant character of the divine love, and its sublime superiority to human love.

To the free outflow of God's love, the Old Testament writers trace the promise to Abraham, the covenant of Sinai, and the oath to David. When the prophets indict the people, they refer to God's loving guidance and protection in the past. God in his generosity forgives sinners, who have no claim against him. God's love is sovereign and he will someday gather his people from among the heathen.

The spontaneity and gracious condescension of this love is often expressed in the Old Testament by the use of the word *chen*. The root meaning of the word is to bend or to stoop. The action passes from a superior to an inferior, and so carries with it the idea of unmerited favor. But the Old Testament term which comes closest to the New Testament conception of grace is *chesedh*, the loyal or steadfast love of God. *Chesedh* does not refer to an act or relation of kindness which is shown indiscriminately, but to one where there is some definite relationship. It is bound up with a two-sided relationship between God and Israel. The whole covenant-society is grounded upon God's everlasting mercy and loyalty.

It is quite clear that *chesedh* and *chen* do not refer to any physical thing or process. *Chesedh* is really the self-giving of God to Israel, God himself in his good will towards men. The grace of God in the Old Testament "is not something separable from God, but is a personal relationship which God establishes between himself and men." [1]

When the writers of the New Testament sought to interpret the experience of God's love, which their ancestors had described as *chen* and *chesedh,* they made use of the Greek word *charis*. As we have seen, classical Greek used this word to signify the human qualities of charm, sweetness, and attractiveness and had extended it to include these same qualities, especially kindness and helpfulness, in the gods. In 250 b.c., the Greek version of the Old Testament, the Septuagint, used the word *eleos,* mercy, to translate *chesedh*. Mercy refers to God's pitying regard for man as weak and helpless and thus bears the meaning of unmerited favor. The Septuagint tends to use the word *charis* in its ordinary Greek meaning.[2]

The New Testament writers fixed upon *charis* rather than *eleos* in order to express the full meaning of *chesedh,* the undeserved, everlasting love of God towards sinful men. There is a special Christian sense of the word *charis* or grace. In the light of God's self-disclosure in Jesus Christ, Christians coined a new sense of the word in order to make it convey something quite unique.

By the grace of God the New Testament means his unmerited love toward man which takes the initiative in freely giving and forgiving, in receiving sinners and seeking the lost, in restoring the fallen and the unworthy, and in giving comfort and strength to the afflicted and oppressed. This grace of God has been revealed in the person and work of Jesus Christ, with whom it is so intimately bound up that it can be called "the grace of our Lord Jesus Christ." Grace is in fact identical with Jesus Christ in person and word and deed. He is the self-giving of God to men. "Later theology thought of *charis* as a divine attribute, but it would be truer to the New Testament to speak of it less abstractly as the divine love in redemptive action. . . . Here the Greek word *charis* seems to pass from the aspect of disposition or good will which bestows blessing to the action itself and to the actual gift, but in the New Testament neither the action nor the gift is separable from the person of the giver, God in Christ." [3]

Jesus is never said to have used the word "grace," but it is quite clear that he was in himself the source of the conception. It is seen in his initiative in seeking the lost, welcoming and forgiving sinners, and in his teaching in such parables as the Lost Coin, the Lost Sheep, the Prodigal Son, and the Laborers in the Vineyard. In his teaching about grace, Jesus emphasized that God's love is not drawn forth by anything in his creatures, but is given spontaneously and utterly without regard to merit. Moreover, he associated the gracious redemptive movement of God with his own person. All of God's kindness is available in Jesus Christ to save men. So there is no distinction between saying that Jesus brings grace and saying that he *is* God's grace. It was above all in his death, especially as interpreted in the Last Supper, that Jesus set forth the grace of God in a new, inward covenant of grace extending the divine forgiveness and renewal and restoration to believers. Jesus asks his disciples to show the same God-like initiative in generosity, in the overcoming of evil with good, in the love of the hostile and undeserving, in the conferring of benefits on those who cannot return them, and in unlimited forgiveness.

The first Christians knew that they lived in the atmosphere of grace. It was clear to them that the saving initiative was with God who had given himself fully to them in the death and resurrection of Christ, and had done so quite apart from any human virtues or plans. But the word *charis* in the New Testament is primarily Paul's word. It is Paul who most thoroughly develops the theme of grace. In the non-Pauline books the word appears only 51 times, and of these occurrences 27 are in Acts and 1 Peter, which are thought to have close links with Pauline teaching. "In contrast with this, 101 instances of it occur in the Pauline corpus of letters, twice as many as in all the rest of the New Testament together, and in much smaller compass. The 101 instances in the Pauline writings occur in 156 pages, and the 51 instances in the rest of the New Testament in 512 pages." [4]

The numbers alone prove that *charis* is a Pauline word, but the rich development he gives the idea also shows that it is central to his understanding of the gospel. Paul sees grace both as the objective activity of God in Christ and as the subjective indwelling power in the Christian life (Galatians 2:20-21).

In writing about the objective reality of grace, Paul describes it as "the grace of God," "the grace of Christ," and "the grace of our God and the Lord Jesus Christ." The variety of phrases makes it clear that "God is the source from which grace comes to man, and that Jesus Christ is the God-ordained means by which this grace reaches man in his need." [5] Because of what God did in Christ, a quite new relation to God has been established, so new that it entails a complete reversal of previous attitudes and ideas (2 Corinthians 5:17).

In the primary sense grace has to do with the act of divine intervention rather than with our receiving of it. At the same time, however, Paul thinks of grace as actualized among men. In Christ grace has really broken through and now operates in this world. In describing the subjective reality of grace or the manner in which it effectively meets human needs, Paul sees grace from two or three points of view.

First, it is related to the reality of salvation. In Paul's teaching grace is related particularly to justification, God's acceptance of man as "righteous" and free from guilt. By the grace of God sinful man may be forgiven. Grace is in no sense a reward for good conduct, but is rather a means of rescuing man from his own deep failure and from his helplessness to overcome it. This theme is treated at length in Romans. In Ephesians the blessing which God confers on man through Christ is called "salvation," rather than justification. But with even greater emphasis salvation is ascribed solely to the action of God's grace. Since man's acceptance with God is all God's doing, it is natural that grace is sharply contrasted with such words as "law" and "works," which describe man's own efforts to achieve status with God.

Second, the grace of God in Christ not only brings salvation, but assigns to those who respond in faith special tasks in the service of God and man. Paul said he was commissioned to be an apostle by the grace of God and since he was both unworthy and inadequate for the task was also given the equipment which he needed as the gift of grace.

God had indeed equipped the corporate life of the church with "gifts of grace" *(charismata)*, of which love was by far the greatest (Romans 12:6-8; 1 Corinthians 12:28-31). Paul understands the inward power or subjective side of grace as the personal working of the risen Christ imparted by the indwelling Spirit of God. This indwelling power is often associated with victory over affliction and weakness and with the gift of spiritual peace.

There is a third aspect of grace which may include the aspects of salvation and service. Paul speaks of "this grace in which we stand" (Romans 5:2) as though the whole status of a Christian in his utter dependence on God in Christ may be described as "grace." That is, a Christian can say that he is "saved" and that he is a "servant." That is his identity. In a world divided between Jews and Gentiles, or Greeks and barbarians, this status was so unique as to lead Paul on occasion to refer to Christians as "a third race."

We have observed that Paul speaks of the objective deed of God in Christ, and of the subjective or indwelling power of Christ in the believer. The grace of God is actualized and made effective for the needs of people. But there are tantalizing suggestions, if no more, that in Paul's thought the grace of God extends beyond the religious and moral needs of people. There are roots, at least, of a view of grace as the redemptive power of the divine working in history. God's deed in Christ gives an entirely new perspective to human history. Grace discloses a new world which has broken through by the cross into our world (2 Corinthians 4:6; 5:17; Colossians 1:13). There is a strain in Paul which sees "the end of the world" as coming soon and catastrophically to usher in the future age of righteousness (1 Thessalonians 4:16ff.). Alongside the apocalyptic view, however, stands another, more existential, picture which sees the end or fulfillment as having already occurred in the death and resurrection of Christ (2 Corinthians 5:17).

But Paul speaks, especially in Ephesians, of God's gracious purpose for the human race. This line of thought is not easy to fit into the apocalyptic and existential formulations. Paul says that "by grace men are not simply reconciled to God but to one another, that the racial barrier between Jew and pagan, which had hitherto divided men, was now abolished in the light of a vast cosmic purpose, and that the reconciliation which had taken place in the church was the initial phase of a world-wide reconciliation to be worked out through God's grace in Jesus Christ. This, the apostle argues, has been in the mind of God from all eternity." [6] The insight which believers now have into this divine purpose ought to warn them against any tendency to isolate redemption from either history or creation, as though reconciliation to God were no more than an extrication of the individual worshiper from material conditions. Paul wants Gentile Christians in particular to appreciate the fact that their election is not casual or individualistic, but "is a vital part of God's eternal movement towards his ends in history." [7]

It is doubtful whether Paul saw history as stretching forward twenty and more centuries. But even though he may not have had a vision of history as a panorama of progressively better things to come, it does seem clear that his confidence in a ground of existence which is eternal, yet is involved in man's historical striving even to the very point of suffering with and for him, implied a faith that history is not meaningless and prompted him to accept his historical responsibilities gladly. To believe that the meaning of life is to be found at least partly in man's involvement in historical tasks and obligations is actually supported by Paul's preaching of the resurrection, which will fulfill and not cancel out the value of individual life and the richness and variety of human action in time.

Paul's thoughts about the cosmic extension of grace, are, if not clearer, at least more frequent and explicit. In thinking of Christ as preexistent, Paul seems to hold that Christ is at the center of the divine order of the universe and is therefore connected somehow with creation. "For us there is one God, the Father, from whom all being comes, towards whom we move; and there is one Lord, Jesus Christ, through whom all things came to be, and we through him" (1 Corinthians 8:6 NEB). Paul is surely affirming that Christ is the vital center for nature as well as for human nature. What the Father is and does in Christ furnishes the ground of the cosmic system and the clue to the ultimate meaning of the universe.

Although Paul sees the world as God's world and alive with reminders of him, he never suggests that the grace revealed person-to-person in Christ can be deduced from any natural phenomena. Yet, alongside Paul's focus on the grace of Christ in meeting the needs of persons, we must place his conviction that the incarnation was not an intervention of the good God in a world which was essentially alien to the divine love. In saying that Christ actualized the reconciling purpose for which history and the universe had been created, Paul implies "that the reconciling aim had been implicit in providence ever since the world began." [8]

We must surely record enthusiastic agreement with Joseph Sittler when, in calling attention to Romans 8:18-25, 35-39; Ephesias 1:2-14; and Colossians 1:15-20, he says: "The grace of God whereby 'Christ Jesus has made me his own' establishes the center. But the center is not the circumference; the circumference of the grace which is redemption is not smaller than that theater of life and awareness which is the creation." [9]

There can be no doubt that the Pauline usage of *charis* became normative for the whole church. There is little in the other New Testament writings to suggest any divergence. There are some passages in Paul and elsewhere which correlate *charis* with the Holy Spirit. But this is understandable since the Spirit is associated so closely with the person of Christ, and is indeed very often interchangeable with Christ. "It is the unanimous testimony of the New Testament that the fatherly love of God expresses itself in that redemptive activity, free and unmerited, which is summed up in the inexhaustible richness of the grace of God and of our Lord Jesus Christ." [10] But it is Paul who has highlighted the freedom of grace, the abundance of grace, the correlation of faith with grace, the effectiveness of grace, and the unity of grace.

The distortion of grace in patristic and medieval theology

In the centuries following the New Testament, almost everything that *could* happen to the doctrine of grace, *did* happen to it. It was at the very least subjected to addition, subtraction, multiplication, and division. This is not to say that the doctrine of grace was ever totally misunderstood, much less that the actual grace of God ceased working out the divine purposes against the cross-purposes of men, including Christian theologians. What happened to the concept of grace could be described in the language of Hebrews 11, where we read of those witnesses to God, "of whom the world was not worthy, wandering over deserts and mountains, and in dens and caves of the earth." This unhappy fate befell other doctrines as well. But the misfortunes of the doctrine of grace were especially troublesome for the future of the church, although not beyond God's power to redeem and restore. In general, the doctrine of grace went astray in the western church when theology deviated from Paul's central themes: the freedom, the abundance, the faith-correlation, the effectiveness, and the unity of grace.

Christian teachers in both the eastern and western sectors of the young church began to think of grace not as the dynamic, freely-given personal presence of God in Christ, but as a form of supernatural assistance given by God to those qualified to receive it. Grace was thought of primarily in terms of man's acts towards God. Grace was something to be acquired as an aid to the work of sanctification. It was detached from the person and work of Christ and was associated with the Holy Spirit, understood in a sub-personal way as a kind of divine energy, akin to electricity, that overcame the power of evil. Thus grace and moral strength came to be thought of as cause and effect, rather than as personal fellowship. Moreover, grace was taken under the wing of the church in an official way. Grace was transferred from God to the Spirit, from the Spirit to the church, and within the church was found mainly in the bishop and in the sacraments.[11] Thus the primitive community became a divine corporation, with a monopoly of the world's supply of grace.

The story should not be given too sinister a cast. The theologians involved were dedicated, decent, and often heroic men, doing their best in difficult circumstances. Paul, after all, had left them with a paradox, when he said: "Work out your own salvation, for it is God who works in you." So free will and guiding grace went side by side in the thought and lives of Christian people.

Some Christians, mainly in the Greek-speaking church, were convinced that freedom of the will is an indispensable condition of all moral life. Sin is a desperate problem, but it is not of the essence of human nature. It is rather a specific decision of the will. Grace, therefore, does not overwhelm or replace man's freedom, but encourages its independent and positive activity. Other Christians, in the Latin-speaking church, saw the human will as mortally wounded, its freedom nearly destroyed, and saw grace as the infusion of a divine energy or force which aids the will in working for the rewards of eternal life. But, whether pessimistic or optimistic about human nature, most theologians saw morality and religion as parallel with each other. The nature and origin of sin, and the relation between free will and grace were not reasoned out.

The division between optimistic and pessimistic views of the human will did not come to a head until the fifth century. By that time Pelagius, a British monk, and Augustine, the North African bishop, were equally alive to the danger of a rather cheap conception of what it means to be a Christian. Pelagius was an ardent, early-day "campaigner for 'moral rearmament.'"[12] Moral freedom is the universal birthright of mankind. Sin has not wiped out God's gift. God in fact has shown men what is good, in the life and teaching of Jesus. Only those who try honestly to live according to the law of Christ will enter the kingdom. Grace is the gift of the gospel which enables Christians to know what they ought to do. It is for sincere Christians to make up their minds to do it! [13]

Augustine saw clearly that this is a return to the religion of good works. It is telling men that they can and must earn their own salvation, qualify themselves for eternal life. Against the Pelagian reduction of grace to the plane of nature, Augustine insisted that grace liberates from a nature that is sinful through and through. Salvation comes only through grace, which heals and restores the will and creates a new nature. Christ, the God-man, brings to the earth not good advice but the powers which give us back liberty to express the new nature. The contrast between Augustine and Pelagius goes back to a two-sidedness in the very conception of salvation. Redemption implies at the same time a sense of moral insufficiency and a sense of moral choice on the part of those who seek it. The believer recognizes his own guilt and appropriates the means of redemption. "According as the one or the other sense is the more active, Christianity appears either as a new creation, a new element in life, changing and ennobling the entire nature, or, as a higher power, calling out all that is best in human nature and freeing it from impediments. . . . The two courses and tendencies are represented in Augustine and Pelagius respectively." [14]

Augustine maintained that grace, the power to recover life, which is really a new gift of life, is entirely the free gift of God. He uses the Latin word *gratia* to describe God's redemptive work. The very word expresses the idea that grace must be free, *gratis*. It is clear that the first move toward salvation must necessarily come from God. Therefore, Augustine calls grace "prevenient" because it comes prior to and apart from any human choosing. If we say that redemption depends on faith, then it must also be said that faith itself is a gift from God.

Grace enables one to turn to God and beyond that it continually upholds the will in living the new life. Augustine therefore calls grace by a second name—"following grace." The believer is dependent on God at every single point for the life of redemption. Augustine also uses the terms "operating" and "cooperating grace" to distinguish between the initial emphasis and the sustaining power, and both are one act of God. But a man is not yet saved nor has he any guarantee of final salvation unless he receives a further gift in addition to "operating" and "cooperating" grace. He must also receive " 'irresistible grace,' which imparts to him the 'gift of perseverance.' This is not given to all, even of those who receive the earlier instalments of grace, but only to those whom God has predestined for eternal salvation, and who are known to God alone." [15]

Augustine's theology of grace, in the brief form in which we have seen it, agrees with Paul insofar as salvation is attributed exclusively to God. But it diverges from Paul insofar as it brings grace only into a loose connection with Jesus Christ and sees the essence of grace not so much in the forgiveness of sins as in the communication of moral power to produce good actions. Thus the religious dynamic consists in an ineffable divine energy rather than in the personal presence of God.

Augustine and Pelagius were the center of a fierce controversy. Pelagius received much support in the eastern church. But Augustine's theology, in one form or another, was approved by several western councils. The official position taken by the Synod of Orange in 529 could be called either semi-Pelagianism or semi-Augustinianism, since it took a middle way through the dispute. It held that God must begin the work of grace, but man has a certain ability to cooperate with God thereafter in producing meritorious works. The Synod agreed with Pelagius in saying that sin has impaired but not destroyed freedom. Yet, it agreed with Augustine in affirming that man requires divine grace for good action. Augustine's notion of "irresistible grace" was ignored, but unconditional predestination was rejected, probably because it would seem to make the church with its means of grace superfluous.

In the thirteenth century the doctrine of grace was given a most elaborate form by the greatest of the medieval teachers, Thomas Aquinas. Most theologians of that age had developed a concept of grace which avoided the extremes of Augustinianism and Pelagianism, even while reflecting the influence of both. Aquinas preserved the priority of God for which Paul and Augustine had struggled. Only God, as the Prime Mover of all things, can convert the sinner. No merit of any kind prior to the gift of grace can make one acceptable to God. But man's free will can cooperate with the "assisting grace" which prepares him for the sheer gift. Since Aquinas retained the older idea of predestination, he held that "assisting grace" is not given to all men. Where it is given, it has nothing to do with merit. Nor does human cooperation have anything to do with merit, since the will of man is moved ultimately by the will of God. But once he is suitably prepared, man receives the gift of "habitual grace" which, through an "infusion of love," enables him to regain the "original righteousness" lost at the Fall, and so becomes acceptable to God.[16] Throughout his subtle treatment of the doctrine of grace, Aquinas failed to make any clear connection between the saving activity of God and Jesus Christ except that Christ alone secures for us the original gift. Thus the action of grace on the soul is not seen in terms of personal presence or influence, but rather as a divine force or energy impinging on the soul, appearing most characteristically in the sacraments.

Paul had, as usual, created certain problems for later theologians. He had said that God's grace and power *for* man became operative *in* man. Thomas Aquinas and his successors looked at the double pattern of grace from every angle and attached various adjectives to the aspects they saw. Their intention was to describe different operations or effects of grace, rather than to say there are different kinds of grace. There is *uncreated grace,* the freely-imparted movement of God; *created grace,* a supernatural habit infused into the soul and constituting the new nature. There is *assisting grace,* by which God turns man towards conversion through his free will. *Operating grace* is grace from the standpoint of divine causation, while *cooperating grace* is the same grace from the standpoint of human consent, and deeds earn merit only as they flow from this grace. *Infused grace* actually gives the power to will the good and bring one to eternal life. *Actual grace* is help given by God to enable a person to avoid sin or to do some particular thing. *Habitual grace,* also called *sanctifying grace,* is the relatively permanent grace which heals the soul and places it in a state of salvation. Prevenient, subsequent, irresistible, sufficient and efficacious grace could be added to the list.

This was surely a complex and subtle chapter in the interpretation of grace. Grace was there both in idea and actuality. But the central themes of the New Testament have been modified almost beyond recognition. God is the source and Christ the bringer of grace, but grace itself is essentially a divine energy which activates the soul, making it worthy of salvation.

The reconception of grace in Reformation theology and beyond

At the dawn of the Reformation Luther was an Augustinian monk. He had in his background both the teaching of Aquinas and the position of Duns Scotus, an opponent of Aquinas. Scotus argued that man is the sovereign ruler of his will. Sin has left the natural freedom of man intact. Grace does not infuse any supernatural habit into the soul. It merely heightens the privately-achieved goodness of man. Human merit is required even for the initial gift of grace, and beyond that the scope of merit broadens out indefinitely.

As Luther pondered the tradition he had inherited, he began to find in Paul the idea that the real blessing of grace is the forgiveness of sins through Christ, not moral transformation qualifying one for salvation. He broke definitely with the conception of grace as a supernatural energy or quality imparted to the human soul, and saw it as the gracious dealing of God himself, quite personally, with men. It is God's mercy and favor in Christ, brought home to us by the Holy Spirit, working in and through the Word or Gospel, in which God himself deals with us and gives himself in Christ to be our own. Grace is simply the loving will of God made alive and revealed in Christ, and the sacraments are efficacious signs of it.[17]

Luther's break with the traditional doctrine of grace grew out of the new insight that came to him during his intensive study of Psalms and Romans. When it struck him that the "justice of God" meant not the power of a sovereign to impose punishment, but the righteousness or right-ness given by God as a free gift, he saw that God need not be seen as man's enemy, but as the One whom man can simply trust. In seeing faith as the sort of trust or confidence one would have toward a dependable and gracious power, Luther was rediscovering Paul's understanding of Christianity. Luther deliberately ignored the philosophical categories that had been taken for granted for a thousand years, and read Paul with a new and radical directness. He saw that communion with God was not the end-result of a laborious climb up the ladder of perfection, but was simply a gift of grace given to the unworthy. It was God's love, not primarily his power or his expectations, that was revealed in Jesus Christ. In this personalistic context, Luther saw grace not as an infused power, but as personal presence in the act of forgiveness. Right-ness with God is calculated not in terms of virtuous acts, but in terms of wholehearted trust.

Luther's directly personal understanding of God's gracious action made it impossible for him to accept the medieval picture of God as the relatively remote and impersonal sovereign of the whole universe whose interaction with men must be conceived in terms of the most elaborate intellectual and ecclesiastical structures. Consequently, Luther broke with the traditional theology point by point as he saw more clearly the implications of a thoroughly personal and unified concept of grace.

The insight that grace is not an infused quality, but the personal presence, favor, and will of God influencing another personal will, is common to Luther, Melancthon, Zwingli, and Calvin. This marks the restoration or resurgence of the long-obscured theology of Paul.

The return to Augustine's ideas of the priority of God and the gratuity of grace, together with the rejection of the element of meritorious works, led the Reformers to focus on the doctrine of justification by faith. In response to this new situation, the Council of Trent (1545-1563) reconsidered the whole subject. As a result, the Augustinian features of the doctrine of grace were retained, but in such a way as would allow a semi-Pelagian or Scotist interpretation. It is plainly said that man's free will alone is insufficient and that without prevenient grace he cannot be justified. But it is equally plain that man has something to contribute to the process of salvation. He can receive or reject out of his own free will the inspiration of the Holy Spirit. Roman orthodoxy thus recognizes prevenient grace, cooperating grace, and the human power of self-determination.

Roman Catholic theology since Trent has continued to see justification as the fruit of divine-human cooperation and regards the sacraments as the instrumental cause of grace seen more or less as an infused substance or some kind of supernatural assistance given to man. In recent years, however, so many new accents have appeared within Catholicism that it is no longer safe to assume that the massive tradition is still representative of its actual theology or that the once typical Roman Catholic-Protestant disagreements are still significant. In the writings of Karl Rahner, Peter Fransen, Jean Daujat, Gregory Baum, and others, grace is said to be synonymous with God's love or personal presence; it is a pure gift; it is God's way of giving himself; it is a single reality; it is universal. Salvation is the divinization of the soul, the freely given introduction into the life of the Trinity.[18]

Since the Reformation, Protestant theology has continued to develop the theology of grace expounded by Luther and Calvin, as that theology has been modified by the impact of science and biblical criticism. The liberal wing of Protestantism was most affected by the intellectual and social revolutions of the last few generations. It modified many classical Christian doctrines, but continued to see grace not as a quasi-physical force, administered by the church, but as the fully personal influence of a loving God, consistent with the moral structure of human personality. Grace is seen as "the free active love of God to sinners, so personally present in Christ as to elicit faith by its intrinsically persuasive content." [19]

Theologians within the so-called neo-orthodox wing of Protestantism recovered the central themes of Paul, Augustine, and Luther as over against the humanitarian Christology and social optimism of many liberals. The recent ecumenical synthesis of many traditions has made the grace of God central and has sought to reinterpret the relation of grace to personal existence, to social and historical process, and to physical nature.

The development through the centuries of the doctrine of grace has not been a uniform movement of thought with balanced attention given to all the components involved in this form of Christian witness. To get even a bird's-eye-view of the ongoing discussion of grace is to see a great variety of ideas, language, and motivations. Themes related to grace take turns being dominant and recessive. In every historical period the interpretation of any doctrine will reflect a multitude of intellectual, moral, social, and political factors.

The authentic marks of grace in the Christian tradition

Against the background of this long history of devotion, controversy, and confusion, can we give a meaning to grace which will be true to the New Testament without neglecting the experience of the centuries? Five authentic marks of grace can be identified within the Christian tradition. These indispensable features of grace can be grouped under five headings: essence, operation, goal, unity, and scope.

The *essence* of grace can be stated quite simply. Grace is God himself in his good will toward men. It is not something separable from God, but is God's personal attitude toward man, his action and influence upon him. For Christians grace is concretely embodied in and communicated through Jesus Christ. This means that grace comes very close to being a synonym for God's love. The words personal, attitude, action, influence, and relationship are almost universally used in recent theology in order to exclude an interpretation that arose in the Patristic and Medieval periods, and may still be present in the popular mind. This is the tendency to conceive of grace in a mechanical, almost semi-material fashion as a mysterious substance or force that could be injected or "infused" into the soul, especially by the sacraments, enabling men to achieve what by nature they could not achieve. Against this, we must say that grace is not an impersonal force, like a charge of electricity or a dose of medicine or a transfusion of blood. It is understandable that many people will think of the soul as something within the body, of sin as a corruption of the soul, and of grace as a healing medicine, because when we ponder the inner life we use physical images and spatial divisions in order to think at all, and we tend to separate and label activities of the personality. Many people in this way use metaphor with no sense of its metaphorical character.[20]

This kind of thinking gave rise to those apparently insoluble problems about the irresistibility of grace, the relation of divine grace to human freedom, monergism and synergism, and so on. The Reformers went a long way toward recovering the exclusively personal New Testament sense of grace, but they were not able to clear away all the long-standing problems that arose from thinking of grace not as God's generosity in personal action, but as a supernatural "something"—strength, assistance, influence—which God gives. There is no sound alternative to thinking of grace simply as a gracious personal relationship, to be thought of on the analogy of the influence of a good father upon his child. "Grace is not something God himself gives us; it is the way God gives us himself."[21] The words "influence" and "relationship" safeguard and express the completely personal character of grace. Both terms imply that one person acts upon another, that Giver and receiver are united in some sense, that one unfolds in the presence of the Other. Grace, as favor or kindness, establishes unity. Love is a unity, and the God who is love creates the unity that is salvation. Influence implies inter-action. The great divergences in Christian teaching about grace have sprung from the tendency to isolate one from another, Giver from receiver, "to consider grace *either* in its source *or* in its direction, *either* as a property or activity of God *or* as a gift which he has conferred upon man." [22]

The *operation* of grace is consonant with its divine and personal character. It is prevenient, that is, God's gracious action precedes man's awareness of and response to it. As God precedes and is prior to his creatures, so his gracious presence is prior to faith as that which prompts it. The first move toward redemption comes necessarily from God, and infant baptism expresses the fact that God's initiative is the source of all blessing. God has always been at work in the world. God loved us when we were still his enemies. Man lives in God's world and God is always there before man because he has created him in love and for love. Wherever the Christian or the church goes in the world, God has been there first.

Grace is not only prevenient, but is also personal. God's gracious presence or love evokes from the believer the response of faith. This response is evoked or elicited from us by the persuasion of our wills, not by the infusion or injection into us of a new faculty for reception. Grace calls for faith, but does not compel it. "Grace *cannot* compel, if it be the activity of love, for love and compulsion are incompatible." [23]

Since grace is personal, it is also free, since it is characteristic of personal action that it is truly self-expressive, that is, free. Grace is free in the sense that it is unmerited.[24] It is given freely, not earned, as Paul says repeatedly. The good will of God is not something that we can earn by our merits. It comes freely to those who are most unmeritorious and unlikeable, as the stories of Zacchaeus and the prodigal son make clear. The good will of God is extended without any conditions, except the condition that it be accepted. Grace is gracious.

Grace is free in the sense that it is unrestricted. Paul links grace with the mission to the Gentiles, thus indicating its unrestricted nature, its universality. God's gracious favor is not directed only to Israel, but to all mankind. "His redeeming activity in Christ transcends not only the deep division between Jew and Gentile, but all divisions whatsoever of race, class, culture, creed, or sex." [25] In Christ love goes forth ignoring and overcoming all conventional barriers erected between good men and wicked men. "Behold, he eats with sinners and publicans." And when this love of Christ grasped Paul, he said: "There is no longer Jew or Gentile." Not only does grace move unselectively through human society, but it also courses freely through all the forms and structures of creation, testifying to the power and goodness of the gracious Creator.

Grace is free in the sense that it is unpredictable. Grace is not only gracious, but gratuitous. It twists and turns and is full of surprises. Since it is God's grace and not ours, it comes to us on his terms. To say that grace can be manipulated or managed from the human end is always a grievous mistake. It comes to us as a gift. Therefore we can never claim it as a right or set up proper rules for its working. So many things about grace are surprising and unexpected that many of us are tempted to tamper with the project in the interest of sound administration.

The *goal* of grace is consonant with the essence and operation of grace. Grace is favor, kindness, generosity, love, and bestowal. Bestowal of what? Of personal relationship. Grace is not a means to the achievement of some end other than itself. Grace is ultimate and bestows itself in ever fuller measure, until at long last it comes to completion in grace unlimited, which is to see God face to face, the fullest amplification of personal relationship. That is precisely what religion is—communion or fellowship with God. Grace aims at fulfillment. It is the operative power of God's personal action, moving us toward that which God intends us to be. The purpose of creaturely existence is that each of God's creatures achieve the fullest excellence of which its nature is capable. Any thwarting of fulfillment, therefore, is really a wrong against the basic purpose of creation itself. But there is such a thwarting and human nature can be set in sharpest opposition to the holy and fulfilling Spirit of God. But the unholy spirit which is *in* human nature is not *of* human nature. It can be cast out and replaced by the Holy Spirit. When that happens, the corruption of the flesh is healed, and man becomes what in the purpose of God he is meant to be—truly and fully human. Within human experience, the aim of grace is to bring about the kingdom of God, a universal community in which the love revealed in Christ seeks the fulfillment of all things in such a relationship to one another that what flows from the life of each enriches the life of all. Beyond human experience, the "resurrection of the body" means that "this mortal" will not be lost. It will "put on" immortality. Things earthly will not be abolished, but fulfilled.

The *unitary* character of grace is fundamental to an understanding of its scope. First, there is only one grace. We must beware of thinking that there are various kinds of grace. All grace is divine favor, and it is one. Its operation is manifold and it is a matter of convenience that the several purposes and results of the bestowal of grace should be differentiated by a variety of terms.[26] But the biblical revelation of the oneness of God makes it clear that a single, undivided will lies behind our many words. The Christian idea of God is not a mere jumble of contradictory elements. It is centered about the grace of God that is known to us in Jesus Christ, and all else that we say about God should be united to and expressive of this central concept of love. "The unity of God implies that there can be no conflict between the different forms of the divine activity towards the world and the human race. Christians have sometimes spoken of God's action as though his love and his wrath, his mercy and his judgment, were opposed to each other." It has also been thought that God's attitude to his creatures changes from a mood of severity to one of mercy. "It is true that the vividly pictorial imagination of Hebrew prophets and teachers has encouraged such ideas. . . . Such language is due to the fact that the relations of God with man can only be expressed in terms of analogy with human experience. The final revelation of God in the New Testament shows that his love and judgment, wrath and mercy are not opposed. They are aspects of the same unchanging attitude of God." We must see that God's attributes are not at variance with each other. "We must not suppose that the death of Christ was a means by which God's justice could be reconciled with his mercy, nor may we think that his justice is opposed to his forgiveness, so that the former has to receive satisfaction before the latter can operate freely." [27]

Secondly, just as there is only one grace, so it must be said that every work of God is grace. These are two ways of saying the same thing. God's love is over all his works and there is no part of the divine activity in calling the universe into being and in sustaining and restoring finite existence which falls outside the scope of love or which can be called by any other name. It is true that in much Christian thought the themes of power, judgment, and love have seemed to be in tension and rather independent theologies of each have been developed. Scholastic theology has always sought to adjust the tension through compromises which distort the true character of each theme.

But if the attitude of God is single and unchanging, and if his attributes are not at variance with each other, then it follows that all of God's actions must be seen as expressions of an ultimate and unified thrust—the power of love. Therefore, "every affirmation about God becomes an affirmation about his love. Nothing can be said about God, his power, his opposition to evil, or anything else, which is not in the last analysis a statement about his love. . . . No other divine attributes can be coordinated with love, nor can these express something that would cancel love." [28] We should see God's opposition to evil, which we call "judgment" or "wrath," as his love maintaining its unbroken opposition to everything that ruins the beloved. God's love is not sentimental, but purifying and renewing. Rather than seeing the justice and mercy of God as expressive of a dualism in God's nature, it would be more accurate to say that the judgment of God is instrumental to salvation. For God can be my savior *only because* he is my judge. If God were not the ultimate critic of the evil I do, he would be involved in that very evil and would himself need to be saved. And if God needs to be saved from complicity in the selfishness, injustice, folly, and even the peccadilloes of life in a fallen world, then he can hardly be *my* savior. It is of vital importance, therefore, to say that every work of God is a work of restoring love, and that grace means the whole of God's love in action.

Now we are in a position to look at the *scope* or pervasiveness of grace, the way in which every work of God is the expression of one grace. As we do so, we will also see what is meant by saying that to explain the doctrine of grace is to give an outline of the entire Christian religion.

We speak of the grace of creation and preservation. All created things owe their existence to God. He is the sole source of all reality. But the world could no more continue in existence without God than it could take its origin without him. We literally move and have our being in God's grace. In one of his sermons, Augustine said that before we were created we neither deserved nor desired anything, either good or bad, and therefore "it is grace by which we have been created." Grace, therefore, becomes also a word for our thanksgiving to God as when we say "grace" at the table.

We speak of the grace of election and covenant. In Old Testament times, the god of the Moabites was bound by nature to his people, not by choice. But the relationship of Israel to God was totally different. This was not of nature but of grace. The people depended on God, but God in no sense depended on them. He had chosen them and he could reject them. They were bound to him, not by a natural tie, but by a covenant relationship. God of his own sovereign grace elected Israel. The idea of grace more than any other idea binds the two Testaments or Covenants together into a complete whole, for the Bible is the story of the saving work or grace of God.

We speak of the grace of Christ, the grace of the incarnation and of the atonement. In Paul's language, grace means incarnation and atonement. "God was in Christ" and "Christ died for the ungodly." Here is favor shown by a superior to an inferior. In Jesus Christ God has "for us men, and for our salvation" come "down from heaven," to call "not the righteous, but sinners." Thus, we see in Christ that "God is love." That is the "nature" of God. That is the "substance" in which, according to the Creed, Christ is one with the Father. In Christ God has spoken to his creatures, and God's word in Christ is the same as his word with which he called creation into being. It is intriguing to place the first chapter of Genesis and the first chapter of John alongside each other and to suppose that the author of the Fourth Gospel is deliberately rewriting the Genesis story. God created the world by speaking a "word." He externalized in creation the innermost thought in his mind. A "word" is essentially an uttered thought, a communicated meaning. What intelligible and operative meaning did God utter in the "word" of creation? The Fourth Gospel sees a connection between creation and incarnation. For the innermost purpose in the mind of God when he embarked on the experiment of creation has now been embodied in a human life. Jesus Christ is what God "said" at creation. "In that life . . . we have seen what God was really aiming at in making man, in making the universe. . . . It is the very life of God himself expressed as fully as it can be expressed in terms of a human life." [29]

We speak of the grace of the Holy Spirit. In the Epistle to the Hebrews, the Holy Spirit is called "the Spirit of grace." It is through the Holy Spirit that the grace of Christ is mediated to men. In both Scripture and Creed, the Holy Spirit is represented as the Lord and Giver of life. He is the life-giving presence, power, energy, activity of God in the world and the lives of men. Indeed, he is God himself, for God *is* Spirit. The Holy Spirit is also known as "the Spirit of Jesus." That is, the Spirit is the mode by which Jesus is present in and among his people, now that his bodily presence has been withdrawn. The operations of the Spirit are directed to the ministry of Christ's reconciling work to all the world.

We speak of the grace of faith. Faith alone, in the sense of personal trust, is needed for man to lay hold of the sonship which is freely offered to him in Christ. Grace is the ground of justification, but faith is the means by which man catches hold of what is offered him. As Luther said: "Faith is a lively, reckless confidence in the grace of God." But grace is so all-encompassing that we regard faith itself as a gift of grace. Faith is a gift in that it is evoked by prevenient grace; it is not generated by man's willing.

We speak of the grace of justification. Little need be said to make the point that justification does effectively formulate the essential content of the gospel. The repentant sinner who trusts the promise of God is graciously brought into a right relationship with him.

We speak of the grace of forgiveness. God visited us with his grace "while we were yet sinners" and forgave us. The righteousness which man cannot achieve for himself is offered to him by God in Jesus Christ. The work of Christ is a work of love, and it is love that offers the gift, and prompts man to trust that he has received it.

We speak of the grace of renewal. We are united with God by "the grace of our Lord Jesus Christ." But the new relationship to God and men is also grace. It is "the grace in which we stand." To be made "new creatures in Christ" means that we receive the gift of a new life, in which grace becomes not only mercy but power. Christ can do nothing *for* us if he does not also do something *in* us. Paul testified that grace had become a power in his life, seeking to accomplish its universal aim through him. In one of his sermons, Augustine said: "The Way itself has come to thee; arise and walk. Walk I mean not physically but morally." Grace at work in men's lives produces a similar grace in them. There can be no good news of Christ apart from the possibility that in some measure the life of love can actually be lived on this dark and bloody battlefield of human history.

We speak of the grace of the church and its ministry, and of the Word and sacraments, the "means of grace." The church is the "body of Christ," who is incarnate grace, the embodiment of God's will. Thus, the preaching of the Word and the administration of the sacraments are acts performed by Christ himself through the instrumentality of his body. Through the "ministry of reconciliation" God continues the work of Christ's incarnation, death, and resurrection. Were it not for the church with the Word and sacraments, the work of God in Jesus Christ would scarcely be more than an ancient tale.

We speak of the grace of final consummation. The atonement which Christ has accomplished has as its ultimate goal the new creation, "a new heaven and a new earth," in which all things are recreated in him, and all men and all things will be restored to perfect harmony through the perfect love of God.

Looking back, we have described grace in terms of many ideas. Although these ideas can and must be related to each other in a careful and consistent way, the end result of our thinking is not a neat system. The grace of God is too large for our finite minds. We can but dimly apprehend one aspect of it at a time. The full reality and mystery of grace strikes us as something incredible and impossible, yet made possible and actual in Jesus Christ our Lord.

3

Grace and Creation

An awareness of the character and comprehensiveness of grace has the effect of stretching one's mind and heart and of driving one in the direction of inclusiveness. To focus on grace as the single and all-embracing work of God leaves one quite dissatisfied with exclusiveness of any kind. Exclusiveness may be forced on us by circumstances or by human actions, and in a tangled world both courtesy and strategy may require exclusiveness, yet we know that it is contrary to grace and ought by all means to be overcome.

The drive toward inclusiveness shows itself in many tendencies in the life and faith of the church. In theology it is to be seen in the desire to recover the sense of grace in certain broad areas toward which much of Christian thought has been rather negative—physical nature, the structures of human personality, the dynamics of social process. If many Christians have not ignored or ruled out these areas, they have at least regarded them with suspicion as being inferior or hostile to the specifically "Christian" and "spiritual" operations of divine grace. But there is a marked disposition today to reconsider the scope of grace and to discern the gracious presence of God in areas often thought to be merely natural, sinful, or worldly.

"Creation" as a theological word

We have described grace as the single and all-embracing work of God. There is no part of the divine activity in calling the universe into being and in sustaining and restoring finite existence which falls outside the scope of love or can be called by any other name. If grace means the whole of God's love in action, then grace is the central and the most comprehensive thing we can say about God. The word "creation" comes very close to matching grace in its breadth. The belief that the whole world and all that is therein is the creation of God is proclaimed on the first page of the Old Testament. But biblical scholarship has concluded that this belief belongs historically not to the infancy but to the maturity of Hebrew faith. The people of Israel were conscious, first of all, of being members of the nation whom God had rescued from slavery and called to be his own people. Gradually they came to see that the God who had redeemed them was sovereign over all nations. His rule was seen to be universal *because* that over which he rules derives its very existence from him. Belief in God who is the creator of the universe was derived, as a logical inference, from the primary experience of God as redeemer. In the order of biblical thinking, creation-faith followed after exodus-faith as Israel saw that the same divine action at work in the deeds of salvation is the secret of the entire created world.

When the Christian creeds place profession of belief in God as the Maker of all things before the affirmation of belief in God as the redeemer of the world, they are following a logical order. It is often the case that the order in which we come to know things is the reverse of the order in which we seek to explain things. The logical order of explanation usually begins with the most comprehensive ideas and moves step by step to more specific elements which fit within the wider framework. Thus the belief in the God of Israel and the Father of Jesus Christ took its place within the wider faith in the God who is the creator of the universe. God's relation to creation is not, therefore, the starting point, but the widest perspective of biblical faith. It is with respect to this unusual breadth that the words "grace" and "creation" are correlative.

Nature, world, universe, creation—these are all comprehensive words. By "world" we mean the total environment that all men have in common. We use the word "nature" to designate the whole economy or system of observable phenomena and things, including man, existing in time and space, and held together in a field or web of cause-and-effect relationships. When we speak of the "universe" we have in mind the most ultimate context of life, an encompassing reality of stupendous proportions and of incredible age. The term "creation" is similar to the other comprehensive words since it too refers to the general cosmic order, the aggregate of all observable or potentially observable entities. But "creation" is a theological word, for it is at the theological level that nature is recognized as the realm of created things. Faith affirms that this world in which we live has its being only because of God's activity, and that it will eventually be brought through his activity to the goal originally intended when "in the beginning" he made it. Faith is aware of a dimension of depth in nature which is not empirically discerned and thus not the concern of scientific inquiry. To speak of "nature" as "creation" implies that everything there is issues from the being, the power, and the will of God. If the one Source of reality has a single, undivided will of love, then it follows that "creation" is a realm of grace, since grace is the whole of God's love in action. The totally affirmative character of grace makes the created order a totally positive concept.

An affirmative reappraisal of the world as the sphere of God's gracious action is dominant in recent interpretations of the doctrine of creation,[1] as well as in longer works of systematic theology.[2] This note has never been completely absent from the Christian tradition, although British theology, since the publication of *Lux Mundi* in 1889, has been most consistently positive in its assessment of the natural order.[3] But the new accents, both more comprehensive and more dynamic, in the treatment of the doctrine of creation could hardly have emerged apart from a consensus that the doctrine itself must be distinguished from a "religious" account of the early history of our planet.

Interest in the origin, nature, and operations of the physical world is ancient and universal. The biblical view of "origins" was inherited by the early church along with Greek philosophy and science. Many elements were combined to form the traditional Christian doctrine of creation. This is a complicated chapter in the history of western thought. But it can be said that confusion and conflict with respect to the idea of creation were largely due to the *form* in which this doctrine entered the modern world.[4]

Throughout Christian history, ancient cosmology, an account of physical origins, and religious affirmation, a witness to the ultimacy and transcendence of God, were woven together into the one Christian belief that God created the world. In the New Testament, the Church Fathers, and medieval theology the religious affirmation was predominant. To believe in creation meant to acknowledge the priority, majesty, sovereignty of God. In the Gospels we see this religious affirmation coupled with a sensitiveness to the beauty and worth of the physical world. Jesus takes as his themes the simplest events: the sowing of fields and the growth of plants, the breaking of bread and the catching of fish. He asks his hearers to see in them signs of the care and purpose of the Creator.

Due to many unhappy circumstances, the glad acceptance of nature seen in the Gospels became in the days of the persecuted church and the collapsing Roman empire, a renunciation of the physical realm as evil. The order of nature was thought to be under the dominion of Satan. Insofar as theologians of the ancient and medieval periods thought about the earlier history of the universe at all, they assumed an anthropomorphic shaping of the earth and their concepts were drawn largely from Egyptian and Greek cosmology. The church did nothing to encourage a careful and reverent study of the natural order. Students of nature were forced to do their research outside of, and under suspicion from, institutional religion.

But when valid scientific accounts of the earlier history of our universe began to appear in the last two or three centuries, most churchmen responded by emphasizing the cosmological strand in the traditional doctrine. It is only in quite recent years that Christians have rather generally seen the importance of separating out the ancient cosmology from the profound religious affirmation contained in the biblical account of creation.

Before this separation was accomplished, the church took a wrong turn, without thereby being guilty of stupidity or of wickedness. The fact that so many Christians bitterly opposed any scientific hypothesis that seemed to conflict with a literal reading of Genesis indicates that in their minds the traditional account of creation was a *factual* record, a theory of secondary causation which had as its subject matter semi-scientific information about the date, order, and method of the process of creation. As such it provided a revealed alternative to scientific theories of natural causation. By presenting Genesis as a record of facts about the origins of the earth and man, the church made it almost inevitable that those who regarded Genesis as "good science" would turn their backs on the modern natural sciences, while those who regarded the biblical account as "bad science" would simply reject Genesis as ancient mythology.

There were, however, mediating theologians, especially toward the end of the nineteenth century, who would turn their backs neither on science nor on the Bible. They saw the biblical writings as having proceeded from both God and man. They held that the biblical writers accurately interpreted the nature and will of God but expressed their religious message in a variety of literary forms, including poetry and symbolic language, and within the framework of the world-picture then current. This school of thought saw the message of Genesis as a *religious* message. It tells us that "man and the world are dependent on God, that the created order is purposeful and good, and that God is free and sovereign." This religious message, expressed through the medium of ancient cosmology, is "compatible with various scientific theories of how the details of creation were and are being accomplished." [5] These theologians found it possible to accommodate a divinely-guided process of evolution within the Christian perspective. They tended to think of evolution as part of the mechanism of creation. Faith apprehends the invisible background and science observes the visible foreground. A distinction can and must be made between *factual* statements about the physical universe and *religious* statements about the meaning of human existence under God. Religious affirmations can be detached from the ancient forms of thought and can be coupled with whatever cosmology is scientifically most tenable at the moment.

Langdon Gilkey remarks that "if there is anything upon which contemporary theology agrees, it is that the biblical belief in creation derives from an answer to this 'religious' question, rather than from an answer either to a scientific or a metaphysical question." The religious question to which the doctrine of creation speaks is the question about the goodness and meaning of our life here and now as finite, transient creatures. "It asserts above all that our present existence is in the hands of the One Almighty Lord whom we know as love." [6] The doctrine of creation is a statement about grace since it expresses in theoretical language those positive religious affirmations which bear on our conviction that we can trust in the source of all being.

The priority of God

The idea of creation cannot be treated here in all its complexity, but certain elements of the doctrine which give clear expression to the grace of God may be underscored. To say that God is the creator of the universe is to say that God is prior to creation. The priority of God is called "transcendence." This means that in contrast to beings whose lives are derived and dependent, God is the self-sufficient and independent source of all things. He "exists" in a different way than do all the objects and persons we know. He is eternal and cannot gain or lose existence as we do through the passage of time. We must think of God "not only as 'beyond' the world, but even more as 'outside' the world in his real nature." Such language "implies a *separation* between God and the world of finite things, as well as a *difference* between God and that world. . . . In his essential nature, God is 'outside' the world in the sense that at no level is the world God or God the world." [7]

Such spatial images and abstract statements appear to make God completely remote and totally unrelated to the world as we know it. There is a deep concern felt by many churchmen today that God should be seen in closer relation to the temporal, imperfect world of human affairs. But the otherworldly strain in theology does not remove God from the world. Talk about the "beyondness" of God, while it uses the language of locality, simply says that man's life with God is a relationship that is beyond place. "The 'otherness' of the other world is not that of a structure standing over against this world." [8] It is the "otherness" of our transaction with God, described in symbols which transcend locality altogether. No image, parable, or dogmatic definition can suffice to convey God's reality. But our experience of God, while it happens within the world, has a "beyondness" or "otherness" that points to the supreme and independent reality of the One who meets us as we reach out for support.

No creature shares in this essential "otherness" or divinity. Nothing transcends the passage of time to share God's eternity. The "difference" or "distance" of God from the world is the basis of his power to launch it into existence and to come into it as One who rules and redeems it. We cannot think of grace apart from the transcendence of God. "If grace is to be found anywhere, it must come from beyond the world of things and the society of human beings, though it may indeed come through these. . . . 'God' is the word which the religious man uses for the transcendent source of grace." [9]

Many Christians have recently reacted against the classical notion of divine transcendence on the ground that it makes God appear to be absent, remote, or unavailable. They have stressed God's immanence or presence *in* the world. But an emphasis on God's priority or transcendence is indispensable. The affirmation first arose out of the concrete religious experience of encountering the eternal "Thou" who saves man. But the affirmation took its shape and occupied its place in a theological structure in response to alternative religious views that reduced or domesticated the divine to the level of merely natural forces. Thus, the theological formulation was never an end in itself. It was always the expression of a deep religious intuition. For religion is essentially communion with God, a practical and personal experience of salvation. The affirmation of God's transcendence is necessary because only a transcendent God can *save* his creatures. God must be present in the world if we are to meet him there, but he must be present as *God,* the One who is from beyond the world, if we are to trust our lives to him and to him alone. It has become very important today to say that the encounter with God takes place in the center of life and not just at the edges. But if faith is to be spoken of as a response to God's actions, then we must be able to speak of God and his acts in a way that is not simply a transcription of statements about *man's* response. The independence of God *from* the world, and his sovereign freedom *over* the world, is the indispensable condition for the kind of relatedness *to* the world in revelation, in judgment, and in salvation of which the Bible speaks.

That the transcendence of God was never meant to stand by itself as a logical inference or as an intimidating article of belief is clear from the effort the Christian tradition has made to maintain the closest possible connection between the ideas of creation and redemption. These two ideas are "mutually dependent in the most intimate way; neither one can be made intelligible, or even affirmed, without the other." The absolutely basic Christian affirmation is that Almighty God had come in Jesus Christ to save men. Thus, "the identity of God the Creator and God the Redeemer, of the almighty power of existence with the love of Christ, is the theological axis of the Gospel of good news."[10] Langdon Gilkey goes on to argue that if these doctrines are separated, "then the almighty power of existence remains a cold and forbidding mystery, and life is dominated by fate, by sin, and by death. Correspondingly, the love that reveals itself in Jesus has only the pathetic frailty of a defeated liberal . . . the astounding union in God of creative power and redeeming love . . . was the basis for the Christian confidence in victory over all forms of evil."[11]

Although the belief in God as Creator of the universe was derived from belief in the reality of salvation, and is thus dependent on it in a chronological sense, there is a sense in which the doctrine of creation is logically or theologically prior to all other Christian beliefs. It is the foundation on which other doctrines are based because "it affirms what Christians believe about the *status* of God in the whole realm of reality: He is the *Creator* of everything else." We recount the many works of God. But we indicate *"who* has done these things through the important affirmation that the Creator of all has done them." [12] This is what is meant by saying that God is prior to the world. It is a *priority of being* which is discerned through experience, is demanded by thought, and is expressed in theology.

The priority of God to creation is expressed in a dramatic and pictorial way in the first chapter of Genesis. God confronts this world in sovereign freedom. He is not identified with any part or power of nature. He is completely independent from the watery chaos. His only connection with the material world is through the imperative of his spoken word. "There is no wrestling with primeval matter, no struggle against other divine beings, as in the Babylonian myth." [13] Even the stars, which were considered gods by other ancient peoples, were the creation of God. The creator comes forth in freedom out of his hidden being in order to draw man into communion with himself within a world of space and time.

There is a sense in which the doctrine of creation is really very simple and portable. It can easily be carried about in one's head without recourse to theological or scientific textbooks. *Whatever exists, does exist because God existed first.* That is the essence of the doctrine. Nothing that an investigation of the physical world can say about it can be anything other than a description of that which exists subsequent to God's decision to create. Even the synthesis of life in a laboratory would be nothing other than the correlation of pre-existent materials, and it is precisely the priority of the Creator to such materials that is affirmed by the doctrine of creation.

How the world has come to be what it is now is not a question the biblical writers can answer for us. But affirmation of the doctrine of creation does not rest on any particular theory about the mechanics of nature's working, nor is it destroyed by any such theory. It is advisable, therefore, for Christians to reject the so-called "gap theory." [14] It is a serious mistake to hold that faith in God as the Creator of the universe depends on the discovery in the world-process of mysterious gaps that cannot be explained by science. To hold this view would imply that the gaps in our scientific knowledge serve to make room for belief in God. It would then follow that as scientific knowledge gradually fills in the gaps, belief in God would become progressively less necessary. G. W. H. Lampe comments: "On this view the relevance of harvest festivals to the life of the farmer would become steadily less as agricultural knowledge increased, and would probably vanish away altogether as soon as physical science devised a satisfactory method of controlling and organizing the weather. Belief in the Creator . . . is an attitude . . . which the Christian adopts toward the world as it actually is, by whatever sort of process it has emerged and however completely its mechanism can be explained by the scientist. The farmer's devotion to God in an unscientific age may indeed be evoked by a sense of dependence upon an unseen power for all the processes of nature which he himself can neither fully understand nor control; but the Christian farmer would experience a deeper sense of dependence upon God, in the sense of a calling to fulfill, obligations to perform, and a Father's love to which to respond, even if the very soil of his fields were produced synthetically and he himself, or perhaps the Ministry of Agriculture, controlled the weather." [15]

The priority of grace

To say that God in his essential being is prior to the created order is also to say that grace is *prior* to creation, since grace defines the nature and activity of God. We express this truth by saying that God is the "Father Almighty." The biblical record of God's revelation indicates that the God who reveals himself as Father must be in a relationship of Fatherhood to the whole world and everything within it. The care of the Father for the birds and the rest of animate and inanimate creation is mentioned by Jesus (Matthew 7:26). Thus, the "almightiness" of the Creator is a "fatherly" almightiness. Or, to put it another way, *nature is included in grace.* Grace is the *ultimate context* within which all created objects, persons, and events have their being. The created world can have only one context since God is one, not many, and since God's will is a single gracious will, not a jumble of conflicting purposes.

To say that God in his power and goodness is prior to the world is to say that the world is radically dependent. Not only has God brought the world into being by an act of his will, but his presence and power sustain in being the order which he has created. The earliest creation-stories devised by the Babylonians describe creative activity as a conflict against hostile forces. The idea that creation is a cosmic struggle left its mark on many Old Testament passages (Psalm 74:12-17; Isaiah 51:9). Yet, in the later forms of the story there are no hostile powers with whom God has to struggle. The element of conflict has been eliminated and the whole creative process is the result of the deliberate purpose of God. Out of the primary chaos order and life emerge at the command-ment of God.

In Isaiah 40-56, it becomes very clear that "the dualistic idea of a conflict between the Creator and some hostile power co-existent with him-self was untenable." [16] The phrase "creation out of nothing," although not used by the biblical writers, expresses what is implicit in their witness. It says that "God is the sole source of everything. There is no substance, such as matter, which exists independently of the creative will of God . . . God was 'there' before there was matter or a world or anything else except God himself." [17] Thus, the idea of creation "out of nothing" does not tell us *how* God made the world, but only *that* God made it. He did not struggle against other divine forces or give shape to already existing substance. If he had done only that, he would not be an abso-lute creator and the union of power and love which is essential to the good news of a gracious and saving entry into the world would be lost and with it all hope of finding life trustworthy.

The deep religious insights in the first chapter of Genesis express the convictions that God is the sovereign power upon which all nature de-pends, that God has guided the development of the world through all its stages, and that the world is the creation of a good God and is itself good. The statement that God made the world "out of nothing" is a necessary implicate of monotheism and is consistent with the first com-mandment. But it also says that "the creation of the world is an act of God's outgoing love, and therefore must be entirely free: nothing can have 'obliged' God to create. He could have done without the world if he had so willed." [18] The free and gratuitous character of God's creative act is said by H. H. Farmer to be "a way of rejecting once and for all any notion that the world is somehow God, or even a bit of God, or a sort of unconscious emanation from God like the filament from the belly of a spider, or a by-product of some procreant life force which has no awareness of what it is doing or where it is going. . . . The world is in existence, and we are in existence, because God in the fullest possible sense of the term intended it and us." [19]

If grace is prior to creation, it follows that the world and our life in it is sheer gift. It is of grace since God was not compelled to create but did so freely, and we ourselves had nothing to do with it. Not one of us, from the first man on this earth to the baby born this morning, has brought himself into existence or equipped himself with such powers of body and mind as he possesses. Still less have we provided for ourselves the vast and varied resources of the world in which our life is set.

The created order as God's self-expression: the goodness and intelligibility of the world

God is prior to creation and independent of it, but he did create. Since God is the only Creator, the created order is God's *self-expression* in some mode other than his own substance. Creation is not God. It is created reality that has been given independence by its Maker. The doctrine of the goodness of creation follows from the belief that creation is God's self-expression.

The goodness of creation flows from the undivided good will of the transcendent Creator. Nothing in creation can be intrinsically evil since it comes from a single good source. That is to say that everything in creation is essentially good. There are indeed bad things in this world, but the badness of a bad thing cannot be the work of God, nor can it be the essence of that thing. A bad thing is always a good thing spoiled. No created thing is evil "by nature," nor is it essentially separate from God or removed from his control. The doctrine of the goodness of creation was used by the early church to rule out any tendency to ascribe the origin of evil to material existence as such or to define salvation as the escape of the spirit from the conditions of personal existence. Christians see nothing evil in the limitations of earthly existence. It is not limitation as such that is evil, but the resentment of limitation. Christians should avoid the practice of drawing a line through the center of reality such that everything above it—the spiritual—is good, while everything below it—the material—is bad. The New Testament specifically forbids such a practice (1 Timothy 4:1-5).

The goodness of creation flows also from the continuing and intimate presence or immanence of the Creator in all objects, persons, and events.

God is present "within" the world in his wisdom and power just as he is "beyond" the world in his priority. Were God to cease to be in things, sustaining and recreating in every moment, they would simply cease to be. So long as things exist at all, they have an essential relation or point of contact with God. God the Creator is inescapably present in all of nature and in all of mankind.[20] The dependence of the world upon God for both its existence and its sustenance is the common belief of the biblical writers. Just as the creative act of God brought the world "out of nothing," so his sustaining act keeps it from relapsing into the nothing from which it came. "But the acts which we so distinguish are not to be separated. God's power is constantly active. To the charge of violating the Sabbath day on which God 'rested from his works,' Jesus answers: 'My Father has never yet ceased his work, and I am working too.' (John 5:17 NEB). God's world is still in the making." [21]

To say that God is perpetually present and active in nature is to speak of "continuing creation." This is a thoroughly biblical idea. To think of creation as continuing rather than as instantaneous, makes it possible to interpret evolution as the means of creation. To think of God as a watchmaker standing over against his finished product is a mistake. Today the world known to science is dynamic and incomplete. Ours is an unfinished universe which is still in the process of appearing. We see nature as a single continuous process in which there are threshold transitions from matter to life and thence to mind and society. There is flexibility as well as structure in nature. We know that the activity of a species does influence its own evolutionary development. This is especially true on the human level where man's thoughts and decisions have much to do with the direction of his evolution. In all of this, the Creator is an integral and sympathetic participant in the process, yet not simply a part of the process itself. Man is God's co-creator, cooperating with God in the completion of an unfinished universe. Eric Rust suggests that this unfinished aspect of the universe is the area in which human freedom can operate.[22]

If the transcendent and immanent God of grace is present to and in all things, then finite reality is good. If created reality is good, then no creature or thing is deserving of scorn or hate because all have received their existence from the same loving will. As C. S. Lewis put it: "God likes matter; He invented it." He not only invented it, he uses it. God uses material things to convey the reality of his grace—bread, wine, and water in the sacraments, human flesh in Jesus Christ, wood and iron in the cross, paper and ink in the Scriptures, moments of time in the performance of deeds of love. Matter is not alien, but is essential, to God's ways with men. The incarnation is the paradigm or supreme illustration of God's use of materiality. "In the incarnate Christ all the processes of nature are summed up and fulfilled. The various levels of the evolutionary process minister to the creative emergence of man, and each of them is constitutive of his psychosomatic wholeness. The chemistry and structure of the physical order, the organic patterning and genetic ordering of animate things, the instinctive behavior, the memory and the capacity of psychic beings to learn—all are built into the structure of man with his self-transcendent spirit." [23]

In asserting the goodness of our natural environment we should avoid a false sentimentality and should not ignore the cruel and darker side of nature. Yet, amidst the travail of creation there is the tender nurture of life. We experience God's grace in the order of the stars and seasons, the rhythm of work and rest, the repeated miracle of birth, growth, death, and new life. But the reverent acceptance of the natural conditions of life has practical consequences. We cannot in good conscience pursue knowledge and control in the mood of rapacity or exploitation. The good earth is good only as we love it in the responsible using of it.

Since God is the source of all things, the dependent world is not only good, but it is simply natural. It is not divine. Just as nothing in the world is deserving of scorn, so nothing is worthy of our worship, "for there is nothing that is not finite, partial, and transitory. The doctrine of creation is a great bulwark against idolatry—the worship of a creature, or of one partial aspect of life, in the place of God." [24] The first commandment is a moral way of affirming the doctrine of creation. It asserts the priority of God and asks that we give God effective priority in living. Tracking down one's idols is a necessary part of trying to be a Christian. Only God is absolute.

If we can distinguish between aspects of God's gracious omnipresence, we can say that just as the goodness of God is reflected in the existence of created reality so the wisdom of God is reflected in the intelligibility of the world. Since the world reflects intelligence, it is a possible object of study. Since it is not divine, it is a suitable object of study. Confidence in the intelligibility of the world is basic to Western culture. We tend to forget, Langdon Gilkey contends, that "this confidence is not so much the result of science as it is the long-term basis of science. Only because men were already convinced that they were surrounded by a world of real and orderly relations would they ever have embarked on the arduous enterprise of understanding that world." [25]

It is no accident that science has arisen on monotheistic ground and has never appeared within the context of pantheism or polytheism. Against the background of the conviction that the will of God was beyond human understanding and was yet rational rather than irrational, Western scientists avoided the search for ultimate causes and focused on an inquiry through sense perception into the actual details and order of the world of nature. Many historians have pointed out that the Christian idea of creation provided the presuppositions that made modern science possible.

The mystery of creation

Although it is important to say that the created order is God's self-expression and that it reflects his goodness, power, and wisdom, it is also important to acknowledge the profound mystery of creation. For the created order does not always conform to our ideas of divine goodness, power and wisdom. In fact, the universe presents elements of mystery and sheer irrationality that make it something less than a cozy neighborhood for human habitation. It is easy for us to read the first chapter of Genesis "as though the whole structure of the universe had no other purpose but the production of the human species and that all things in it had been made for the use of man. And we may slip from there into the further assumption that the 'use' of man can only mean his happiness or even his material comfort." [26]

It is salutary, therefore, to take note of the fact that the Nicene Creed adds to the phrase, "God is the Maker of heaven and earth," the further clause, "and of all things visible and invisible." The added words imply that the range of God's creation is not limited to the world we can see. It widens out to include things beyond our perception.

This reference to "things invisible" cautions us against thinking of the world too narrowly as a home for man. And if God, in his self-disclosure in Christ, has shown us what man is meant to be, it should be impossible for us to believe that the created order exists for the sake of satisfying natural desires. An anthropocentric view of the world runs the risk of defining the meaning and use of created things in terms of the visible alone.

A second mistake to which we are liable is to regard the universe as man-centered in the sense that nature has no meaning of its own. John Keats suggested that this world should be called "a vale of soul-making." But are we to suppose that the natural order is merely a framework and stage for the fashioning of men? That "soul-making" exhausts the meaning of the world for God? The doctrine of creation affirms that the natural order has a significance for itself. It is also eminently fitted to be a place in which values can be won, in which character can be made, and in which souls can be tested and tempered. But, as H. H. Farmer remarks, "it is not in the least necessary to Christian faith to maintain that all creation should be a means to the end of human personality, but only that it should include all that is requisite to that end and nothing that should make its final achievement impossible." [27]

It is presumptuous to believe that this universe is solely for us. It surely carries other meanings and is meaningful in itself quite apart from any functional purposes that it may serve. The Nicene Creed's reference to "things invisible" fits in with the impression, so difficult to resist, that nature expresses some aspect of the divine purpose which serves God's design for man, but goes far beyond it. This thought becomes quite irresistible when we lift our eyes to the infinite extent and majesty of the heavens. But it is not only the sheer splendor of sky, and sea, and mountain that amazes us. There is also the impression of sheer mystery and irrationality which the physical universe makes upon us. W. Macneile Dixon writes: "If there be a sceptical star I was born under it, yet I have lived all my days in complete astonishment. . . . Expound to me . . . how, for example, a stimulus to a nerve produces a sensation, by what process we recall a name or a fact, how a peacock's tail builds up a series of perfect eyes out of hundreds of separate feathers, each with its thousands of separate branches." [28] Explanations in terms of natural selection do make sense, but the most interesting feature of the explanations is not their content, but the bright-eyed simplicity of the human mind.

In affirming that there are things to be seen the eye has not seen and things to be heard the ear has not heard, we should want to take our stand with Luther rather than with Erasmus. Roland Bainton claims that Erasmus could never have written this sentence from Luther: "If thou couldst understand a single grain of wheat, thou wouldst die for wonder." In commenting on Psalm 139, Bainton uses language that Luther could have used—and probably did: "The trouble with Erasmus is that he is not stupefied with wonder at the child in the womb. . . .

He does not praise and thank God for the marvel of a flower or the bursting of the peach stone by the swelling seed. He beholds all these wonders like a cow staring at a new gate." [29]

Whether such animadversion is proper in the case of Erasmus, it was not thus with the Lady Julian of Norwich. In the fourteenth century, she wrote in the fifth chapter of her *Revelations:* "He showed me a little thing, the size of a hazel nut in the palm of my hand; and it was round as a ball. I looked thereon, and thought: What may this be? And it was answered thus: It is all that is made. I marvelled how it might last, for methought it might suddenly have fallen to naught for very littleness. And I was answered: it lasteth, and ever shall, for that God loveth it. And so All-thing hath Being through the love of God."

When we look at nature it gives every appearance of standing as an independent system over against human purposes. It is simply the case that much of nature cannot be understood in terms of God's design for human life. How can divine providence be related to the incredible and wasteful fecundity of life on this planet, to the enormous busy-ness of an ant-heap, and to all the enigmatic creatures in the zoo? [30] The temptation is strong to regard nature as having a life of its own which is only partially intelligible and relevant to man. We should want to say that God has a life of his own, and that our physical environment also has a life of its own. Nature has some intrinsic significance and a permanent place in the purpose of God. It is not merely a stage setting which will pass into nothingness after the last act of the human drama.

The parasitic character of evil

To say that the created order is God's self-expression and that it reflects the goodness, power, and wisdom of God, while remaining mysterious, seems to give a false picture of the world as we know it. For much of human experience, some would say most of it, reflects some reality other than divine goodness and wisdom. But the omission or postponement of any reference to sin and evil has been deliberate. It is a most important step in Christian thinking about the world to see the fact of sin against the background of creation. If this is not done, the doctrine of sin is distorted and, in turn, distorts everything else.

We must say that God made a good world and that evil is present within it as an intruder. In commenting on the motives that lay behind the healing ministry of Jesus, James Stewart writes: "In God's world Jesus always regarded disease as an intruder. It was not part of the plan. It was not directly devised by God's good will. It was not native to God's kingdom. It was alien. Therefore Jesus, whenever he met it, set himself to destroy it." [31] John S. Whale describes sin as a surd factor in the structure of reality. "Man's sinful will cannot be explained: it must remain as the one completely irrational fact in a world which God created, and saw to be 'very good.'" [32]

Nothing in creation is intrinsically evil. If God is the sole source of existence, then evil is a parasitic growth upon existence and being. Since creation is essentially good, a bad thing is a good thing spoiled. Evil can exist only by feeding on the good and is thus like a parasite that cannot live unless the host lives. To say that creation is good is not to deny evil, but to say that anything in creation is subject to perversion, distortion, abuse. Since evil is a perversion rather than the essence of nature, it can be removed. Thus human existence is redeemable.

So we must say that sin is a disturbance of the divine order, but the order is prior to the disturbance or there would be nothing to disturb, nothing to go wrong. In this sense, sin can be understood only against the background of the idea of creation. Sin occurs within the ultimate context of grace. Luther often warned: "Though man may be diseased, he is not the disease. We must distinguish between original sin and the creature." Through the Fall sin has become "natural" to man, but it does not proceed "from nature," Calvin argued. Man still remains the creature of God. Luther and Calvin had much to say about the goodness of man's native powers of reason, emotion, and will even in his "fallen" condition.

The doctrine of sin, is, therefore, neither the first nor the last, but rather the middle word which Christian faith has to say about man. The concept of man as a sinner presupposes the concept of man as made in the divine image, and it points to the contradiction in man between that image in which he was made and the perversion of that image, not its loss, in his actual existence. Christian faith goes on to stress the possibilities of the new life created by the redemptive love of God. Evil is real, but it is not intrinsic or ultimate. It is a serious error, even a heresy, to say that the doctrine of sin is the starting-point of Christian theology, or to preach or live as though it were the most fundamental reality.

The Holy Spirit as the dynamic and processive divine presence in creation

We have seen that God's relation to creation is the widest perspective, although not the starting-point, of biblical faith. This perspective, when seen in its full breadth, has the power to provide a new appreciation of the grace that is in creation. The word "grace" expresses the giftlike character of existence itself. This grace of existence is prior to any particular experiences of grace. In acknowledging this grace, man is responding in all the dimensions of his existence to a reality that transcends his own. In his faith, man accepts and commits himself to the ultimate reality that has brought forth human life. Faith thus implies the conviction that God has provided a meaningful context for human life and for moral striving in relation to oneself, to one's neighbors, to the structures of society, and to the physical environment.

But the benefits of this fruitful perspective have been obscured by certain misplaced emphases in the traditional Christian understanding of God. If we are to provide a suitable horizon of understanding for a doctrine of grace in creation, we must re-conceive the nature and work of the Holy Spirit and do so in such a way that grace in creation is seen in the light of the single, out-going, universal divine thrust, God in gracious mission to the universe.

Why should it be necessary to re-examine the nature and work of the Holy Spirit? The doctrine of the Trinity is the most complete and profound understanding of God available to Christian people. Yet, it is difficult to resist the impression that a good deal of what passes for Christian faith is not really trinitarian, but binitarian or tritheistic in nature. For many Christians the focus of faith and worship is God the Father, but often conceived less as Father than as a remote King, Judge, Creator. For others, the focus is the person of Christ, either in his ministry or in his resurrection and ascension. The Father-oriented focus does establish a connection with the world through the idea of providence. But the remoteness of the Father-figure made the providential ordering of nature and history a rather static idea. The Son-oriented type established a connection with the world through the omnipresence of the Word or Logos, or through the Lordship of Christ. Both types of faith fail to represent that element of dynamic and processive divine presence and inspiration which is expressed so powerfully by a proper doctrine of the Holy Spirit. The result of ignoring the Third Person of the Trinity was that for centuries the focus of the Christian religion has been away from the world of nature and of real life as it is lived from day to day.[33] A re-conception of the doctrine of the Holy Spirit is needed if we are to see grace as God's self-bestowal throughout the whole range of reality.

The doctrine of the Holy Spirit is widely regarded as a difficult and neglected theme in Christian thought and life. Some speak of this area as "a vacuum in the dogmatics of the contemporary churches."[34] We have seen that in the New Testament the word "grace" is associated with God, with Jesus Christ, and with the Holy Spirit. But, in subsequent Christian thought, grace was understood almost exclusively in relation to God the Father, the source of being, and in relation to God the Son, the mediator of forgiving grace. At times, grace was seen as a favor or power distributed by the church. But it was rarely related to the Holy Spirit.

The neglect of this doctrine has a long history. There is a general vagueness of teaching about the Spirit in the early church. Down to the fourth century, all creeds had the simple phrase "I believe in the Holy Spirit," without any addition or elaboration. The Spirit is mentioned in the classical creeds in one sentence after many sentences about Christ. The theological attention of the church during these early centuries was focused mainly on other aspects of the faith. So far as the doctrine of the Spirit is concerned, theologians for the most part confined themselves to elaborating the evidence provided by Scripture.

There are reasons for the lack of clarity and fullness in this doctrine. Confronted by threats to the unity of the Godhead, by evasions of the fact of God's incarnation in Jesus Christ, and by a vague and unregulated spiritualism, the early theologians chose to follow the lead of some aspects of the New Testament teaching. They used ideas available from such sources as the Wisdom literature, which might have been properly employed in working out a theology of the Spirit, and applied them instead to the elaboration and enrichment of the doctrine of the Logos, the Second Person of the Trinity.[35] "The enthusiasts of all ages—the Montanists, the Anabaptists, the Quakers, the Pentecostals, and many other movements which emphasized the presence of the Spirit—discouraged the official churches because they feared a loosening of the ties between the Spirit and the letter of the Scriptures, or between the Spirit and the institutional church life."[36]

This neglect or misplaced emphasis has continued down to the present day. By focusing on God the Father and God the Son, the larger churches have incurred the risks of making faith seem to be merely an intellectual phenomenon, of forcing Pentecostal movements to organize outside the churches or as special-interest groups, and of failing to relate the dynamic grace of God in creation to the Holy Spirit. Wolfhart Pannenberg complains that by neglecting to emphasize the Holy Spirit as the origin and principle of all life, contemporary theology has produced "a curiously watered-down conception of the Spirit. . . . The original breadth of the efficacy of the Spirit in the sense of the Bible and the Christian tradition has been . . . forgotten or at least pushed into the background." [37]

If we are to develop a doctrine of the Holy Spirit which corresponds to the breadth of the biblical witness and allows us to speak theologically about the phenomenon of life, we must emphasize two ideas: that the Holy Spirit is *God,* and that the *whole creation* is the field of his operation.

The doctrine of the Trinity enshrines the deepest truth of Christianity and it is certainly the most difficult of all doctrines. It has always been known as the "central mystery" of Christian faith. Christians resist Unitarianism but often themselves fall into a kind of tritheism. Trinitarian doctrine speaks of One God in Three Persons. The Latin word *persona* did not mean what the English word "person" means today. That is, it did not mean either "person" or "personality" in the sense in which we commonly use these words, as implying a distinct center of consciousness. "Originally it meant the mask which the actor in the theater wore to indicate his role. The next significance was: the role itself, which led to a more general meaning: the role or function which a man performs in his social context. Finally, it came to mean: man's character. In theological terminology, *persona* meant at any rate more than an external mask or a mere function, but less than our word 'person' contains. It was a word which became a source of embarrassment and confusion for many centuries." [38]

It is extraordinarily difficult to find an exact English equivalent to the Latin *persona*. The words "aspect" or "mode" are inadequate. They imply too much the partial expression of a person's full individuality and would suggest "that the one God plays three separate . . . parts, like an actor who plays Hamlet, Macbeth, and Othello on three successive nights." [39] The ancient church called this view "modalism" and rejected it as a heresy. On the other hand, "person" is misleading. It suggests too much the idea of an "individual," as though there are three personal divine beings in the Godhead. Since most modern Christians tend to think of "person" in the sense of an "individual" rather than as a "mode" or "aspect," the common understanding of Father, Son and Holy Spirit sees the Triune God as three distinct and separate personalities, "in the sense that Smith, Brown, and Robinson are three separate and distinct persons. Such a view . . . would leave us with a mental picture of three kings trying to sit on the same throne." [40] Or, it could leave us with a picture of a divine committee of three. This would not be Trinitarianism, but tritheism.

When tritheism prevails in popular religion, the Father and Son get most attention. The Father is associated with creation, providence, and the last judgment. The Son is associated with atonement and the church. The Holy Spirit is relegated to third place. "In Roman Catholic theology, the Spirit is mainly the soul and sustainer of the church. In Protestant theology, he is mainly the awakener of individual spiritual life in justification and sanctification. So the Spirit is either institutionalized or individualized. . . . The Spirit in this way is the builder of the church and the edifier of the faithful, but not the great mover and driving power on the way from the One to the many, from Christ to the world." [41]

When a division of labor is applied to the doctrine of God, under the influence of an almost unconscious tritheism, the Holy Spirit is restricted to the function of applying or reproducing the action of the Second Person of the Trinity in the primary areas of ecclesiastical and personal life. There is little in this conception to prevent the individualistic and institutionalistic introversion of Christian faith.

The Third Person of the Trinity can be seen in proper perspective if we bring into close relation the unity, the action, and the grace of God. It is beyond question that monotheism, belief in *one* God, is the primal presupposition of Christianity. The church has fought many battles against the suggestion that there could be two gods or that Jesus was or is a second god. When Christians have known what they were doing, they have directed their concern to *God,* even as they sought to understand the meaning of Christ. [42]

In affirming that there is one God, the Christian faith has also affirmed that the unity of God is not a bare mathematical unity. It is that, in the sense that unity is the opposite of multiplicity. But the unity of God is an organic, complex, plural unity. In our experience we know of biological and sociological entities that are single, yet multicellular. Perhaps the nearest we can get to a middle way between "mode" and "person" is to say that "the nature of God is personal, existing and expressing itself in three eternal characters and activities which together constitute the divine being." [43] With its origins in Jewish faith as a constant reminder and incentive, the church found it very important to preserve the unity of the Godhead against any tendency to distinguish the operations of the three "persons" in such a way as might open the door to the possibility of tritheism. J. N. D. Kelly describes this theme in early Christian doctrine as follows: "The divine action begins from the Father, proceeds through the Son, and is completed in the Holy Spirit: none of the Persons possesses a separate operation of his own, but one identical energy passes through all three." [44] This emphasis not only fixed the unity of God but also ruled out any tendency to regard the Holy Spirit as in some way subordinate, a mere emanation from deity, the junior member of a divine committee of three. There can be no doubt about biblical monotheism. One might say that Father, Son, and Spirit are *relational* terms. They point to the complexity of relations that the one God maintains between himself and man and within himself to himself.

Some of the Church Fathers understood the relation between identity and diversity within the Godhead in this fashion. "There is, within the being of God, pure Godhead, God as he is in himself, wholly transcendent. But if this were all that God is, if he were nothing else, there could be no going out from himself in creation: he would remain a bare self-contained and self-sufficient 'unit.' There is also present within the being of God his Logos, his Word, reason, power of self-communication. . . . But this again, by itself, is not sufficient. It is, in itself only the potentiality, even the necessity, of expression, of communication, but not the action itself. That is the work of the Spirit, whose characteristic description is that he 'proceeds,' goes out in creation and inspiration, from the Father and the Son." [45]

Further emphasis on the unity of God is found in the Augustinian conception of the unity of the action of the Trinity—*opera trinitatis ad extra indivisa sunt*. This formula, known as the canon of Trinitarian orthodoxy, lays it down that "the works of the Trinity, directed outward from itself, are undivided." The Trinity is "a single source of activity, one subject at least in relation to the created world." [46] This means that there can be no act of God that is not the act of all three Persons. If we are to associate creation with the Father, redemption with the Son, and sanctification with the Spirit, it cannot be in any such way as to imply that creation, redemption, and sanctification have separate agents in the three Persons of the Godhead. In the epistles of Paul (1 Corinthians 12:4-6), the essential unity of the divine action is such that the three names are interchangeable. George S. Hendry comments: "Since God was in Christ, every relation to Christ is at the same time a relation to God; and since the Holy Spirit is the Spirit of God and of Christ, the presence of the Spirit in us is equivalent to the presence of God (Ephesians 2:21) and of Christ (Romans 8:9f.). And the gifts of the Spirit are at the same time the ministrations of Christ and the operations of God." [47]

Classical theology is open to criticism for its neglect of the doctrine of the Holy Spirit. But, in all fairness, it must be said that there was good reason for identifying the Spirit with Christ. The New Testament itself does identify the Spirit with Christ and says in many passages that the Spirit is the risen Christ himself acting in his congregation. The Spirit is Christ's new way of existence and action, the continued presence of Christ in another mode. This identification of the Spirit with Christ rules out the heresy that the presence of the Spirit supersedes the presence of Christ, and guarantees that Christian faith is centered in Christ, whose finished work gives specific content to the work of the Spirit. [48] But, in taking this course, classical theology has tended to make the Spirit's work *instrumental*. In so doing, theology has presented the Spirit as "a second reality beside Christ, but entirely subordinate to him, serving in the application of his atoning work, in the realization of justification by faith." [49]

Hendrikus Berkof argues persuasively that this classical picture of the Spirit does not do full justice to the New Testament teaching about the Spirit. For there are themes in the New Testament which suggest that the Spirit's work is far more, or other than, instrumental. The Spirit's "coming to us is a great new event in the series of God's saving acts." [50] Those who, in every century of church history, have protested against the lack of spiritual reality in the life and teaching of the official churches, had this in common, that they considered the Holy Spirit as a center of new actions. Is the Spirit merely instrumental to Christ, or an independent reality with his own content?

Berkhof contends that this antithesis can be overcome if we recognize a tension in the New Testament presentation of the relation between Christ and the Spirit. One line of thought describes Jesus as the bearer of the Spirit. This is dominant in the synoptic Gospels which stress the prophecies that the Spirit will rest on the Messiah, and say that the Lord has anointed Jesus with his Spirit. Here the Spirit has divine priority over Jesus. But, mainly in Paul and John, there is another line of thought. Here Jesus is not so much the bearer as the sender of the Spirit.[51]

These two pictures are really complementary, not contradictory. "Jesus can be the sender of the Spirit only because he is first the receiver and bearer of the Spirit." Our traditional theology has one-sidedly stressed the fact that Christ has the Spirit at his disposal in order to guard against a merely humanitarian Christology which sees Jesus only as a man supremely endowed with the Spirit. It is possible to "understand the person and work of Jesus Christ as the result and starting-point, as the center of God's life-giving presence, of the work of the Spirit among men" without denying the deity and centrality of Christ.[52] To do this would enable us to recover the emphasis on Christ as the bearer of the Spirit and thus strengthen the affirmation of the unity of the divine action. It is important to avoid the tritheism which restricts the Holy Spirit by dividing up the work of God among the three Persons.

From a clear conception of the unity of God we can conclude that the Spirit is not the third, and least important, member of a divine committee with only special tasks to perform. Whatever God does, the Spirit does. If God is active in the world at large, that is the work of the Spirit. This conclusion is strengthened by an analysis of the relation between the Spirit and God's action. Recent biblical and theological studies agree in using the formula: "the Holy Spirit is God in action." On what grounds do they say this? The etymology of the biblical words for "spirit" provides the main basis. The Hebrew *(ruach)* and Greek *(pneuma)* words refer primarily to wind or storm. The meaning shifts to the movement of air caused by breathing, and from breath it is a short jump to the principle of life or vitality. "Spirit" means that "God is a vital God who grants vitality to his creation."[53]

Vitality becomes associated with power, since power is actually an aspect of the original metaphor. In the Old Testament, the term "spirit" is associated with God's world-making activity and with God's activity in relation to his people. The Spirit of God is a mysterious power which possesses certain men, filling them with a divinely-sent energy which enables them to function as warriors, leaders, rulers, craftsmen, and poets. The Spirit inspires the prophets to see the meaning of God's acts in history. Most importantly, the Spirit is God's very presence among his people. In the New Testament, the Spirit is the link between Jesus and the Father, and on the day of Pentecost it is the Spirit that brings fulfillment and power. Thus, biblical usage stresses action as the central meaning of Spirit, but weaves the ideas of vitality, power, and presence into the content of divine action.

The New Testament associates with the Holy Spirit such words as life, love, liberty, power, unity, fellowship. All these words have reference to the practical effects of the presence of God in our human life. The rich variety of the Spirit's work is further indicated by the terms vocation, cleansing, regeneration, election, illumination, conversion, justification, and sanctification. To use all these words, or even to narrow them down to justification and sanctification, is to obscure the fact that these are all works of one Spirit and are thus basically one work. An all-inclusive category should be chosen carefully in order to see the unity of the authorship of these works. Berkhof suggests that "the word which best expresses the unity and totality of the Spirit's work is the word 'regeneration.' " [54]

Regeneration focuses on *life*. The term is in harmony with the name given to the Spirit in the third article of the Nicene Creed: "I believe in the Holy Spirit, the Lord and giver of life." The concept of life goes from the creed back into the New Testament, and beyond that to the Old Testament where the Spirit had come to be regarded as the source of all life, the giver of physical, mental, emotional, artistic, and religious vitality. Birth, rebirth, new birth—these terms express the essence of God's work in creation and in redemption. God is in action to transmit life to created reality. This *is* the divine mission: to give life, to bestow being, to exert steady pressure against all the forces that spoil and destroy life. Spirit is the outgoing and active power of the living and life-giving God.

When we move from the unity and action of God to the grace of God, the full breadth of the doctrine of the Holy Spirit becomes evident. For grace is essentially God's bestowal of his personal presence throughout the entire created order. To be in God's presence is to be *alive,* in a far deeper sense than the medical. To be in God's presence with and through Jesus Christ is to have "the life which is life indeed" (1 Timothy 6:19). It is to be alive in, through, and with God and one's fellow-creatures. For it is of the very essence of grace to be inclusive. Grace thus reflects the nature of God who is both complete and inclusive. God's being or value expresses without qualification or exclusiveness whatever is of value anywhere. The existence of God is the affirmation, the *ruling in* of all significant possibilities. To love God is to affirm the value of his being and also to love the world, and particularly our fellow-creatures because God himself affirms the whole. His interest and concern are all-inclusive. Thus the First Epistle of John: "If anyone says, 'I love God' and hates his brother, he is a liar" (1 John 4:20).

The Spirit is not only the giver of life on the levels of creaturely being lower than that of man's "spiritual" being. But "the unitive movement of the Spirit" brings beings "into a reconciling unity with Being, yet without destroying their diversity." [55] The Spirit is the expansion of the divine saving presence over the earth. The movement, expansion, or mission is from the One to the many. The aim of the mission is incorporation. Grace or presence goes out from the One to the many, incorporating the parts into the whole.[56] John Macquarrie insists that "grace is to be understood as the overcoming of alienation and as the reconciling of what has been thrust apart. . . . We may say that grace is at work wherever that which has become isolated and fragmented is incorporated into a larger whole, but incorporated in personal terms, rather than being merely absorbed or annexed into the whole. . . . The work of grace is to build up wholes out of fragments, to overcome separations, to effect reconciliation." [57]

The line of thought we have followed in making the point that the Holy Spirit is God, fully God, and that in every act of God we have to do with one and the same God, is well summed up by Berkhof: "God is a living, acting God. In creation he transmits his life to a world outside of his being. In the act of creation, he therefore becomes a life-giving Spirit. As Spirit he sustains and develops his created world, he elects and protects Israel, he calls and governs her leaders. In the fullness of time, God himself becomes man. Incarnation is the highest act of his Spirit. From now on the world has the center of God's activity in its midst. Jesus Christ is the acting God present in our world. God's spirit from now on is Christ's spirit, without ceasing to be present in a more general way in the created world. God's action in Christ is his more specific operation, in the light of which his general operation is revealed in its ultimate meaning." [58]

In seeking to recover the biblical breadth of the understanding of the Holy Spirit as God's grace in action, we have emphasized the unity of God. To this should be added the declaration that *the whole creation* is the field of the Spirit's operation. It is necessary to say this because we have a history of restricting the work of the Spirit to the building of the church and the edifying of the faithful. If we are going to think productively about the Spirit in relation to grace and creation, we must go beyond the church and the believer without implying that they are unimportant.

In the early church, theologians pondered the relation of the closer and more intimate presence of God in the church to the widest perspectives of divine activity. Origen used the figure of three concentric circles to illustrate the respective spheres or ranges of activity belonging to the three Persons of the Trinity. He confined the range of the Spirit to the "saints" or church-members. But the early apologists of the second century made no clear distinction between the Logos or Word of God and the Spirit of the pre-existent Christ. "They boldly claimed for this Logos-Spirit, not only the inspiration of the Hebrew prophets, but all and any enlightenment of the human mind . . . and especially the development of Greek philosophy and its trend towards monotheism." [59] One sees here an effort to extend the sense of the Spirit's work beyond the sphere to which classical theology has confined it.

Hendrikus Berkhof, in his most valuable study of the Holy Spirit, has made fascinating use of the image of concentric circles. He suggests that we can understand the relation between the Spirit and the whole range of created reality if we think in terms of three circles. After discussing the relation of the Spirit to Christ, to the mission of God, and to the church, Berkhof says that we should try to think of God the Spirit drawing "wider and wider circles around Christ." God in Christ is at the center. The church and the believer are "somewhere in the middle between Christ and the universe, as a partial realization of his goal and as representative of his deeds and purposes toward the world." [60]

Thus, we can think of the work of the Spirit as having a narrower and a wider circumference. Within the narrower circumference the works of the Spirit are the church and the individual, the "first fruits" of the Spirit in the world. Within the wider circumference the works of the Spirit are to be seen in the creation, in history, and in the consummation of the world. The works of the Spirit in this wider circumference are all more or less neglected in our traditional theology.[61]

Our chief interest is in the work of the Spirit in relation to the whole creation. But a brief look at Berkhof's conception of the narrower circle throws much light on the content and goal of the Spirit's work in the wider circle. The narrower circumference includes, first, the church. This means that a choice has been made as to the ordering of things.

We start from God in Christ as life-giving Spirit engaged in a mission of grace. The mission, outgoing, or movement is the first and most basic act of the Spirit of the risen Christ. The mission is more than a practical instrument in the expansion of the church. The mission, in fact, is not at the disposal of the church. Both mission and church are at the disposal of the Spirit, whom we know as the gracious movement of the One to the many.

The fundamental shape of this movement is mission. The mission is therefore prior to the church, and the church is not more than the instrument in the great mission of the Spirit. The church cannot consider itself as an end in itself. It is the instrument of the ongoing movement. Yet, the church is at the same time a partial or provisional result of the movement. Thus, the church has a double aspect: it is both realization of the mission and instrument of the mission. Christ's mission is first. The neglect of the mission of Christ's Spirit in our theology has caused the introversion of the church about which so many Christians feel uneasy.[62]

If mission is the basic activity, the upbuilding of the church with ministry, Word, and sacrament is the next step. The church comes after the mission, and the individual believer comes after the church. The church is prior to the individual. In calling his disciples, Christ makes them enter into the community with him and with one another. The same entrance into the church occurs in Acts 2. The Spirit is poured out on a community, making it the witnessing church into which individuals are invited. This does not mean that the work of the Spirit in the individual is subordinated to that in the church. Perhaps the highest work of the Spirit is his dwelling in the lives of individuals, but this work presupposes the work in the church. As long as we put the individual first, we cannot get the right view on the church as the ground of the individual life. But, if we put the church first, we can see the individual as born out of her. The logical order is that Christ points to the mission, the mission points to the church, and the church points to the individual.[63]

If we move from the narrower circumference to the wider, we can see that the same divine action at work in the deeds of salvation is the secret of the entire created world. In the Old Testament the Spirit of God is thought of as a mysterious dynamic power. The Hebrew word *ruach,* translated "spirit," primarily denotes "wind" or "breath" and the ideas signified by the word stand for power and life-force. Although thought of mainly as an impersonal force, it is plain that the term "spirit" points to the immanence of the transcendent.

On the cosmic level, the Spirit is seen as the origin of all life. In the creation stories, the creative word is equated with the breath or spirit of God, which brings movement and order out of chaos (Genesis 1:2) and quickens man into life (Genesis 2:7). The Spirit of God sustains the life of nature, and particularly the life of man (Psalm 104:30; Job 33:4). The Spirit is so intimate to man's life that when Job says he has the Spirit of God in his nostrils, we feel we are close to pantheism (Job 27:3).

Apart from references to the Spirit's activity in world-making (Psalm 33:6), most Old Testament passages present the Spirit as a potent and mysterious force from God which seizes upon and possesses certain men, filling them with a divinely-sent energy. Samson, Gideon, Moses, Saul, David, Bezalel and others were all raised above themselves to display strength, courage, wisdom, justice, skill, and inspiration (Judges 14:6; 6:34; Numbers 11:17; 1 Samuel 16:13; Numbers 24:2; Exodus 31:3). Pannenberg comments: "The extraordinary (charismatic) powers which are ascribed to the Spirit of God in particular cases are also to be understood in the light of this general efficacy of the divine Spirit as the origin of all life: these are special, unusual capacities . . . which demand a particular degree of vital energy." [64]

Through the inspiration of prophets to formulate God's ethical judgments upon his people, it came to be realized that the Spirit is something more than a divine energy. The Spirit is the "holy" Spirit and is seen to be identical with the presence of God. The Spirit is the bond between God and his own people. The prophets look forward to a time when the Spirit will inspire a whole people, and not merely certain individuals (Joel 2:28). In certain quarters it was thought that the Messiah would be the agent of God through whom the general diffusion of the Spirit would be brought about.

The New Testament shows Jesus to be conscious of the coming of the Spirit at the point of his baptism as the messianic Son of God. Throughout the Gospels, the Spirit is the link between Jesus and the Father. The day of Pentecost was seen as the anticipated outpouring of the Spirit, with the result that all God's people would share in the gift of prophecy (Acts 2:16ff.). The New Testament depicts the Spirit as the principle of Jesus' life and work and as the motive-force in the church's mission of extending the saving work of Christ to the whole world. G. W. H. Lampe points out that although the New Testament does place the distinctive work of the Spirit within the community of Christian people, it does not in any way "deny that the Spirit of God also operates outside the fellowship of those who consciously live as members of Christ's people. The Spirit who re-creates men's lives in the community of those who belong to Christ is none other than the creative Spirit, the breath of divine life by which all things were vivified in their first creation. The Creator-Spirit cannot be concerned with only a part of creation. He is the giver of all life, both physical and spiritual." [65]

The Holy Spirit as the giver of life, must be conceived as present and working in the cosmic process at all its levels. Unity is at its lowest in the sphere of inanimate matter. The line of creation which leads up to man shows the Spirit in action as unifying power. Simpler unities are transformed into higher and more complex unities. In man, organic life is raised to the level at which personal fellowship with God has become possible through the power of self-determination.

Some theologians like to say that when scientists and philosophers speak of the "life-force," they are describing in non-religious language the work of the Holy Spirit. And why not? If the divine Creator-Spirit is perpetually moving out in gracious mission to the created order, to all that is not God, then his work ought to be seen and affirmed in the starry worlds in space and time, in the pageant of the seasons, in the constant uprush of new life, in the ceaseless growth of things, in the richness and variety of our world—the movement of planets, the beauty of the flowers, the flight of the bird, the instincts of animals, in all enlarging life and in all devoted and responsible search for truth, justice, mercy, honesty, and beauty. The Spirit of God is to be seen in that striving of all things to be their best and to fulfill the end for which they have come into being. All this, and more, must be seen as grace in creation.

4

Grace,

Personality,

and Social Process

We noted in the previous chapter that the concept of grace drives one toward inclusiveness and that much contemporary theology is seeking to recover the sense of grace in areas traditionally regarded as merely natural or worldly. We looked at grace in its widest possible perspective by seeing it as the active and generous self-expression of Ultimate Reality, or as the mission of the Creator Spirit toward the universe. We observed that much is to be gained by seeing the full scope of the Spirit's action in terms of Hendrikus Berkhof's image of concentric circles radiating outwards from the gracious mission of God the Creator Spirit in Christ to the church, to the individual person, to the physical creation, to the events of history, and ultimately to the grand consummation of God's purpose for all that he has made.

Even though our hopes and speculations may extend to the remotest galaxies, our focus at this point must be on the earth, with all its furniture, inhabitants, and events. Within the sphere of a grace-full created order, we become aware of ourselves as persons, enmeshed with other persons in the structures and processes of social life, and involved in the flow of historical events. Where is grace to be found in the dynamics of personality, in the structures of society, and in the pageant of historical development? These topics are too large to be encompassed in one chapter, but some directions of thought may be suggested.

Grace and Personality

The goodness of creaturehood

Christian thought must take as its starting-point the basic axiom that the God of grace is a moving God. He is a movement of love. He is God in action moving into created reality, bringing all that he has made to fulfillment. As the living God graciously transmits his life to a world outside his being, he moves into human personality and establishes the goodness of creaturehood. It is the conviction of those who witness in the Scriptures that God's Spirit creates and sustains the life of nature and particularly the life of man. The first page of the Bible declares that "the Spirit of God was moving over the face of the waters" (Genesis 1:2). The Genesis account goes on to focus on human life: "Then the Lord God formed man of dust from the ground, and breathed into his nostrils the breath of life; and man became a living being" (Genesis 2:7). The prophet Isaiah sets the presence of God in the life of man within the context of the whole process of creation: "Thus says God, the Lord, who created the heavens and stretched them out, who spread forth the earth and what comes from it, who gives breath to the people upon it and spirit to those who walk in it" (Isaiah 42:5). The same theme occurs frequently in Job and is given a strongly personal emphasis: "The spirit of God has made me, and the breath of the Almighty gives me life" (Job 33:4). It is clear from the biblical witness that the spirit is to be regarded as the source of our life in its totality, including our body, our vitality, our mind, our emotions, our creative gifts.

But the human life of which God is the source is *creaturely* life. God did not design us to be deities or semi-divinities, but to be finite, free, and dependent persons in this world of space and time. The first-hand, concrete, unsystematic utterances of daily experience tell us plainly enough that we are finite and limited. Man can see that he is a very small item in the universe, a mere segment of the whole of humanity, with restricted powers and perspectives. He is limited by geography. He is confined by the limits of his senses, which perceive only a small range of the total spectrum of available impressions. He is capable of knowledge, yet is acutely conscious of his ignorance. Able to plan, he is the constant victim of disappointments. Men and women who have been involved in the effort to discover and be themselves have found the struggle very often a long succession of defeats, perhaps because some natural or social factor hinders them from reaching particular goals, or because goals that are reached are seen to be not worth the cost, or because they cannot focus clearly on any goal and live in continual inner turmoil.

Human existence is insecure not only because of subtle inward tensions and contradictions, but also because of great external forces beyond our control. There are rigidities of substance, shape, and sequence in the created world and these must be respected if one is not to court disaster. Apart from human folly and error, there are natural calamities that descend on man's life and on all that he labors to create. When earthquake, flood, or incurable disease wipe out human hopes, even the congenital optimist is likely to see the destruction as meaningless. Man's boundless imagination makes all limitation seem irksome, if not desperate. There is something in the general constitution of man's mind and of his world which subjects him not only to recurrent needs and tasks, but also to something like permanent frustration and defeat. The very powers which fit man to his world also "misfit" him because in the process of solving problems they create others.

No one has surpassed the remarkable catalogue of ills, sufferings, accidents, and aggressions compiled a millenium and a half ago by St. Augustine:

> That the whole human race has been condemned in its first origin, this life itself, if life it is to be called, bears witness by the host of cruel ills with which it is filled. Is this not proved by the profound and dreadful ignorance which produces all the errors that enfold the children of Adam, and from which no man can be delivered without toil, pain, and fear? Is it not proved by his love of so many vain and hurtful things, which produces gnawing cares, disquiets, griefs, fears, wild joys, quarrels, law-suits, wars, treasons, angers, hatreds, deceit, flattery, fraud, theft, . . . pride, ambition, envy, murders, . . . cruelty, ferocity, . . . luxury, insolence, . . . fornications, . . . blasphemies, perjuries, oppression of the innocent, . . . plots, falsehoods, . . . violent deeds, plunderings . . . ? These are indeed the crimes of wicked men, yet they spring from that root of error and misplaced love which is born with every son of Adam. . . . Why is it that we remember with difficulty, and without difficulty forget? learn with difficulty, and without difficulty remain ignorant? are diligent with difficulty, and without difficulty are indolent? . . . What fear and grief are caused by bereavement and mourning, by losses and condemnations, by fraud and falsehood, by false suspicions, and all the

crimes and wicked deeds of other men? For at their hands we suffer robbery, captivity, chains, imprisonment, exile, torture, mutilation. . . . What numberless casualties threaten our bodies from without— extremes of heat and cold, storms, floods, inundations, lightning, thunder, hail, earthquakes, houses falling, the stumbling and shying of horses, countless poisons in fruits, water, air, animals. . . . What disasters are suffered by those who travel by land or sea! What man can go out of his own house without being exposed on all hands to unforeseen accidents? Returning home sound in limb, he slips on his own door-step, breaks his leg, and never recovers.[1]

The calamities and misfortunes Augustine records are still with us, even though in some parts of the earth we have learned to control and cushion their impact. Life remains precarious and painful. If by good fortune or wise management we make our way through several decades of life, yet death cannot be avoided. "The ultimate sadness is that nothing lasts; that the bloom so soon disappears from all things that are young, that the vigor of maturity is so short-lived, while age brings weariness and forgetfulness and decay such as presage the oblivion of the grave. . . . To call to mind the care-free days of youth, to see the friends of youth disappear one by one from our earthly company with hopes only half-fulfilled and work only half done, and to know that no task of our own can ever be completed nor any joy held in possession for more than a few fleeting years—this is our great heaviness of heart." [2]

All this we know from first-hand experience. But knowledge of a wider sort, more accurately informed and more coherent, although less vivid, also tells us that man is a part of nature. The biologist sees each man as a community of millions of cells living together more or less successfully as one individual. The body cells which are constantly being born are specialized in form and function for an intricate division of labor. Co-ordination of cell numbers and functions must be nearly perfect or the life of the body will be destroyed. Within the body a complex chemical laboratory utilizes, makes, and distributes a variety of products. The compounds that provide the essential internal conditions of life are often balanced within limits of incredible precision and sometimes endure for more than a century. If the internal and external conditions of life are properly matched, a continuous interchange goes on between man's body and its environment.

The sciences tell us that man is a highly developed mammal and that his life, like that of his animal cousins, is deeply immersed in the river of natural events. Like them, he depends at every moment on the sustaining cross-currents of an intricate physical environment that binds him even while it bears him up. Man is no mysterious stranger, but a genuine member of the physical order. He belongs in the system of nature, and shares in the creatureliness of all the things, organic and inorganic, around him.

Yet, man is a unique part of nature, an exceptional animal. He is set off from the earth, buildings, machines, plants, and animals by the fact that he uses them deliberately to build an artificial physical environment for himself in the midst of raw nature. In the construction of his human world, man behaves as none of his animal neighbors seem able to do. With his upright posture, movable thumb, and enlarged brain he is able to use tools and fire, to communicate in elaborate ways, to keep historical records, to respond to obligations and rational insights, to pray, and to enjoy fellowship with other men and with God. In all these ways he serves distinctive human needs. He is immanent within nature, involved in the give-and-take of his environment. Yet, he transcends nature in his ability to rise above the animal and physical world, and even above himself—to plan, to set goals and reach them, to criticize, repent, and worship.

It is man's double status as physical and mental, or as natural and moral, that gives him the relative but sufficient freedom within his environment to express his human uniqueness. The creation accounts in Genesis 1-2 show man poised between heaven and earth, occupying a position that no creature can share with him. Yet, he can never be anything but earthly and finite. He is not separable from his environment. "Without its perpetual support he could not exist for a moment. . . . With all his power and freedom, man is dependent on a reality far greater than he . . . on the other hand, the nature of that reality is itself defined in part by the fact that it has brought man to birth, sustains him, and to an impressive degree supports his efforts at understanding and purposive action. In it man appears to be not an orphan, but a child at home. He and his world belong together." [3] He can try to deny his limitations, but he must fail. His denial is sin and his failure causes him to live out a falsehood. The world is his proper home.

Man's life in this world with all its ills and accidents, joys, and achievements, has been determined by God's grace. The Creator does not scorn man's natural environment. The fundamental conditions of creaturely life were in biblical faith seen to be "good" because God created the totality of all these factors. God has made nature the way it is. Just as grace is present in nature in general, so it penetrates the structures of human nature. Since the Creator has invented and endorsed nature and human nature, we must say that it is in this world that man is related to God. In and through its many structures, man is to express his God-given humanity. Christian faith attributed reality and value to concrete creaturely life. It saw that each finite being in all its aspects was called into existence by God's purposive will. Thus material being is not meaningless or negative in character, for God made the whole person, mind and body, feelings and thoughts. Every facet of man's life is potentially creative and is not to be denied, but affirmed, purified, and reorientated. God even willed that the life of Jesus Christ should unfold within and transfigure human existence in this world.

Salvation as the fulfillment of creation

Grace does not destroy or contravene humanness. Since the gracious God is the source of all that exists, no aspect of creatureliness can be intrinsically evil any more than it can be worthy of ultimate respect and loyalty. The basic structure of the world is good. The presence of limitations, or of evil in the widest sense, does not contradict this claim since Christian faith sees evil as a perversion rather than a necessity of our existence. Humanness is, therefore, not alien to grace whether that grace be expressed through creation, judgment, or forgiveness. Grace aims at fulfillment, not at deprivation and frustration. Love gives. It is not the nature of love to take away, to dispossess, to hinder, to degrade.

If finite things have fulfillment as their goal, then it is God's purpose for each created reality that it achieve the fullest excellence of which its nature is capable. Man was made to be fulfilled, to realize the inherent possibilities of the created spirit and to reach the ultimate goal of trusting reunion with his creator and loving fellowship with his neighbor. Christian faith sees salvation as "the restoration of creation, not its destruction; and the created self is enhanced and perfected, not overwhelmed, by grace." [4]

The theological insight that any thwarting of fulfillment is a wrong against the basic purpose of creation itself takes the shape of an ethical imperative to reduce human suffering, to seek justice, and to promote a sense of well-being. In describing the Christian responsibility for eco-

nomic growth, Richard Dickinson relates the doctrine of creation to a
"theology of development":

God has created nature and man, and works through history to
bring his creation to fulfillment. Part of his providence is to grant
men freedom and creativity of their own. The earth is given for
man to inhabit and subdue. Its riches are given for *all* men, irre-
spective of national, racial, religious, ethnic and other barriers which
men create to arrogate to themselves special privileges. This self-
seeking corrupts the real purposes of creation. It deprives both those
who covet power and advantage, and those who are deprived of the
natural riches of the earth—which are also theirs, of their true fulfillment. This deprivation appears in undernourishment which crip-
ples the body, malnourishment which deadens the mind and nervous
system, ignorance which shackles the intellect, deprivation of beauty
which deforms and atrophies the spirit, ostracism which poisons
personal relationships, greed which obliterates sensitivities. Not only
is personal freedom stifled in these ways, but endemic tensions rooted
in inequities poison and frustrate *koinonia*. Gross differences in the
living conditions of men are a corruption of God's creation.[5]

Christian faith affirms the reality and value of creaturely being. Creatures are real, relatively independent, spontaneous centers of being and
power. They are made to be creative in a creaturely way, as God is
creative in a divine way. It is, after all, not finitude but the resentment
of finitude that is evil, and judgment is directed against man's sin, not
against his existence as a man. Seen in this light, the demand (when it
is productive rather than destructive) for autonomy, authenticity, and
integrity is the demand for the right to be a human being. In the cry
for justice there comes to expression the demand to be accorded full
significance as a person, the claim that one should count in whatever is
going forward as one whose personal life and history and destiny are
entitled to the fullest and most sympathetic consideration in their own
right, and not merely so far as profit, expediency, or personal predilection
may dictate.

Biblical creation—faith and the central Christian theological tradition
express a positive evaluation of nature and of human nature. This can
be said despite the sombre implications of the Christian belief that man
and nature have a "fallen" character. The Protestant Reformers are often
thought to have said that man lost the "image of God" in the Fall and

that the effects of his sin extend to all the powers of body and soul, spreading disharmony and corruption through the whole of man. Luther and Calvin did say this, but they said more. The full picture of human nature set within the environment of physical nature was too complex to be exhausted by any one theme or statement. Luther and Calvin both contended that we must "distinguish between original sin and the creature," and remember that if, through the Fall, sin has become natural to man, yet it does not proceed "from nature." Man still remains the creature of God. The "natural" life, even of fallen man, "is a bit of eternal life and a beginning." Man's reason, too, is a "natural light" that is kindled from the "divine light," and it still retains some knowledge of God, even though it is prone to misinterpretation and error. It remains an excellent instrument for conducting the affairs of this temporal life, in which it is the discoverer and governor of all arts and sciences. Similarly, all the natural human affections, and not least love between the sexes, are implanted by God and in themselves are excellent, even though they are tainted by the self-seeking which is the essence of original sin. Furthermore, there remains in fallen man sufficient reason and will to enable him still to exercise a real measure of that "dominion" over the earth, which was part of his original endowment as created in the image of God.[6]

The fact that Luther, Calvin, and others could find no contradiction in saying that man both is, and has lost, the image of God shows the pull of creation—faith as the most primordial of biblical affirmations. Despite its recognition of both finitude and evil, Christian thought sees creatures as essentially and potentially good, as entities enjoying the possibility of the genuine fulfillment of their natures. In the case of human nature, this fulfillment involves the "filling out" of man's distinctive capacities of freedom, intelligence, and love. Historic Christianity, at its best, stands for and works toward the highest and fullest development of human selves. The church is, or ought to be, a community in which the possibilities of human existence are affirmed absolutely.

The well-being of the whole person

The Christian message is that man is God's creature and that "it is God's design for him—and, therefore, the human possibility—that he should grow up into sufficiency and fulfillment in God's providence and through his own trustful responding to God's grace."[7] The language of "growing up" is consistent with the psychotherapeutic insight that the basic direction of the human organism is forward. Albert Outler writes: "The aim and pattern of this forward motion is maturation, understood as fulfillment at every level of the organism's capacities. Men are born to grow up, to develop, to become mature and productive persons, capable of object-love and rational management of their lives, without phobias and anxieties, without regressions and illusions." [8]

It is surely the case that most people do not make it to the goal of maturity. Yet, the Christian life of grace and confidence looks in hope to the well-being of the whole man. "It sets a high value upon health—of body, mind and spirit. But health is not a terminal value in and of itself. . . . The value of health is to supply an efficient agency for the projects of the total self, to provide a fit instrument for the growth and maturation of men and women in community with others and communion with God." [9]

Such an estimate of growth and health is in harmony with the Christian idea of creation, according to which "each finite being in all its aspects was called into existence by God's purposive will. Thus every facet of an entity and every significant factor in man's life is potentially creative, and involved essentially in any real human fulfillment. . . . The whole man included body as well as soul. . . . The basic problem of life, therefore, was no longer the achievement of the victory of one factor of man's nature over another. Rather the central issue of life hinged on the relation of every aspect of man's being . . . to his Creator. In a positive relation of creature and Creator, all the aspects of life, including even the physical and emotional, become essential parts of human fulfillment and human meaning." [10]

William Lynch translates the theological idea of wholeness into psychological language: "There would be little reason for hope and much reason for hopelessness if reality were constructed on basically conflictual lines, in such a way, that is, that if one absolutely necessary human goal were reached another would have to be lost. Then we could not have any good thing without tragedy or without illness. It is not true that one human value is at war with another. All the great human contraries are meant to be at peace and to support each other. . . . There is no basic conflict between any of the basic, permanent elements of the human reality. An organic view of things will make basic conflict impossible. . . . Actually, the human reality, like reality itself, is structured and organic; it nowhere submits to the dominance of one single form and always allows the rights of many elements." [11]

The paradoxical character of human nature

We do not need to be persuaded that "many elements" assert their rights or that the human reality "nowhere submits to the dominance of one single form." Our awareness of this fact often gives talk about wholeness, integration, and forward movement a hollow sound. Man's characteristics and capacities are so ambivalent, unsimple, and two-directional that individual wholeness and social maturity seem impossible dreams. The same human power makes for both advance and retreat, achievement and failure.

Man is conscious of individual selfhood. This quality makes him a special sort of creature, significantly different from every other item, process, or level in nature. Endowed with self-consciousness, man is aware of himself as an organizing center of ongoing experience. The awareness of being an individualized self lies at the root of the sense of personal responsibility. It also supplies man with some of the most indispensable categories of his thought, such as time, substance, cause. Yet this same sense of individual selfhood gives "a quite peculiar intensity to man's instinctive loves and affections. . . . The relationship between 'selves' is a unique relationship, as individual and unrepeatable as the two distinctive individualities which enter into it. Hence, if a man loses his wife or child he loses something which quite literally cannot be replaced. . . . One consequence is that death becomes a far worse problem and affront than it ever is to the brutes." [12] Not only does consciousness of individual selfhood make man a misfit in a world where death is a permanent fact, but the very power to unify the self in space and time enables man to pervert the self by organizing it around base purposes. Each individual is singular, a mere segment of humanity. This singularity enables one to make a particular contribution to life, but at the same time it may result in incorrigible bias.

Man possesses intelligence and exercises thereby the power to distinguish between true and false, to grasp universal principles by means of conceptual thought, and to build up systematic structures of knowledge. Yet man's intelligence creates problems it can never solve, for the very attempt to solve them intensifies them. The mind reaches out for a unified apprehension of the world. It is restless in the presence of contradictions. Yet the very effort to reconcile the polarities of thought and to fill the empty spaces in our knowledge of the world causes the intellectual enterprise "to break down the broad unities of our experience into an ever-increasing number of disconnected scraps and departments . . . synthesis is one of the great needs of our time; . . . yet the intellect, it would appear, cannot meet it." [13]

Man alone has the capacity to look before and after and beyond. He has memory and imagination and he lives by hope. Memory is the basis of all systematic knowledge. Memory and imagination together give man the foresight and creativeness which enable him to survive and to manage his material environment. Yet these powers present man with almost impossible tasks in the management of himself. Fear and worry attain a power in human life which is unknown in the animal world. Mental and physical ill-health are brought about by repressions, submerged memories, continual anxieties, and refusals to face facts. It is the very retentiveness of memory and richness of imagination that make sound personal adjustment so difficult. Moreover, the capacity to look before and after enables man to gather diabolical skill out of the past and to plan the future slavery of his own race.

Man is free. He is able to do something "on purpose." He has the power to direct his action intentionally toward previsioned aims. Freedom is surely a slippery word. But general agreement might be obtained with respect to the suggestion that to be free is to be able to make out a course that is one's own and to pursue it on one's own power. Such a notion of freedom requires that we regard a human self as a creature who is able to superimpose a hierarchy of desires and values upon a physical-chemical system which obeys natural laws but which submits also, within limits, to the direction of the self. Freedom and intelligence together give man the power to organize communities in accordance with meanings, so that individuals act in concert through symbols and ideas instead of being at the mercy of instinct. Yet the intelligence and freedom which are the marks of man's uniqueness are also the marks of his misery. The endowments of freedom and creativity carry with them the problem of what is to be done with them. Persons can make bad choices and character can become deeply corrupt through free choices.

Man is a moral being. He can distinguish between good and bad. Unless he were judge of his own actions, as well as doer, morality could not arise. The pursuit of worthy goals and the reconciliation of conflicts and diverse interests requires sympathetic imagination and a vision of the good. Yet the inescapable discrepancy between the ideal and the actual is a source of despair as well as inspiration.

Man is a social being. To think of man at all apart from his group is to think in a most dangerously abstract way. De-socialized man does not exist, and could not exist. Man's capacity for community enables him to find his highest destiny in organic entirety with his fellows. His interdependence may be, and often is, the occasion for creative and helpful interchange in human affairs. But man's social nature makes him pay dearly for the gifts it brings him. Endless problems are created for him by the combination of intense individuality and intense sociality. It is the very blessing of interdependence that leads to interpersonal conflict. The capacity to love carries with it the capacity to hate and to create the countless ills of strife.

So strange is the ambivalent and paradoxical character of human nature that we can readily ask with the Hebrew Psalmist: "What is man that thou art mindful of him?" (Psalm 8:4). And we can understand why Sophocles should say: "Much there is that is weird, but naught that is weirder than man." Blaise Pascal gave classic expression to the awareness of the ambivalence of human nature: "What a chimera then is man! What a novelty! What a monster, what a chaos, what a contradiction, what a prodigy! Judge of all things, imbecile worm of the earth; depository of truth, a sink of uncertainty and error; the pride and the refuse of the universe!" [14] Both Alexander Pope's *Essay on Man* and Edward Young's *Night Thoughts* echo Pascal's sense of amazement and resignation.

> How poor, how rich, how abject, how august,
> How complicate, how wonderful is man!
> How passing wonder He, who made him such,
> Who centred in our make such strange
>   extremes! . . .
> Dim miniature of greatness absolute!
> And heir of glory! a frail child of dust!
> Helpless immortal! insect infinite!
> A worm! —a god! —I tremble at myself,
> And in myself am lost! [15]

Man's literature has as one of its major themes the thought that this world yearns for a good which in its very nature it cannot embody. There seem to be permanent conditions which stand against the achievement of maturity and mutuality. Nature sets life against life. "Human values split into a thousand varieties of incompatible ideals. We find ourselves divided by our very efforts to realize the wholeness of life." [16]

The hopefulness of creation-faith

One is tempted to coin a new Beatitude: "Blessed is he who seeks to understand and overcome the ambiguities of existence, for he shall have plenty of material to work with." Yet the evidence which points to the contradictions of human nature can be read in two ways. One must make a choice with respect to the weighting or interpretation of the positive and negative features of human experience. In describing these features, one can say that man has such-and-such a positive capacity but that it is unfortunately overpowered or cancelled out by some particular negative factor. Or, one can say that man has a certain negative tendency, but that it is fortunately mitigated, circumscribed, or even transformed by a corresponding positive quality.

A decision as to the priority of one or the other oot of features will be in accordance with one's fundamental vision of reality. Since the Christian view of man grounds human existence in the divine creativity of God and holds that the highest human hope and good is defined by the love of God and that human self-acceptance occurs within the atmosphere created by God's self-disclosure in Christ and immanent presence in the Holy Spirit, we ought to give priority to the positive and hopeful features of experience.

It is interesting to note, however, that an affirmative attitude toward life can coexist with a vision of reality that finds no place for God. Albert Outler comments on the despairing realists of our time: "The most explicitly 'realistic' among our contemporary existentialists (e.g., Sartre, Camus, Heidegger) assure us that their unblinking, morbid gaze at the ordeal and horror of human life is the precondition for recognizing the role of freedom and decision by which man may wrest or salvage more valid meanings than would otherwise be possible in his existence in an idiot world. The uses of pessimism are finally hopeful." [17]

If affirmation can be squeezed out of pessimism, and if courage can be born of anxiety, then how much more should the creation—faith that human existence is intelligible, meaningful, and purposive in its essential nature because its source and origin lie in the will of a gracious God, be able to spawn an unquenchable confidence. Langdon Gilkey argues that "the massive forces of existence, which seem so thoroughly to dwarf human meanings and so frequently to snuff out human purposes, are not the final power in reality, since they are not its ultimate origin. Man is not a tiny, rational, and purposive mite, floating like flotsam on a vast irrational and blind sea. . . . However mysterious they seem to our finite and sinful gaze, the depths of our existence are neither blind nor cold. And since by faith we can know the nature and purpose of the divine will in which is our ultimate origin, we can have a confidence in the underlying order, goodness, and meaning of our finite lives, that could not be derived from any other assumption." [18]

In the light of creation-faith, the Christian can affirm that there is a legitimate hope for good in every human situation. For any situation, no matter how riddled with evil it may be, is subject to the creative transformation through which the human spirit is turned toward its true good. This is so because the universe as a whole is the expression of the beneficent mind and will of God who created the world and man on purpose. This purpose cannot be thwarted because there is no other being with power and ingenuity sufficient to frustrate the divine intent. Bad choices, vicious character, and tragic events are part of an order that allows genuine freedom. But these facts, no matter how desperate, do not impair the soundness of the comprehensive created order within which they occur. Therefore we rightly celebrate the capacity of the power of faith to make man face any experience with the hope that out of it some real good can come.

The cosmic creativity and the personal struggle for wholeness

A positive evaluation of human nature is intrinsic to the Christian faith. Western cultural life has been greatly influenced by this fundamental assumption. Western man, because he has been "Christianized" by his cultural tradition, has the sense that in producing food, comfort, security, in fostering the personal relations of the family, and in improving his society, he is doing something worthwhile.

At the same time, this perspective enables us to give a positive interpretation to the personal struggle for wholeness and harmony. We must hold that such a struggle is an integral part of the cosmic creativity. David Roberts suggests that the image of primitive integrity and innocence associated with Adam and Eve should be taken as indicative of every man's capacity and striving for such integrity and harmony.[19] This striving takes the form of a deep, absorbing desire for identity. The strength of this desire is emphasized by William Lynch in his description of "negative identity": "It is instructive that those of the sick who have not yet fully yielded are inclined to hold on to any kind of actuality, so long as it is actual, rather than make the final break with reality. They, and we with them, will hold on to anything rather than yield entirely to the substitute life. They will hold on to bad parents and bad friends rather than none at all. They will hold on to unpleasant feelings, and even to hate itself, rather than to nothing at all in the feelings. An unpleasant fact is better than no fact at all, and anything is better than having *no* interior life and no self. . . . Negative identity represents a hold on reality. And a human being will hold on to any scrap and the last scrap of reality. . . . It is amazing what people will cling to in the name of existence." [20]

The universal struggle for integrity and wholeness includes, in addition to the deep desire for identity and the tenacious hold on actuality, a primordial sense of the need to belong. Daniel Williams describes the will to belong as "the core of selfhood." The will to belong designates that psychic and organic craving which constitutes our humanity and points "to what we observe in human motives, cravings, sacrifices, satisfactions, and perversities." Williams writes: "The self is thrown into an incomprehensibly vast creation, a world teeming with other creatures, and other selves. Each self tries to find where it fits in this immense and threatening confusion. . . . The power and stubbornness of the self to maintain its being against the onslaughts of an overpowering world is one of its most amazing characteristics. It will grasp at anything, use anything, defend anything in struggling to maintain its poise and strength. . . . The autonomous self wants to be recognized as a self, and it seeks response in the other. . . . There is, therefore, a kind of self-giving in the most elementary level of selfhood. It is the self-giving which offers communication to the other, and craves, waits for, and is rewarded by the response of another. . . . The self must participate in being with its environment and thus begin to belong." [21]

The psychotherapist, and all others who promote healing and wholeness, can take for granted the ultimately positive character of these natural vitalities, drives, and loves. From the Christian point of view, man's effort to achieve wholeness and harmony is not a brief, lonely struggle to create *ex nihilo* some satisfactory meaning, for, as David Roberts puts it, "this struggle is an integral part of a cosmic creativity." [22] The drive toward integration, which man can see in himself, runs beyond man and moves through all levels of creation. This is the point at which the doctrine of the divine immanence connects with all human efforts to reach wholeness. "The destiny of man cannot be conceived apart from his linkage with processes at every level of nature. In this sense God moves *through* His creation." [23] If the human struggle is "an integral part of a cosmic creativity," then we can say that in the struggle against illness, insanity, and evil, man's drive toward health can be counted on because "his essential nature is suited to an appropriate role in this scheme of creation, and because nature is suited to the emergence and sustenance of man." [24]

Grace and the therapeutic process

If resources for healing, harmony, maturity are immanent in human nature, then the therapist—and we are all therapists insofar as we help each other to satisfy the need to love and be loved and the need to feel that we are worthwhile to ourselves and to others—can be seen as one who mediates something much greater than himself. The therapist-professional or amateur—is not himself the source of the trust that unifies and heals. He merely points to a trust which has its source beyond himself and he works with capacities resident in the patient, especially the drive toward fellowship, wholeness, and honesty which is deeply rooted in human life.

As the therapist seeks to discriminate between what is constructive and what is destructive among the forces that work on the human scene, he will seek to formulate a norm of "the good for man" which is not merely a projection of his personal preferences, but is a faithful and realistic reflection of "the status of human values in relation to cosmic process as a whole." [25] Thus, he must place some confidence in what has produced human nature. He assumes that there is no final threat in reality itself, no ground in being for compulsive anxiety. Consequently one can realistically embrace and receive into awareness one's present experiencing no matter how threatening it may seem.

If we say that reality—existence itself—is ultimately curative in all its wide forms, then we are saying that the therapeutic process, taken in its narrow or broad form, involves the mediation of the kind of faith in the ultimate meaningfulness of life which is at the core of religion. Whenever constructive people operate with an active confidence in the curative forces at work in persons and society and rely upon these therapeutic powers to counterbalance the factors of disorder and disablement, they are making an important assumption. Implicit within a concrete therapeutic relationship in which one finds oneself thoroughly accepted and feels the impact of an unconditional positive regard is the assumption that *"being itself* is accepting, that reality is not just a void, . . . but that reality itself in some sense is reaching out to affirm and support the healing process." [26]

In discussing the relation between hope and help, William Lynch argues that while "hope is truly on the inside of us," it is in fact "an interior sense that there is help on the outside of us." [27] In the therapeutic process, the client's quest for meaning and wholeness is met in and through the counselor or friend by a trust which is somehow rooted in reality. Courage is born of the conviction that the final reality which we confront in life is trustable.

The theoretic and operational moves made by the therapeutic disciplines have a remarkable affinity with the traditional idea of grace in Christian theology. For the Christian perspective wants to say that when powers are unleashed which put an end to conflict and enable a person to achieve wholeness and internal harmony on a new level, these powers come from "beyond" the individual's own thought and will. As David Roberts puts it, "healing power is latent in men because it is latent 'in the nature of things.'" [28] The buried resources for healing "are 'there,' so that they can be drawn upon, only because of a divine strategy which reaches back beyond the appearance of man upon this planet." [29] Whenever genuine love occurs in interpersonal relationships, it occurs on the basis of a larger assumption that reality itself is the ground of love, care, and acceptance.

Christian faith points to a power at work in life and history which moves in us and draws us into its mysterious workings. It calls this power God's grace. The generic meaning of grace is that of some help communicated from the outside—the presence and intent of God operating in the complex web of personal life and the human community. The Christian proclamation has said that God moves with power and wisdom and love in our human history to redeem the world from its evil, and man from his sin. In the history of Israel, in Jesus Christ, in the ongoing life of the church, and in all of life, the gracious God makes available to us resources which are our defense against the despair which comes when evil lays waste to life.

The implicit assumption that being itself is accepting, that reality reaches out with its curative powers to support the drive toward wholeness, is made explicit in the witness of the Christian community to God's self-disclosure. For the explicit subject of the Christian proclamation is the presence and power of God's love in spite of the absence of human love and merit and in the very midst of the loneliness and fragmentation of human existence. Thus, we may say that the energy which fuels the power to be human is from the Holy Spirit who is God at work in us actualizing the possibilities he has already created for us. The gracious presence of the Creator Spirit moving out in mission toward the universe is experienced when, in the life of the individual, isolated and conflicting impulses are integrated into a larger pattern, and when the individual finds his place in a community, and, finally, "when human striving and effort cooperate with and are in turn strengthened by the larger strivings of history and of the whole creative process itself." [30]

The correlation between some basic concepts of psychotherapy and the doctrines which theology uses to interpret the actualities of human experience cannot escape notice. If theology wishes to adapt its principles to growing knowledge and if it intends to acknowledge and use the resources of the modern arts of healing, then it ought to incorporate into its doctrine of sin the therapist's description of bondage to inner conflict, and into its doctrine of grace his description of the healing process. But, such an incorporation of empirical or "secular" materials would require theological revision at important points. Albert Outler contends that "the time is past due for a Christian doctrine of man which holds in balance both classical motifs of original sin *and* original righteousness." [31] John Macquarrie makes a similar claim: "Some Christian theologians (myself included) have held that any doctrine of original sin needs to be counterbalanced by a doctrine of original righteousness." [32]

Much of our traditional theology has given a larger place to original sin—the perverted and negative aspect of existence—than to the common grace which is present in the created order and gives it a positive and curative character. Yet the classical doctrine of "the image of God" speaks of a dialectic within which sin and grace are seen as real and existential, not substantial, realities. But in this dialectic, grace is seen as more fundamental. Biblical faith affirms unequivocally the original goodness of creation. Man was created good before he fell into evil. So long as he remains man, some trace of this goodness remains, if only in the form of an image of who he ought to be. Man has undoubtedly disfigured the "image of God" in his inmost nature. But his essential being has not been destroyed by sin, nor can it be since God's power is able to hold in being that which he created in love. Grace penetrates human nature in many ways, not least in the residues of "original righteousness" which constitute the buried resources, the curative forces upon which we draw in the struggle to live, to find identity, to enjoy community.

To affirm that something of an original righteousness remains, even if it is heavily impaired by sin, implies that evil is essentially secondary and parasitic. Creation-faith declares that however desperate evil may be, it cannot be as primordial as goodness. To hold such a view is to take the oneness, the grace, and the power of God seriously. Any other view comes perilously close to the sort of dualism between good and evil which the early church rejected, or to an inverted humanism in which man is seen as a Titan endowed with sufficient power to enable him to defy his Creator in the most radical way.

If we acknowledge the reality of an "original righteousness" that co-exists alongside "original sin" and is even more fundamental, then we may be able to agree with David Roberts' contention that "man's longing to exercise his creative powers should not be regarded necessarily as an indication of pride *(hybris)*. . . .The helplessness to which the doctrine of sin calls attention has far too often been conceived in such a way that the doctrine condemns, as an effort on man's part to 'save himself,' what is really indispensable to man's 'being himself.' " [33] If it is clearly understood that God and man are not active in the same way or on the same level, then it would seem that alterations could be made in the doctrine of sin, in order to develop a positive interpretation of man's natural vitalities, without denying the primacy of grace. Then it could be said that God's power and man's derived power are dynamically related in the ongoing of life.

There is no disposition to suggest that human personality reaches its desired or intended fulfillment when man taps the curative powers resident in nature and human nature. Nor is it our claim that God and man cooperate as partners in the quest for wholeness. Man-on-the-way-to-wholeness is neither a lonely hero nor God's assistant. It is the vital part of the Christian message to say that the potentially grace-full structures and powers of man find their destined fulfillment only when man becomes harmoniously related to God on God's terms. The total constitution of man's being as a creature made "out of nothing" roots his life in the transcendent source of his existence. The human powers of mind, feelings, and will can fulfill themselves only when they point beyond themselves to God. Creaturely life is "good" when the whole existence of man is centered not on earthly securities but expresses its dependence on God in faith and love.

But Christians emphasize that knowledge of the goodness of creation and of the graciousness of God's will cannot be taken for granted, nor does it emerge from an inspection of nature and history. Such knowledge comes through the revelation of God's will in the prophets and in Jesus Christ. "If the Creator's will is motivated by the same love for man revealed in the words of Jesus and by the cross, then the products of his will must exist for fulfillment, and not for mockery and destruction." [34] It is in the Gospel that we see the inmost nature of existence to be love. Through the reconciling love of God revealed in the atoning death of Christ, we understand that the ultimate purpose of God is personal communion with his creature man. In communion with God, man is given back the essential structure of his existence as a creature. In the reunion with God, accomplished by the divine forgiveness disclosed in Jesus Christ, man "learns why he is created: for fellowship with God, for communion with his neighbor, and for the consequent fulfillment of all his human powers." [35]

Grace and Social Process
Man as a being-in-relation

When we consider the manner in which grace penetrates and fulfills human personality, the individual is the main focus of interest. Yet the individual is an abstraction. There really are no individuals. There are only persons and persons are constituted by their relationships. Thus, we must shift our focus from man as a creature to man as a social being.

There are no isolated selves. The human experience is the experience of persons in community. Man is inescapably social, and this means not only that he needs society, but that he is formed and exists in a matrix of social relations. A person is, from the beginning, a life related to others. A person cannot survive, learn a language or achieve maturity in any degree apart from interaction with others. This being-in-relation is not merely accidental to his being, but is constitutive of his being man. He exists only in this way. To be personal is to be interpersonal. Man knows himself *as* a self, and knows what it means to *be* a self, only in relation to other selves which confront him in equal freedom and self-hood. The meaning of his existence is dialogic. He cannot know who he is until he is *told* who he is. Thus he can have only "the vaguest idea of what personality means outside of personal relations. A man knows himself as he is known by another; and, since it is love that opens the one to the other, then the greater the love the greater the knowledge." [36] The truly human life is woven into these social relations. It is in the shared appreciations of social experience that real value emerges. History is the common life of man-in-community and nature is the inclusive environment of history. But our awareness of God's gracious presence in nature and personality depends upon a prior awareness of God which occurs in men's life together. The mutual communication of fellow men is the ground of human experience.

Man is a social being because God has made him that way. Grace is love and love is essentially social. The story of man's creation in Genesis 1-2 pictures man as made for fellowship. Love is social because it is a situation of genuine mutuality, that is, one in which two (or more) persons resolve *to be* for each other. Only in this kind of situation is there fulfillment of personal being. Daniel Williams, in defining an organic as over against a mechanical conception of "the good," describes the social character of love: "The love which is revealed in Christ is a love which seeks the fulfillment of all things in such a relationship to one another that what flows from the life of each enriches the life of all, and each participant in the whole life finds his own good realized through the giving of self to the life of the whole. . . . The fuller good resides where this life and that life, this natural fact and that spiritual aspiration go together in such a way that each person becomes more of a whole person in serving the total order of life actual and possible of which he is a part." [37]

Forms of community as gifts of grace

Since grace is love and love is mutuality, the Creator calls all men to form social structures that will be relatively responsive to the needs and the possibilities of persons. These social structures make up the common life. To say that "God is love" is to say that his unwearied concern is with persons in their aspirations and with their communities as the environments that were meant to support those aspirations. The supportive environments that are penetrated by God's grace take the form of institutions or forms of community which arise out of the nature of man as he is by creation. There are certain forms of life together that are necessary and universal, despite some variations in organization from one society to another. All men are involved in some way with the family, the state, economic activity, and a host of voluntary organizations designed to serve the pursuit of special interests.

The Christian tradition has regarded these forms of community as gifts of grace. Although the New Testament writers affirm the church to be unique among all human institutions, they do not hesitate to describe it in terms drawn from other common social entities, e.g., city, nation, kingdom, commonwealth, race, household, people, colony, tribes, and family. The corporate nature of the believer's relation to Jesus Christ cannot be properly embodied by any one of these social entities. Yet the uniqueness of the church can be meaningfully described in the same terms applied to other and familiar human groups.[38] What God has given to man as creature is not alien to what he has given to man as believer. Throughout its history, the church has given a positive interpretation to the processes common to all human societies, and "at any given time and place it has reflected the patterns and natures of other social groupings in the culture in which it exists." [39]

Luther insisted on the centrality of Christ's atoning work and, therefore, had much to say about the sinfulness of man. Yet he never understood the sinfulness of man to imply the worthlessness of the world. Sinful man is impotent before God, but he is not impotent in the face of social or moral standards. As Edgar Carlson puts it: "The relationship of God to the world defined by the term 'creation' is no less enduring and contemporary than the relationship defined by the term 'redemption.' God confronts man the creature as well as man the sinner. . . . Luther's doctrine of the 'created orders' . . . testifies to an enduring relationship between God and the world which is rooted in creation and which has not been destroyed by sin. . . . There is positive social good involved in the services made possible by social and political relationships apart from and independent of the virtue or faith of the individual who occupies the position or office. A bad ruler cannot alter the fact that government as such is a good, and a bad parent cannot turn parenthood into evil. This good which inheres in the relationship rather than in the person . . . derives from the nature of creation itself and must be regarded as an aspect of the divine Love." [40]

Following Luther, Emil Brunner and other theologians often called "neo-Orthodox" or "neo-Protestant," have used the term "orders of creation" to designate those universal social structures which make possible life in community as opposed to isolated existence.[41] The Christian should look upon these social structures as divine gifts for they reflect the purpose of God in the creation of man for life-in-community.

Theologians of all traditions who affirm the penetration of social structures by divine grace have been able to draw upon biblical materials. The Old Testament is emphatic in declaring that God's spirit goes forth to create and sustain not only nature and personality, but also man's culture. God-in-action, the Spirit, puts forth creative power for the making of the world. The Spirit is a mysterious dynamic power which possesses certain people so as to inspire them and to control their whole personality. But this influence is not restricted to merely temporary accessions of physical strength or of leadership. Kings and other rulers were believed to possess a more permanent endowment of the Spirit, which was thought of as expressing itself in the wisdom and judgment which the holders of such offices in the community needed for the discharge of their duties. The Spirit is said to be especially active in inspiring the prophets and in empowering them to declare the will of God. "The Spirit is the power through which God's sovereign claims and his pastoral care for his people are made effective in the life of the Israelite nation." [42]

In general, the Old Testament treats of a divine righteousness which touches man's life in every dimension: internal and external, spiritual and material, personal and social. Biblical spirituality sets man's life in a firm context of community obligation, and in a responsible relation to the material world. The Deuteronomic Law, which is a product of the prophetic movement, ranges over the whole reach of man's social life. It establishes directions for man's economic behavior as well as for his personal conduct. It guides the God-fearing man when he reaps, harvests, pays wages, loans money, sets prices, sells land, releases creditors, frees slaves, administers justice, wages war, leaves an inheritance, and all the rest. The prophets are also champions of the oppressed and helpless, heralds of the truth that religion and ethics are inseparable and that God requires of his people social justice and public righteousness as well as personal integrity and goodness.

In the New Testament this exhaustive delineation of what the divine holiness requires is not reiterated but is taken for granted. The New Testament adds to the Old Testament vision by grounding the solidarity of mankind in the embodied love of God in Christ. "This new solidarity implements itself first within the *koinonia* . . . but it shortly runs out into political concern and the care of the state, as soon as it becomes manifest that the community of love must coexist with the communities of law, and that the feeding of the hungry and the care of the poor is a political act. It is this coexistence of the community of love with the community of law, and the perception that the law of justice, like the law of God, can be an instrument of love, that sets the problem for Christian political thought." [43]

"Common grace" and the structures of society

The biblical and theological declaration that God's grace penetrates the structures of society was given clear and forceful expression by John Calvin. He used the term "common grace" to designate the sustaining grace of God that is present in civil society, even outside the boundaries of the church. For all of his dark view of fallen man, Calvin had remarkably confidence in man's capacity to create and to preserve a relatively decent social order. He believed that all men could be trusted to know a great deal about the moral law. He says that "man is naturally a creature inclined to society; he has also by nature an instinctive propensity to cherish and preserve that society; and therefore we perceive in the minds of all men general impressions of civil probity and order. Hence it is that not a person can be found who does not understand that all associations of men ought to be governed by laws, or who does not conceive in his mind the principles of those laws." He refers to "that perpetual consent of all nations, as well as all individuals, to the laws, because the seeds of them are innate in all mankind, without any instructor or legislator." [44]

Calvin lived before the moral and social foundations of Western culture were radically shaken. We may think that we have fewer illusions about the goodness of the actual political order. Yet his notion of "common grace," as the power given by God to make this world a better place to live in for all men, both for those who are on their way to heaven and for those who are not, is still a valid and useful concept. John C. Bennett, in commenting on the intellectual ferment in the Soviet Union, says: "One of the most reassuring facts about Russian society is that decades of education, censorship, propaganda and terror have not succeeded in destroying the inner longings for truth transcending the will of the party or the state. . . . Out of the struggles of our period we have learned as one ground for hope that there is a good toughness in the human spirit that often preserves it from dehumanization. . . . Christians may understand this as a mark of the divine image in man or of what Calvinists call 'common grace.' " [45] Reinhold Niebuhr uses the idea of "common grace" to illuminate the tension between self-seeking and self-giving. He argues that common grace, the power of responsibilities and affections to draw the self beyond itself, creates the condition for self-fulfillment which a consistent drive for self-realization can never accomplish. It is a fact, he writes, "that the law of love is indeed the basis of all moral life, that it can not be obeyed by a simple act of the will because the power of self-concern is too great, and that the forces which draw the self from its undue self-concern are usually forces of 'common grace' in the sense that they represent all forms of social security or responsibility or pressure which prompt the self to bethink itself of its social essence and to realize itself by not trying too desperately for self-realization." [46]

Luther did not speak of common grace, but his conception of the "masks" or "veils" of God bears much the same meaning. Luther insisted that God always approaches man through means. There is no unmediated relationship to God. God approaches man in a unique sense through the Word, or through Christ. But he also approaches man through the created orders, for God rules in the order of creation as well as in the order of redemption. "The home and family into which one has been born, the school that he attends, the local magistrate, the job that he is assigned in his community, all the instituted authorities by which his activity is governed—these are 'masks' of God. Luther identifies these created orders with creation itself." [47] The whole created world, as Luther sees it, occupies a kind of mediatorial position between God and man. The various callings, occupations, roles, relationships, and responsibilities constitute the channels through which God acts to minister to the needs of men and through which Christian love flows out to others. All the good that is done to us by other men, according to Luther, we receive in the last resort not from them, but *from* God *through* them. Luther even contended that the law as set forth in the Decalogue and in the Sermon on the Mount has meaning for men because it is fundamentally the same as the Law of Nature that they "naturally" know.[48] Men misuse and pervert the orders and offices of life, but they cannot turn them into evil realities, for the center of hostility to God is in the human heart, not in the institutions and relationships of social life, and "all the created orders, which constitute the environment, are means that God employs to overcome the entrenched evil of the human heart." [49]

The grace-full penetration of the structures of society is thoroughly consistent with the fundamental affirmation that the Creator Spirit moves out in mission to the universe, from the One to the Many, seeking to actualize wholeness and integrity and mutuality on every level of creation. The New Testament picture of the special operation of the Spirit in the Christian society is presented as the restoration and fulfillment of his work in creation and in community. His work in creation is, in fact, the presupposition of his work elsewhere. Thus, in the moving into and through the structures of society the Spirit is not coming to an alien sphere but to his proper home. Therefore, we are encouraged to discover his traces with joy and gratitude everywhere in the natural, personal, and social structures of our world.

In declaring its freedom from some of the rather negative stereotypes of traditional theological systems, recent Christian scholarship has found in the ministry of Jesus a new mandate to look for signs of the kingdom of God in the broadest possible context. Jesus announced by word and deed that the kingdom of God was revealed in and established by his presence. The disciples, transformed into his normative image, become agents of healing in the world. They become whole and free and are empowered to exist for others and joyfully to affirm life. But Jesus identified these same signs of new life outside the circle of disciples, even among those who consciously reject God. "It is as if the power of life that is focused in himself is reflected in various ways throughout creation, and he is at pains to affirm these reflections wherever they occur and to teach his followers to recognize and affirm them also." [50] Thus, in the parable of the Good Samaritan, one who is identified as an unbeliever is the very person in whom grace is manifest and the reign of God is established. "Here Jesus instructs those who would follow him to break through their narrow version of reality and to discover, celebrate, and be nurtured in the power of life wherever it manifests itself." [51]

Whether or not this interpretation of the parable of the Good Samaritan goes too far in its effort to emphasize the free-ranging, universal character of grace, it is certainly true that many Christians draw from the theology of the Reformation the principle that the "law of creation" is not alien to man but is expressive of his essential nature. The Lutheran tradition has specified two "uses" of the Law. The "second use" or function of the Law concerned its power to convict of sin. The "first use" or function referred to the foundation that God established through Law for human fellowship. When speaking about the "first use" of the Law, the theologians meant primarily the biblical commandments. Yet they knew that God had not left himself without witness even for those who were ignorant of the biblical commandments. They saw the "law of creation" as a universal law through which God works to realize love and justice in human fellowship, partly by fighting the evil and destructive forces in human life ,and partly by constructive work for genuine neighborliness and community.[52] The fulfillment of the "law of creation" represents the fulfillment of man, and its defiance is the perversion of man's nature. To think in terms of the "law of creation" means that we meet the will of God in the demands which life imposes. These demands meet us in the family, in society, in work, at every point where men have to do with one another. We cannot escape these demands because we know in our minds and hearts that the needs of our fellowmen have a legitimate claim to satisfaction. But these imperatives do not often take the form of divine commandments; they usually appear as anonymous demands to serve the growth of community.

If we understand "community" as that order in which the members of a society are so related that the freedom, uniqueness, and power of each serves the freedom, uniqueness, and growth of all the other members, then we can see that the God of grace calls man to be a creative participant in the social and historical process. Wherever humane values are realized, man has answered this call, whether or not he acknowledges God.

The call to be a creative participant in community as social process has often been ignored or suppressed by Christians. Some theologians and moralists discount the significance of the general quest for humane values, especially when the channels and instruments are such impersonal factors as institutions, laws, political structures, and the power of technology. Many Protestants find it difficult to understand that the Creator Spirit has anything to do with the organizational character of the church because they have such an individualistic, spiritualistic, and personalistic conception of the Spirit that they fail to see that God created structures as well as persons.[53] Yet, a sound understanding of grace implies a positive interpretation of the structural and impersonal elements of human life.

Grace and social organization

Such a positive interpretation grows out of the necessity and universality of social organization. If important human needs were not being met by systematic cooperation, man would never have invented organizations. And man could not have invented them if the Creator had not endowed him with the capability of forming structured institutions. The fact that human beings always develop some kind of organization leads us to regard this form of life together as an "order of creation." Whether men live in primitive tribes or in complex societies, they have their practices, customs, and institutions. When many people live close together in a high-speed, technological society, they need intricate organization. It is through organization that we provide for economic security, for a high standard of living, for health and education, for dependable transport, and for protection against various misfortunes. "Modern man survives within organization. . . . If he wants to fight the organization, he probably joins an organization for the purpose. To be an individual he depends upon organization." [54]

Our dependence upon institutions often strikes us as a form of bondage. Every organization poses some threat to free personal selfhood. Teachers, students, employers, employees, clergymen, doctors, judges, parents, children—all sense the tension between the actual needs and interests of persons and the impartial demands of the "system." Some of the profound literature of our time records the search for authentic personal life in the midst of all the forces which threaten to depersonalize man.

Institutionalism is like most other things in life in that it involves a tradeoff. It does threaten free personal selfhood. But it is also a fact that "in human life the growth of wholesome personal relations depends in part on the existence of certain impersonal elements. The impersonal factors in laws and institutions . . . are not merely concessions to sin. They enter into and support the growth of the personal factors. We miss the wonder of human personality if we look for it solely in the factors of consciousness and mentality and moral freedom. The most wonderful thing is that these factors appear within and are co-ordinated through the vast world of structures and processes which are not personal. It is the creative work of God which achieves in personality a unique organization of impersonal structures which becomes a new center of power and direction reacting upon the impersonal order." [55]

Daniel Williams' "theology of institutions" offers a positive framework within which we can see beyond our frustrations to the necessity and even the benefits to be found within the system's demands for conformity. It is the very impersonality of the public order that contributes to the making of mature men and women. The bracing demands of a larger world exert steady pressure against sentimental individualism, friendly domesticity, and the idolizing of good fellowship. Adulthood requires impersonal struggles with refractory raw materials, work schedules, legal requirements, constitutions and by-laws. "One can outwit, cajole, or argue down a human opponent, but not a spirit-level nor a time-clock. Either the job gets done or it does not. Either the joint fits, the wall is plumb, the engine runs, or it does not. And meeting this sort of test is indispensable to personal maturity. To be a grown person means not only to be a good companion. It means also to be a disciplined worker." [56]

Impersonality also characterizes the larger patterns of community life that surround the individual. Each man is a member of various organized groups. These groups form the massive structure of organized society. We find that even though the institutional forms of the social order are less impersonal than the physical order of matter, space, and time, they yet have something of the same factual character and call throughout for a more objective kind of behavior than that which is suitable in private personal relationships.

Social organization brings the advantages of large-scale cooperation. Many of the human services we cherish would not be available apart from organization. Yet many contend that efficiency can be purchased at the cost of freedom, identity, and warm personal relationships. It is true that one may lose all personal integrity if he becomes a weak reflection of the system within which he works. But organization need not, and does not, always enslave individuals. Roger Shinn argues that "organization by its nature impresses men with the interdependence of human life and the need that people have for each other. Cooperation, as truly as individualism, has moral value. It is not clear that the old-fashioned rugged individualist, who eyed every man as his competitor, had richer human relations than the modern man, who must work with many others in an organization." [57]

The church must be included within the general claim that most great human concerns are necessarily maintained and propagated by means of institutions. In the depth of its being, the church is a community of faith responsive to God in Christ. Yet the church is also a fully human society that can work only through social and institutional structures. "In its doctrine of the church, the Christian faith is again declaring, as in the doctrines of creation and incarnation, that it is only through earthy entities and structures that God becomes present and manifest. . . . Christianity without a body could be only a ghost." [58]

The church as a visible institution alongside others in the world is essential. It is also sometimes necessary for the church to express itself in elaborately organized forms. But these forms can easily become a conspiracy against God unless the church recognizes the temptation to lead its members in a religious retreat from faith by becoming an end in itself. Thus, there is always a tension between the "event" character of the church and its institutional heritage. The churches in our day have had to change or abandon many of the institutional forms that were characteristic of the past. This means that the "event" character of the Christian life has priority, and when institutional forms stand in the way of new obedience to God's call, they must be given up. Yet, we never escape the problem of deciding what is the continuing institutional life that we need. The Lord calls the church to leave behind all securities, to stretch out beyond institutional forms, and to go out as a pilgrim people in mission to the world. Yet the same Lord equips the church "with continuing forms which express both his care for it and his purpose for it." [59]

Grace and legal structures

A positive evaluation of the institutional aspects of community must also extend to other impersonal channels of common grace, such as legal and political structures. All human societies have laws of one kind or another. Laws are designed to provide the order without which life would be unpredictable and the justice without which no person could ever be safe from harm or seek relief from aggression. Law has a built-in tendency that is favorable to justice, unless the law is perverted by political or economic forces or is vitiated by corrupt administration or by insensitivity to changing social needs. Edwin S. Corwin defines legality: "Law must be general; it must afford equal protection to all;

it may not validly operate retroactively; it must be enforced through courts." [60]

A legal system designates certain ways of life and, by giving them collective sanction, declares that they are entitled to the loyalty of all members of the society regardless of private preferences. The Bill of Rights, for example, establishes the basic legal guarantees of freedom. It defines the rights of freedom of speech, of press, of religion, of petition, and assembly; the right to trial by jury and treatment in accord with due process of law. The courts are guardians of these rights and if these rights are infringed, the impersonal and impartial processes of the legal system come to the aid of the victims.

It is clear that law is closely related to morality. There is a pre-legislative level of moral awareness. Human beings are not neutral. They value certain objects and actions and disavow others. There is a legislative level on which moral values are enacted into positive law, with a coercive element present to guarantee compliance. In this sense, the conscience of the community is expressed through its laws. The laws are sometimes lower and sometimes higher than the private convictions of the citizens. The laws do not often, however, rise above the moral opinions dominant in the community. A law is likely to be obeyed only if it does not make demands which are too far above the moral level of the community as a whole. Yet it is also the case that decisions of the Supreme Court and congressional legislation sometimes run counter to the habits of the majority and the preference of the power structure. But, on the whole, legislatures reflect public opinion and when the courts make law the judges are guided by their own moral convictions and by their interpretations of the conscience of the community. Justice Benjamin Cardozo has written that in deciding difficult cases a judge may have to be guided in his determination of the public good not by considerations of "mere expediency or prudence" but by heeding demands which are "those of religion or of ethics or of the social sense of justice, whether formulated in creed or system, or immanent in the common mind." [61] There is, then, a pre-legal level on which morality precedes and underlies law. There is a legislative and judicial level on which specific laws come to embody and enforce some of this morality. And there is a third level on which morality goes beyond law, calls it in question, demands the recognition of new rights, and recommends ethical behavior that is not subject to any law at all.[62]

No one is likely to believe that in actual practice the legal system embodies purity or perfection. The actual law of any state depends upon the complex of powers and interests which establish it and which are responsible for its enforcement. Laws can be corrupted by those who wield political and economic power. Justice can be frustrated by incompetence, willfullness, or the cost of litigation. Every law represents a compromise between conflicting interests. Law is further limited in that it cannot enact genuine mutuality.

Yet the law has a remarkable capacity for self-correction, if there is no deliberate interference with its workings. The process of self-correction "includes the following elements: the procedures in the courts, the limited roles of the various participants, the rules of evidence, the publicity, the carefully kept records, the appeals to higher courts, the establishment of precedents which become guides for the future but which later experience can overturn, the emphasis in all this on 'due process' so that actions can be invalidated if this process of self-correction is not faithfully observed." [63] After assessing the benefits and the limitations of the law, John C. Bennett affirms that "justice under the law" is "one of the highest human achievements and one of the most precious gifts of 'common grace.' " [64]

If systems of legal control are universal and, for the most part, beneficial, then we should give law, like organization, a positive interpretation and recognize it as one of those necessities of our human life that serves love. The common structures and principles which stand impartially beyond the particular wishes and passions of individuals provide the stable common ground in which personality can exist and social interchange can flourish. Law offers one of the conditions of personal freedom and growth "when it imposes an element of impersonal principle upon all the members of society." [65]

Grace and political order

The collective political structures of the human community should be given the same positive interpretation as channels of common grace as that which has been given to the institutionalization of life and the development of legal controls. When we consider the massiveness of the state and the ambiguities of its use of power, ranging from tyranny to sensitive caring, can we say that the grace of existence moves through the political order? The long and consistent tradition of Christian thought has held that the power of the state and the instrumentalities of politics are "ordained of God" for limited but none the less vital and beneficial ends.

This tradition is rooted in the attitude of Jesus to the state. In some typical texts, Jesus endorses governmental authority because it is intended by God, even though that power is often misused (John 19:1-11). He declares that it is right to pay taxes because they are essential to the state's God-given role of keeping justice, order, and peace. But there is a limit to the subservience the state can demand. Since God has final authority, the state must be denied the right to absolute obedience (Mark 12:13-17).

In the rest of the New Testament one finds two emphases which reflect the polarities involved in Jesus' cryptic saying about God and Caesar. On the one hand, most New Testament writers saw the state as a God-given institution which was necessary for human life and to which Christians owed obedience (Romans 13 and 1 Peter 2). There is a strong sense of divine providence working through political authorities. On the other hand, the positive affirmation of the mandate of government is balanced by a negative emphasis upon the limits of the functions of the state (1 Corinthians 6 and Revelation 13). Christians are not only told to show the provisional character of the state by living on a higher level than its laws command, but they are warned against an absolute state with pretensions that have become demonic. It is not always true that the Christian should obey the governing authorities. While the New Testament does not urge political resistance to unjust government, many Christians have found in Romans 13 an implicit standard by which a state can be condemned as no true state and on this basis they have endorsed not only verbal protest but also revolutionary action. It is a long way, however, from first-century Rome to twentieth-century America. Therefore, says John C. Bennett, "The most that we can learn from the New Testament is that there must be political authority, that the Christian should take a positive attitude toward the order-creating functions of civil government because in and through them the providence of God is at work in preserving essential conditions for human life, and that the state should be kept in bounds and not be allowed to usurp the place of God." [66]

From this basis, theological and political thought in the West have come to agree that a distinction must be drawn between the state and the human community. The state is the most comprehensive organization man has developed. But it is not identical with the community. It is instead a legal association for limited purposes. The purposes of the state are defined by law and are confined to such purposes as can be achieved by law. The state is, therefore, that organ of the human community which lays down laws and enforces them for the purpose of enhancing the common life. "The state presupposes the existence and autonomy of voluntary associations within the community. . . . This limits the function of the state to the coordination and harmonizing of the free activities of its citizens as individuals and as members of voluntary associations." [67]

The coercive power of the state is very real and it can be both irksome and oppressive. Yet, it is necessary that in every nation there be a source of final authority which can act with force. Therefore, citizens have consented to giving the state a monopoly of physical force with the legal right and power to use this force for specified purposes. Thus, consent and coercion are closely interwoven in the activities of the state. The state serves a great variety of needs within the community. It exists to promote order and security, justice, freedom, and welfare. All of these aims are to a remarkable degree interdependent. The healthier a nation is, the less it will have to depend upon force in serving these ends. The state can even function as "the agent of a sensitive caring for the welfare and the dignity of all its citizens." [68]

If the state provides some of the conditions of mutuality in the common life, then we must regard the political order as having the potentiality of mediating the grace of existence. Alexander Miller puts a positive interpretation upon the main function of the state: "Justice is love operating at a distance, amid the impersonalities of the social and national communities; . . . it does not represent that final transcendence of interest which is the fruit of grace and grace alone, but it does achieve that precarious balance of interests which makes human life livable this side of redemption; . . . it is also a mechanism by which love can operate amid the collectivities of life." [69]

Grace and human responsibility in the historical process

If we believe that God calls man to be a participant in community as social process, then we must also believe that human activity in the form of organization, law, and the state have the possibility of providing conditions under which the work of grace may be more fully released. But community as social process moves through time, and we must consider God's call to be creative participants in community as historical development. It is a basic element of the theology of creation to hold that the world is an unfinished world and that its structures and processes are pliable in the hands of the creative God and, to some degree, in the hands of his creatures. But the theology of creation cannot be separated from the Christian view of history since history is the realm in which the depth-experiences of personal creatures occur. Consequently, we must say that the grace of God is operative in human history to achieve a continual victory of good over evil. There would be no world at all, if there were not a continual realization of good.

From the first pages of the Old Testament, it is evident that Israel meets and knows God in the midst of her history, in her involvements in political crises and complex social and cultural problems. In the Incarnation, God relates himself once and for all to man within a dynamic historical process. God meets us in the history in which we live. He has given us the treasure of his grace in "earthen vessels" (2 Corinthians 4:7). The Christian tradition uses the word "grace" to describe the divine presence in human affairs. Seen from one angle, history is a tragic story of what man has made of his possibilities. But from another angle, history is the record of God's unfailing care for his creatures. The doctrine of providence sums up all the effects of God's love in our lives.

The purposive presence of God in human existence must be seen in its widest scope. Daniel Williams has described the mission of grace to the universe with unsurpassed eloquence and precision: "Through infinite time God has been at work to make a world, and to make it a good world. With patience and power beyond our imagination He has made a cosmos out of primordial chaos. He moved through the struggle and surge of the evolutionary process, bringing new levels of life into being, and crowned His work with the creation of mind and spirit. He has created free men who can participate with Him in the ongoing task of world-making. Man has risen from savagery and barbarism to civilization in response to the divine working within him. In the progress of reason, in all cultural expression, and supremely in the growth of moral and religious insight man has had his life opened to the new adventure of partnership with God. God's purpose and power have been revealed everywhere; but it is in the experience of one people, the Hebrews, that the depth of that purpose was clarified and made known with power. In one life, which arose in the midst of that people, God uttered His truth and spirit in such a way that His love, which is His very essence, became known and operative with transforming power." [70]

On the day of Pentecost, the early Christians interpreted what was happening to them as a fulfillment of Joel's prophecy that God's Spirit will be poured out "upon all flesh" (Acts 2:16-17). Although Christian people have tended to limit the Spirit's operation to faithful church members, there have always been those who have insisted that the impact of the Spirit as the active presence of the Father of Jesus Christ has been more widely felt in the world than we are inclined to believe. Such a conviction is consistent with the belief that God's purpose for mankind is one and that God intends all nature, personality, and social process to be penetrated and fulfilled by grace. God does not postpone the gift of his gracious presence to the unevangelized until the end of their lives. He is present to them in grace from the awakening of their consciousness. Thus, there are no grounds for restricting the response to grace to the minority who belong to the Christian church.

The order of grace is present universally throughout mankind. There are secular realities and secular activities, which have their place and autonomy, but there is no self-contained order of "nature" standing over against "grace" or even over against the church. Nor is history in the concrete ever a merely secular history unaffected by grace. Men who are not Christians by name are helped by God's grace to grasp and pursue such values as the dignity of the human person with all the implied freedoms, rights, and duties. The difference between the church and the world, then, is not that God rules in the church but not in the world. The difference is that within the church it is known under whose grace and governance we stand. Charles Forman writes that, according to their own belief, Christians "have no special corner on God's love. God does not love Christians more than pagans. He does not love church members more than atheists. In fact, church members are the recipients of God's love, not because they are a part of the church, but because they are a part of the world. It is the *world* that God has 'so loved' (John 3:16). This includes the Moslems, Jews, Buddhists, atheists, and agnostics along with the Christians. In Christ we know that God loves men no matter who they are." [71]

But *where* do we discern the Spirit's working outside the boundaries of the empirical church? The most adequate way to relate the idea of grace to social process is to say that God's action in the world aims at transformation. Hendrikus Berkhof points out that the idea of transformation has its roots in the New Testament, where conversion includes the creation of a new pattern of behavior, which in the long run influences the environment and transforms the social and cultural structures. The mutual behavior of husbands and wives, parents and children, masters and slaves is a matter of deep concern to the apostolic writers (Ephesians 5:21—6:9; Colossians 3:18—4:1; 1 Peter 2:18—3:7).

Although the New Testament has much to say about moral obligations, we cannot deduce a comprehensive social ethic from the pages of Scripture. Its central thrust is to say that God in Christ has made all things new and that believers are required to share in this transformation of the world. The justified man who has been given peace with God through grace, and to whom God has entrusted fellow humans, is also the man who shares in the active expectation and operation of the Kingdom of God, in the light of which we cannot accept the perpetuation of injustice, tyranny, and war. It was clear to the early Christians that forgiveness sets men free to act for the neighbor and to move ahead, despite conflict, self-interest, and ambiguities of all kinds. It was also clear to them that justice required actions to be taken and structures to be shaped to defend the powerless members of society. They could also rely on the belief that in the midst of struggle and hostility, persons and perspectives can be transformed through the reconciliation of differences. Trusting that every moment of history is shaped by the divine activity, they looked for evidences of God's action and for opportunities to enhance human wholeness along the road to the future.

Many have undertaken to describe the ways in which the church, in the postbiblical period, influenced its environment, and was, in turn, influenced by its environment. Although opinions can differ widely about so complex a process of social and moral interaction, a good case can be made for the claim that when the Roman Empire became nominally Christian in the fourth century, a certain Christianization of society was inaugurated. In some of the "Apologies" of Christian writers in the first three or four centuries, one notices a sense of deep concern for the responsibilities of Christians in their social environment. It is as though many Christians could not believe that God intended all the hard political work, which must be done if tolerable conditions are to be preserved on the earth, to be done by infidels. That would be equivalent to saying that God intended Christians to be parasites on the life of the world at large.

Prior to the fourth century, the church's response to Roman law was expressed chiefly in the principle of civil disobedience: laws that conflict with Christian faith are not binding in conscience. But when the church came to operate within the power structure, it faced the question whether the emperor's acceptance of the Christian faith had anything positive to contribute to his role as a legislator.

In a collection of laws promulgated in about A.D. 740, the Christian emperors of Byzantium expressed their sense of Christian responsibility. The Preamble of the *Ecloga* states in its opening paragraph: "A selection of laws arranged in compendious form by Leo and Constantine, the wise and pious Emperors, taken from the Institutes, the Digests, the Code, and the novels of the great Justinian, and revised in the direction of greater humanity, promulgated in the month of March, Ninth Indiction in the year of the world 6234." [72] The effort to revise the laws "in the direction of greater humanity" had gone through several stages. Harold Berman writes: "Under the influence of Christianity, the Roman law of the postclassical period reformed family law, giving the wife a position of greater equality before the law, requiring mutual consent of both spouses for the validity of a marriage, making divorce more difficult, and abolishing the father's power of life or death over his children; reformed the law of slavery, giving a slave the right to appeal to a magistrate if his master abused his powers and even, in some cases, the right to freedom if the master exercised cruelty, multiplying modes of manumission of slaves, and permitting slaves to acquire rights by kinship with freemen; and introduced a concept of equity into legal rights and duties generally, thereby tempering with the strictness of general prescriptions." [73]

To these humane revisions of the legal system, could be added other references to the ways in which Christianity effected a decisive change in social morality. It deepened the sense of the sanctity of human life not only by discountenancing infanticide, but also by ending the scandal of taking human life for sport and by providing care for the oppressed, the helpless, the deprived. "The discovery of the philanthropy of God gave a new confidence and a new dimension to philanthropy in human society." [74] The maintenance of Sunday, the protection of the church, and the introduction of the concept of the essential unity of the human race as a consequence of the common nature and destiny of men were essential features of the gradual and partial Christianization of society.

In both East and West, reforms and innovations were introduced by Christian kings, by Cluniac monks, and by the Decretals of Pope Gregory IX (1294). The canon law of the later Middle Ages was the first modern legal system in the West. Alongside it there emerged various types of

secular law which emulated canon law in transmuting the complex categories of the obsolete Roman law into abstract legal concepts, such as
the principles of reason and of conscience. In this way, the church sought
over many generations to legalize morality and to moralize legality.[75]

It is a commonly-held opinion that this positive process of Christianization ceased in the periods of the Renaissance and the Enlightenment and
was gradually replaced by the negative process of secularization. Many
contemporary theologians, however, deny this opinion. Hendrikus Berkhof, for example, argues that secularization is "the continuation of Christianization. The difference lies in the fact that in modern times the consequences of the gospel are mainly drawn by those who are outside of
the church and who are not aware of the source of their inspiration."[76]
Ronald Gregor Smith sees the Renaissance as "the new world which was
ushered in with the break-up of medieval civilization. . . . No other
great change has taken place, and in fact a proper assimilation of the
change which then took place is still our main task and way into a
responsible future."[77] The essence of the change lay in man's self-understanding. History was no longer seen as the necessary but tiresome ante-
chamber of supra-history, but as an existent power whose meaning could
be sought in itself. People "discovered all manner of new and autonomous interests and pursuits: the religious experience of the individual,
the independence of intellectual pursuits, the liberated imagination in art,
the liberated individual in political organization, the rise of new political
and economic groupings, the rise of politics as an independent art, and
finally a new philosophy in the attitude of the experiencing subject to
reality."[78] The flowering of these interests in modern science, philosophy,
literature, political science and technology has been due to the change in
man's self-understanding. Smith writes: "All this activity was possible
because man understood his situation in history in a new way. He saw
himself as free, and as responsible for making his own life, and as open
to a future which was not an arbitrary or threatening disposition of fate,
but was awaiting him as his own destiny."[79] Smith sees the Renaissance
as "an efflorescence of the Christian spirit which went beyond the bounds
prescribed by medieval philosophy." He quotes with approval some words
of Luther: " 'The sphere of faith's works is worldly society and its order.'
As Dilthey says, justly, 'With this sentence there enters into history one
of the greatest organizing thoughts that a man has ever had.' "[80]

Charles Davis adds to this testimony that the revolution in human
self-understanding which marks modern history is not in its essence at

variance with Christianity. In discussing "the dechristianization of the modern world," he writes; "The faith lost by the average man in the West was an imperfect faith, what might be called a cultural faith. The Christian tradition, superficially understood, was simply accepted as part of the culture in which one lived. . . . This situation did not do justice to the transcendent quality of Christian faith. . . . The so-called dechristianization of some areas is simply an awakened Christian awareness of the absence of faith there. . . . Is it not truer to say that the great industrial cities were never Christian than that they have lost the faith? So, while no doubt the absorption in the secular has drawn many from the faith and increased the power of secularism, the general dechristianization of the West is not the destruction of faith by secular culture. It is the uncovering of the defects of Christian evangelization, the breaking down of the political and social facade that hid those defects, and the consequent purification of the Church for a renewal of its spiritual mission. In the world situation of today, where Christians are a proportionately decreasing minority, what social context offers the best chance of carrying out the Christian mission? The answer . . . is a pluralist, open or secular society." [81]

An affirmation of secularization obviously implies an endorsement of the essential features of the phenomenon. Secularization may be defined rather briefly as a state of mind and a pattern of relationships characterized by preoccupation with the factual, the relative, the relational, the inclusive, the immanent. Reality is in events. Rational man grasps knowledge and truth by describing accurately what he sees and feels. He does not try to deduce values from a timeless order of reality. He is concerned with life in this world, within the historical process. He sees that communities, ideologies, and cultures are shifting, relative entities. They are not the source of certainty and security. Social advance is the only security. Community is man's task and for its realization he requires freedom and education.

Can this perspective be harmonized with Christian faith? There are Christian thinkers who contend that modern science and technology would not have been possible apart from biblical faith which secularized nature by demythologizing and dedivinizing it. It is seen in the Bible as purely "natural." It has been stripped of demonic and divine forces. It can be studied and manipulated. Biblical faith affirmed the worth of human work, especially by refusing to allow a distinction between the "higher" activity of the mind and the "lower" activity of the hands.

From the psychosomatic unity of man there flow such consequences as the validity of earthly activities, including the use of observation and equipment in the effort to gain empirical knowledge of the world. Biblical faith secularized law by making it the servant of claims and relationships which corrected and modified the very legal systems which protected them. Biblical faith secularized the forms of religious community by making them subservient to the covenant relation, whose constancy lay in the character of God and not in the structure of the community. Biblical faith also affirms culture, that is, the process whereby man creates the values and conditions by which he lives. Biblical man believes that change is both possible and desirable, since he is not trapped within a fatalistic or cyclic historical order. The God who discloses himself in events of social change, notably the Exodus, has ordained that history shall be the theater of human responsibility.[82]

Western Europe and North America were the chief bearers of science and technology because the dymythologizing of nature had taken place in these areas in the most radical way. Without this radical change in man's concept of nature, implicit in the Bible and explicit in the Renaissance and its aftermath, it is doubtful whether science, technology, and medicine would ever have developed in their present form.

A positive interpretation of secularization sees common grace mediated through the humane effects of science and technology. But "the consequences of secularization in social and political areas also have a Christian background."[83] We have already seen that biblical faith secularized law and culture. The early church introduced a significant innovation by drawing a distinction between church and state, between the religious and political spheres. The distinction was based on the conviction that the mission of the church came from God through Christ and was not subject to the authority of the state. This contention radically limited the power of the state, which before had always extended over the whole of human life. The distinction was a clear one, but the conversion of Constantine caused confusion, and neither the medieval commonwealth nor the Reformation territorialism could escape extending the confusion between the two spheres in practice.

In relatively recent times, the spiritual forces within the church broke through and produced a new vision of the faith and mission of the church. Then it became possible to recognize that "the new, democratic freedoms, despite many ambiguities, were a genuine advance in man's political consciousness."[84] A positive interpretation could be given to the state as a secular reality. This means that the power of the state does not extend into the realm of the spirit. The state is not concerned with the transcendent nor with man's eternal destiny. Its function is limited to temporal affairs, and its powers should not be used to further any religion or ideology that claims to possess ultimate truth about man and the world. No state has an immediate divine mandate. "All political systems are relative and changing. They come within the sphere of man's developing understanding, and are subject to his intelligent modification and control." [85]

A further distinction should be made between the state and society. The secular state becomes an agency with a limited role within society. But society is a wider reality, embracing personal and corporate freedom. Whereas the state is concerned with public order, society aims at the common good. "The common good includes all the social goods, spiritual, moral, and material, which men pursue together." [86] A secular society is a human community that has not committed itself to any particular view of ultimate truth. It is a pluralist society, including within itself a variety of attitudes about ultimate beliefs and values. It is not officially grounded upon any religion or upon any ideology hostile to religion. The consensus with respect to the cultural values that must be accepted if the society is to survive, is secular, not in the sense that it excludes the sacred, but in the sense that it prescinds from it "in building a social order on a minimum of common aims and principles acceptable to men who differ on any question concerning the transcendent." [87]

Yet, the concept of grace implies that to speak of the secular state or the secular world is to speak of an abstraction. If we mean by the "world" the totality of the lives and activities of men outside the church, then it is not exclusively secular. It is the effect of grace, the product of the divine presence in history. Grace is at work everywhere. Sin causes setbacks. Yet, the historical process is a working out of God's plan, a plan which is operative through grace and embraces the whole of history, not just the part directly related to the church. There is an explicit disclosure of God through the historical media of revelation. But there is also a movement of the divine through history by its latent presence through the working of grace in the consciences of all men. Thus, ordinary history is not just secular. Underlying its secularity is the hidden presence of common grace. Outside the church, humane values are supported by an "anonymous Christianity." It is clear that many who have no commitment to ultimate truth are capable of promoting human brotherhood "with energy and integrity, often surpassing Christians in doing so. The same may be said of the other values at the basis of a truly open society. . . . Secular society is a *kairos* for the church." [88]

Hendrikus Berkhof extends the notion of "transformation" even to the revolutionary developments in modern history. He urges that the God of the Bible is not another name for the existing social order, but is the revolutionary God, who lifts up the burdened and casts down the oppressors, who resists poverty and promotes equality. This image of social standards, Berkhof writes, "is the primary source of our modern revolutions, in which again and again new groups of oppressed claim their rights. The French Revolution, with its ideals of liberty, equality, and fraternity, had far more to do with Jesus Christ than had those who resisted it in the name of Christ. After the French Revolution we witnessed the emancipation of the slaves, the women, the laborers, the colored races. Since the Second World War this revolutionary movement goes on at an accelerated speed over the whole world. The liberating and transforming power of the Spirit of Jesus Christ is at work wherever men are freed from the tyranny of nature, state, color, caste, class, sex, poverty, disease, and ignorance." [89] It is interesting that Nicholas Berdyaev, who suffered greatly as a result of the Russian revolution, asks in his autobiography if it is possible *not* to see in the uprisings of men against tyranny and callous neglect of human rights an outbreaking of the Spirit of God, who works through judgment as well as mercy.

The shape of Christian obedience in the world

Conversion, transformation, Christianization, secularization, liberation. These powerful words point both to the presence of grace and to the human response to grace. The Christian, who is not only a social being by nature but a member of the "body of Christ" by faith, cannot turn away from the world. Christian experience is essentially corporate for it is the work of the Holy Spirit to reconcile men to God and to each other. What can be said about the shape of Christian cooperation with what God is doing in the world? What picture of Christian obedience is consistent with the full scope of grace?

St. Paul made a careful distinction between law and gospel. A human being is a "Christian" if he hears and believes the gospel. He lives a "Christian life" by doing the works of the law in Christian faith. But the law in question is not a special "Christian" law which prescribes an ideal for church members that is unknown to non-Christians. The works done by Christians in the world must be fruits of faith and deeds of love. They are to be done not for the sake of an ideal, nor for the sake of our own improvement, but simply for the sake of our neighbor. "They are not 'Christian,' but necessary, needful not in order that we may be Christian—for that is something we can only be by faith—but needful for human life." [90]

There is no special "Christian" ethic that Christians are to imprint upon the world. There is only one kind of ethics for the Christian—it commands that our works of love are determined only by the needs of our fellowmen and not by ideals that would confer on those who attain them some kind of moral perfection. If our good works are determined only by the needs of our fellowmen, then they cannot be specifically and uniquely Christian, since human needs have always existed, and will always exist, whether Christians are present or not. The actions that satisfy the real needs of men are not changed in character or aim because they are done by a Christian. These are the deeds that every man, Christian or non-Christian, ought to do for the sake of his neighbor. And all men need basically the same things. The Christian is not commanded to do good works other than those every man ought to do for his neighbor.

There are distinctively Christian components in the moral posture of the responsible believer. The creative and redemptive will of God, the model of obedience found in Jesus Christ, the priestly and prophetic functions of the church, and the hope of ultimate fulfillment have much to do with one's disposition toward the world, with the cultivation of those qualities of life that make for morally fruitful action, and with the enjoyment of certain satisfactions. But a straight line cannot be drawn from such beliefs and attitudes to a special set of "Christian" values.

In the light of the biblical doctrine of the grace of God and the Reformation insight that deeds of love are to have the needs of the neighbor as their sole motivation, it can be said that questions which have to do with daily bread and freedom, with education and conservation, with honesty and fair play, with consideration and generosity, are *human* problems, not Christian problems. "But just because they *are* human problems they are of endless and costly concern to Christian men." As we work out our obligation in society, "there is no peculiar form of Christian duty, but only a peculiar Christian urgency to do our human duty well." [91] The normal human duties that fall to all men, and which the Christian ought to perform with particular energy and diligence, are summed up in justice and justice, in turn, is broadly recognized as equality—equality of opportunity, of possessions, of rights before the law. Christian ethics, then, is the ethics of justice, achieved in the spirit of love. Therefore, we acknowledge the works of justice and love done by non-Christians with as much gratitude as those done by Christians. At the practical level, Christians will find their allies "not on the basis of creedal affinity or community of faith, but among men who love justice and who can agree about what best serves justice in a present and particular case." [92]

The church and the structures of society

If Christian obedience takes this shape for the man or woman who is seeking to cooperate with what God is doing in the world, what can be said of the manner in which the church, as a social unit, is called to service? It is often said that the church today is uncertain about its functions and about its relation to the structures of society. But the confusion may be more apparent than real. Many seem to welcome the alleged confusion because it provides a refuge from the hard necessity of choosing between alternatives or of formulating a multi-faceted concept of function and role. The confusion can be greatly reduced if attention is given to certain factors.

Clarification must begin with a bi-focal perspective. Jesus said of his disciples, "they are not of the world." They are a holy people, called to be citizens in an eternal kingdom of faith and love. On the other hand, Jesus said, "I have sent them into the world." They are also a secular people, called to be citizens of a temporal kingdom of law and justice, knowledge and skill. God is the single Lord of life, whether he rules men as saints through Christ, the gospel, and the church, or as creatures through law, reason, and cooperation.

There may be some ground for confusion in the fact that it is difficult to be *in* the world but not *of* it. Too many fall into the confusion of being thoroughly *in* the world, bound by its horizons, guided by its criteria, restricted or liberated by its prospects. For them, religion merely endorses and confirms the structures of society, the transcendent is domesticated, there is no leverage for an independent criticism of society, and Christianity becomes the culture-religion of Western man. On the other hand, there are too many who fall into the confusion of being *out* —way out—of the world. They are preoccupied with private values and are waiting for the Lord to come and "take them home."

But there is no excuse for thoughtful people to be taken in by such specious alternatives. It is true that from Paul to Augustine to Aquinas to Luther and Calvin and their British, French, and American successors, the dialectic between state and church or society and church has been difficult to manage and has oscillated between state control of the church and church control of the state. Americans can take some satisfaction in the fact that the First Amendment rules out both a state-controlled church and a church-controlled state. In working out a concept of the relationship between the church and the structures of society, of which the state is the most comprehensive and ultimately the most coercive, Americans have been guided by the formula: institutional separation and functional interaction.[93] Jefferson's absolute "wall of separation" has been only relatively absolute. It has been clear enough to prevent a harmful intermingling of political and religious institutions, but it has favored a degree of functional interaction to which most citizens can give their approval.

Americans live in a pluralistic setting which allows the church to relate to the structures of society, and to define its own role, under the rubric of "coexistence and coordination" or of "functional interaction." One further factor affects our present way of understanding the role of the church. "The church in our time is no longer in a position to lord it over the world in the old medieval sense, attempting to draw the whole of the culture under its 'christianizing' influence . . . the church no longer can provide a stable center to culture—a controlling world view or value system to hold society together."[94] Colin Williams explains that we live within an "exodus culture." "Our whole culture is traveling away from its old institutions—leaving all established ways—and is prepared to live in a permanent exodus situation outside the safety of all mental and cultural systems that provide safe structures of order. We live in a situation in which we are moving constantly from one temporary structure to the next."[95]

The "exodus culture" involves a "diaspora situation" for the church. "Christendom" is rapidly dissolving, so that the church is becoming a dispersed people even in the West. As the population explosion continues unabated, Christians each year become a smaller minority in a single world society which is secular in character. This "cultural disestablishment" of the church affects in a most direct way our understanding of the role, and perhaps even the nature, of the church.

If it was ever the case that the church was the arbiter of culture and the only guardian and promoter of human welfare—a claim often made for the medieval period or the sixteenth century—it is so no longer. The minority position of the church in an open, pluralist society means that it has a joint, not the sole, responsibility for social welfare. The church shares the function of commending humane behavior with its associated social and political community. It must guide and shape morality in partnership with "the totality of the ethically involved forces in the community." [96] In a pluralistic society, the church is one member of a coalition of morally oriented agencies, which includes the educational, the legal, the psychiatric, the journalistic, and the governmental sectors. Therefore, the church no longer controls the ethical tradition. In fact, it no longer controls *Christian* ethics, since the church has learned much about needs and strategy from the world and has seen secular agencies exert their parallel pressure on behalf of justice and reconciliation.[97]

Yet the church has a unique role to play in this coalition. The most common designation of this role is to say that the church must assume the position of a "servant." The church must work in the world, for the world's sake, without seeking to establish a theocratic lordship or Christian domination over different spheres of life. There is a difficulty, however, in saying that the church, without claiming anything for itself, exists to serve secular society. This idea raises christological problems, since "if Christ came only to serve in humility and anonymity, his logical goal could only have been oblivion." [98] One could hardly say that the church *is* its mission, since it must *be* a distinguishable entity in order to *have* a mission. The church's mission could be lost in the world unless we stress the independence of the church's own base, its transcendence of the world. The being of the church is lodged beyond itself. Without ceasing to be genuinely human, social, and historical reality, the church has its existence in God who has called it into being in Jesus Christ. In some sense, then, the church must transcend the city, the culture, the state, and any local situation to which it would speak. The church points to the God who is immanent *as* the transcendent One, and something of this character must pass over into the worshipping community.

Despite the human failings of its members, who have no special aptitude for saintliness, the church represents that group of men and women who explicitly define true humanity by what they see in Jesus Christ and who base their prospects of fulfillment upon what humanity becomes in him. The unique role of the Christian partner in the moral coalition is to publicize the symbols of judgment and fulfillment, as these symbols are drawn primarily from biblical images of wholeness-oriented human faith and conduct, and secondarily from secular wisdom about the most effective ways of serving real human needs. Religious vision cannot be embodied in concrete and effective action without translation into worldly language. But secular wisdom, apart from the biblical images of human wholeness and depth, always runs the risk of settling for a shallow anthropology.[99]

In the light of this picture of the situation and mission of the church in a pluralistic society and in a world whose structures are penetrated by grace, we must develop a complex and multi-faceted concept of its functions as it co-exists or interacts with the associated communities it is called to serve. Seven functions can be specified.

First, the church functions as *Worshiper*. Through its services of public worship, including the preaching of the Word, the administration of the sacraments, and especially in its prayers of intercession, the church is related to society. It is simply indispensable that the church witness to its transcendent Source.

Second, the church functions as *Advocate*. It urges citizens to obey the laws and to do their duty. The church affirms human needs and the means of meeting them. This is the church's conserving function.

Third, the church functions as *Critic*. It is a critic for it cannot affirm in an uncritical way anything that is human. It knows that all things human will face judgment. Therefore, the church must proclaim the law of God which requires conduct that is productive of peace, human wholeness, and well-being. But, since individuals and social structures are never fully responsible, there is need for the proclamation of the law in order to make visible the potentialities and the limits of human behavior.

Fourth, the church functions as *Teacher*. The church must instruct, empower, and guide Christian citizens with respect to social action that is in keeping with the gospel. Christians disagree as to the degree of concreteness with which the church should speak. But they are agreed that the church should address itself in some considered way to public issues.

Fifth, the church functions as *Pastor*. It should give pastoral care to its members who are in positions of leadership and influence in voluntary organizations and in public office.

Sixth, the church functions as *Partner*. It cooperates with public and private agencies which care for those in need. Partnership between church and community involves an identification with the cause of those who suffer need as well as those who suffer under social injustice and who cannot win the battle alone for freedom, justice, and equality.

Seventh, the church functions as *Pioneer*. The church must be more than a critic and co-worker. It must also stimulate and inspire. The church should innovate in meeting needs more creatively than they are now being met by parallel agencies, public or private. The church can, for example, undertake many pilot or experimental projects that are not being undertaken by other agencies.

There is little reason for confusion about the relation of the church to the structures of society. Our laws and customs are based on the principle of institutional separation and functional interaction. Governmental and all but a very few ecclesiastical agencies are clear as to this principle. Moreover, all churches do in fact carry out the seven functions we have described. If confusion exists with respect to the role of the church, it is due to a failure to communicate adequately on the part of national headquarters, or a failure to understand or to communicate on the level of the local congregation, or there may be a fixation on one or two of the seven functions on the part of some individual or group. Some people are frustrated, not confused, because the church as they encounter it is busy doing something they are not interested in and is not busy enough doing what they want it to do.

As it seeks to follow the Spirit's leading into a world which exists within an ultimate context of grace and in which nature, personality, social process, and historical events are penetrated by grace, the church should give its critical support to all projects for the improvement of man's life. Support is called for because the church knows that Christ is the Head of the world as well as of the church, that the Holy Spirit is not locked up in the church, and that God wills man's well-being, not his frustration and death. But the support must also be critical because the church also understands the ambiguous character of human life and knows that all things human must face dissolution. Christians are called to involvement, not to other-worldly renunciation. "The gospel is not the enemy of human freedom and fulfillment; it liberates us to find our true humanity, it frees us for creativity and service. Grace is active wherever authentic human life emerges, though every historical manifestation of grace is partial and ambiguous." [100]

The touchstone of authentic social change

It is no easy matter to move with confidence in setting a direction and making hard choices when that which is authentic can never be fully detached from the ambiguity of existence. Where are we to discern the stirrings of the gracious Spirit of God outside as well as inside the life of the church? By what criterion can we distinguish between the working of the Spirit and outbursts of emotional fervor, impatient desires to set the world right by abolishing evil at one blow, claims to final illumination?

We have seen that the Spirit's work in the larger world takes the form of a drive toward the transformation of the age-old static structures of man's life with their dehumanizing effects. But how can a criterion of authentic transformation be formulated? One can say that "the revolution of rising expectations" which is going on in the world today has been caused by God himself, that the winds of change are sweeping across countries and continents, and that it is the blowing of the Spirit of God. Yet, something in us is prompted to ask how one knows whether it is God or the devil who is at work in any given revolution. How can one distinguish the authentic revolution from the pseudo-revolution or the counter-revolution?

What is the touchstone or authentic social change? Is it simply emancipation? Ecumenical councils and moral theologians tend to answer this question in terms of the concept of "humanization." Paul Lehmann has formulated the proposition: "What God is doing in the world is setting up and carrying out the conditions for what it takes to keep human life human. The fruit of this divine activity is human maturity, the wholeness of every man and of all men in the new humanity inaugurated and being fulfilled by Jesus Christ in the world." [101] Jesus Christ himself is the criterion, being true man as well as true God. The image of true humanity found in Christ is related to the ideas of justice and reconciliation, to human dignity, and aspirations. The realization of one's true identity in reconciliation with God and mutuality with fellowmen is central to the content of "humanization." "The power to will what God wills is the power to be what man has been created and purposed to be. It is the power to be and to stay human, that is, to attain wholeness or maturity. For maturity is the full development in a human being of the power to be truly and fully himself in being related to others who also have the power to be truly and fully themselves." [102]

If the content of humanization is spelled out in terms of the possession of freedom, dignity, and certain goods that fulfill man's life in the way that the Creator of all good things intended, and if rigid social and political structures stand in the way, then revolutionary change can be endorsed. Richard Shaull, for example, holds that "as a political form of change, revolution represents the cutting edge of humanization. . . . But revolution is the bearer both of signs of fulfillment and of symptoms of decay." [103] He suggests a set of criteria: "What are the elements at the center of God's humanizing activity in the world? One of them is the fact of forgiveness, which sets us free to act for our neighbor. . . . Another basic element is justice. . . . A third is reconciliation." [104] Again he writes: "In the Christian community we have certain clues to the type of structure that is most in line with God's work of humanization. Revolutions today are basically struggles for justice. But, in God's world, justice and revolution belong together." [105]

Ian Barbour applies the criterion of humanization to the effects of technology upon modern life: "The distinctive task of the servant church is *to safeguard the human*. The biblical message holds up both an ideal of social justice and a model of man as a responsible self. The church must not only help to redirect technology but must keep us aware of dimensions of life inaccessible to technical reason. It can be an agent for the cultivation of feeling, the enrichment and intensification of experience, the development of modes of thought not reducible to computer programs. In a technological age, men and women need an awareness of their own capacities, and of the range of ways of being human. The church should encourage the artist and poet as well as the social reformer. It should present leisure as an opportunity for service, self-discovery, and celebration. Here, once more, the biblical concern for personal and interpersonal existence is an important corrective to the depersonalizing tendencies of a technological society." [106]

The most important and difficult task confronting the church today is to consider the question of the criteria of Spirit-led social change. Christians have always known that the Spirit's work "has a double effect. He 'is set for the fall and rising of many.'" [107] Liberation motivated in some sense by the Spirit can lead to reckless autonomy as well as to freely-chosen obedience to the will of God. We know that the churches' reactions to secularization were largely negative. There was good reason to fear that emancipation as such was ambivalent and that it could turn men away from faith to human autonomy or to nihilism. Most of us think that emancipation has in fact gone into reverse in some sectors of society.

It is not surprising that the churches have been of two minds about the modern temper. The official churches have resisted the currents of secularization, or have at least tried to do so, or have said they were resisting. In the process of doing so, they have narrowed and domesticated the scope of the Spirit's activity for the sake of stability and continuity. This made it almost inevitable that, down through the centuries, a host of dissenters and reformers should have arisen both within the church and outside it to claim that God's Spirit had channels other than the strictly ecclesiastical ones, or that the dignity and rights of men were entitled to a support that was not forthcoming from the official church. At this point in time, one can sympathize with those who have contended that while the Spirit has been the driving force of the church's life, it has had to work most of the time against the dominant trends of belief and practice, an undercurrent of vitality which has revealed itself chiefly when it has burst through to the surface in the form of upheavals and revivals. It would surely be the part of wisdom to listen carefully to those who claim that the church can never be truly "led by the Spirit" unless it is "continually alive to the fact that the world is God's world, that he is always and everywhere present in creation and in the shaping of history, and that the signs of that presence are to be seen, directly or indirectly, in movements which at first sight appear to be unrelated to or even in direct opposition to the religious set-up of the time." [108]

Grace and hope

The commitment of Christians to working with others in secular society for human values is a key part of our mission today. We must go out of an insulated Christian environment and meet God's grace as it is operative among our fellow citizens. As we respond to God's creative, restraining, and redemptive call, we cannot move forward in a mood of pessimism. The ultimacy of grace rules out pessimism. Nor can we be deluded by utopian hopes of abolishing evil at a single stroke. The attempt to establish the right kind of society at a single sweep presupposes a capacity to envisage clearly the ultimate goal and a grasp of the interrelation of an infinitude of conflicting forces that are beyond the reach of man. The enigmatic character of the world and the impenetrable mystery of evil dictate that the only option for the Christian is to obey God in the situation in which he has been placed. This does not rule out attacks on evil on the grand scale. But, it does suggest that our aim should be to pledge ourselves to "the unending positive task of building up a healthy society by a continuous piecemeal attack on particular evils and the progressive improvement of particular institutions." [109]

Can we expect any progress or cumulative achievement in history? Does the movement of grace through nature, personality, social process, and historical events bring about concrete and discernible improvements? Christians are not likely to agree on such a difficult question. Reinhold Niebuhr and Paul Tillich found it very hard to discard completely the conception of a cumulative achievement in our moral and religious experience. Albert Schweitzer, on the other hand, found life to be at the mercy of meaningless happenings. Yet he combined a complete skepticism with an intensely affirmative attitude toward life itself. We cannot understand evil, but we can fight it.

We know that God has his own strategy for bringing good out of evil. Christian hope clings to something deeper than the continuing chance that something will turn up to keep life going. It depends on the fact of the present creative and redemptive working of God in human life. Therefore, the Christian believes that there is no situation in which he cannot find some meaning. There is no social wrong which need remain unreformed. There is no circumstance in which love will not make some difference. "Love hopes all things."

In the light of the grace God has already given, we realize how great is the disparity between the world as we know it and the meanings implicit in that grace. In faith and hope we look forward to a re-created world. God intends to complete what he has begun. The Christian already possesses the indwelling of the Spirit, marking him out as a member of God's people. For the present he is only in part controlled by the Spirit, partially "spiritual." He looks forward to becoming wholly "spiritual." The Christian hope looks forward to the "spiritualizing" (that is, making open to the Spirit) of the whole personality, the whole social order, and even the whole creation. "Eschatological hope holds out the promise that what is now achieved only fitfully and ambiguously will eventually be manifested in its fullness. The hope is that the signs of the kingdom of God, the partial and fleeting realizations of the good that we see today, are not just sports or accidents in this world, but are indicators of its destiny. With this hope to encourage him, man, we may suppose, will be more eager and more persevering in his attempts to obey the command of love and build up the beloved community." [110] Love can indeed hope and persevere if we live in a grace-full world.

Part Two

RECONCILIATION:

THE

CONTENT OF THE

DOCTRINE OF GRACE

5

The Emergence of

the Reconciliation Image

in the Nineteenth Century

When the doctrine of grace is properly understood, it is seen to have a strongly inclusive character. The capacity of this doctrine to embrace the widest range of religious, moral, and intellectual concerns can best be demonstrated by a consideration of one of Paul's great grace-words. The term "reconciliation" has a largeness about it that enables it to express the reality of grace.

Reconciliation is splendidly suited to illustrate the goal and qualities of grace for it signifies precisely the reunion of the separated. Reunion restores lost options and offers new opportunities. By overcoming estrangement, reconciliation restores, expands, and actualizes human possibilities. The dimensions of reconciliation coincide with God's gracious presence in creation, in the dynamics of personality, in the structures of society, in historical events, and in the church. For reconciliation *is* what God is doing. It is the reality he seeks to create among men. It is the ultimate state he aims to bring into being. God is the supreme reconciler and reconciliation is his central and all-embracing work. In this part of our study, we will focus on the primacy and amplitude of reconciliation as a mode of expressing the religious reality of God's grace-in-action. We will conclude with some comments on reconciliation as a theological approach or attitude and on the relation between grace and gratitude.

If we propose to claim that the word "reconciliation" is a suitable and strategic way of expressing the all-encompassing character of God's gracious work and will as well as the corresponding inclusiveness of man's response, we should be aware that we are choosing one image from a variety of formulations which appear in the New Testament. For it is clear that the New Testament does provide different images of redemption and of the work of Christ. God's reconciling act in Christ is variously described as victory over the powers of evil, as payment of a debt, as the ransom of a slave, as the vicarious satisfaction of a legal penalty, as atonement by a priest, as the sacrifice of a lamb, and as a shepherd's life given for his sheep.[1] Paul speaks of the saving work of God as "redemption," a word-picture taken from the slave market; as "justification," a term derived from the law courts; as "reconciliation," a model drawn from personal relations.

Since the New Testament itself offers a plurality of images and expressions with respect to the message of salvation, as well as other doctrines and practices, it is important to go behind the differences found in the writings and the situations out of which they speak. We must seek the constant element or fundamental intention behind the different formulations. But at the same time the theological pluralism of the New Testament legitimates a variety of theologies within the church, subject, of course, to the theological limits set by the New Testament itself. It is quite proper, for example, to interpret the work of Christ through a variety of images so long as the interpretation does not violate the affirmations that Jesus is both Son of God and fully human. In a dialogue of Lutheran and Reformed theologians in America, the theological pluralism of the Scriptures was acknowledged: "The churches of the Reformation confessed this gospel by means of the biblical concept of justification by grace through faith alone. The Scriptures also present the same gospel in other concepts, such as reconciliation, regeneration, and redemption. An evangelical confession accordingly may be, and has been, framed in terms of one or more of these."[2]

The absence of reconciliation imagery from the classical theological tradition

Reconciliation is clearly a legitimate mode of theological interpretation. It is one of a small family of words used by Paul for the central reality of Christian faith and life. Yet the aptness and power of the idea of reconciliation seem not to have been recognized until the nineteenth century. The absence of this theme from the classical theologies and confessions of the church might be attributed to the fact that reconciliation terminology as such does not play a large part in the New Testament. The noun and the two verbs which express the idea of reconciliation are found only in the Pauline epistles and there only in five passages. But it is more probable that the strongly personalistic quality of the reconciliation theme was not considered important during the period between Paul and the nineteenth century.

It is a fact that every age reads the Bible with a special sensitivity to certain aspects of its message and a special insensitivity to others. The norm of interest or importance is largely determined by man's understanding of his own predicament. There can be little doubt that the two dominating conceptions of medieval piety and theology—grace and merit and the adjustment between them—crowded out the idea of reconciliation.

Medieval man was encouraged to believe that grace comes through definite channels. These channels are the sacraments and the sacraments alone. The seven sacraments, as defined by Peter Lombard, were said to have been instituted by Christ, directly or through the Apostles, and all convey grace from Christ to the members of the church. Without them there is no true union with Christ. Every sacrament consists of a material substance and formula conveying its sacred use. The priest must have the intention of carrying out the commands of Christ and the church, and the mature recipient must have a sincere desire to receive the benefit of the sacrament. Where the material substance, the verbal formula, and valid intentions are present, the sacrament conveys grace by the fact of its reception—that is, *ex opere operato*. The sacrament is understood in terms of causality. God is the principal cause and the sacrament itself is the instrumental cause. Moreover, the theory of *ex opere operato* (by its very performance) makes the sacrament an objective event, controlled by the hierarchy. Although the whole of life stood under the effects of the sacraments, the theology of the medieval church never "gave an answer as to how the sacrament and the personal element are related to each other."[3] The determinative theology of the medieval church was unknown to all but the educated class and even for them it had an abstract, legalistic, objective, impersonal character. Paul Tillich points out that it was mysticism, not theology, that introduced personal experience into the religious life.[4]

If this picture of the medieval man's conception of the legitimate means of access to God's saving grace left little room for the idea of reconciliation, it might be thought that Luther's intensification of the subjective element in the sacrament of penance would open the way for an interpretation of the personal element in religion in terms of reconciliation imagery. Medieval theology had treated the doctrine of Christ's redemptive work in a purely objective way, with a view to its effects on God. The impact of Christ's work in and upon man was considered under the heading of the doctrine of justification or inner renewal. Luther, however, "coordinated the two thoughts of Christ's satisfaction (objective) and the sinner's justification (subjective)." [5] This means that Luther saw justification as a personal religious experience, complete in itself and realized solely on condition of trust in the free grace of God proclaimed in the church's message of salvation. On the one side stands the free grace of God and on the other is personal faith whereby the believer altogether disregards the value of his works and relies only on the divine forgiveness. "This coordination of *grace and faith* determines the character of justification in Evangelical theology, in contrast to the conjunction of *grace and merit* in the Roman doctrine." [6]

Yet despite this rejection of the abstract and impersonal theology of grace and merit, Luther and his colleagues worked within the context and limitations of the inherited doctrinal system. Consequently the idea of reconciliation plays a very minor part in Reformation theology. The reality of a deeply personal experience of being restored by grace to fellowship with God was there. But it was interpreted in terms of justification. Reconciliation was occasionally used as a synonym for justification. This was also true of the several Lutheran confessions published in *The Book of Concord* (1570). There the work of Christ and the experience of salvation are spoken of in the language of righteousness, forgiveness, justification, redemption, mediation, and propitiation. Reconciliation is used a dozen or so times but always as a synonym for the dominant terms and always in such a way that it is the Father who is reconciled to sinners by the work of Christ.

In the theological systems constructed by Lutheran scholars during the seventeenth century, reconciliation is a seldom-used synonym for justification, atonement, and satisfaction. To the extent that the word took on a special or independent meaning, it was located within the framework of the doctrine of Christ's threefold office. Calvin had described the work of Christ in terms of the triple office of prophet, priest, and king. As "prophet," Christ proclaimed God's eternal decree of salvation and works continually in the congregation through the Word. As "king," Christ reigns over the faithful and all creation. And as "priest," Christ presented the perfect sacrifice for the sins of the world. The effect of his substitutionary suffering was to "reconcile" us to God.[7] Johann Gerhard, in his vast systematic theology of Lutheran orthodoxy, followed Calvin in referring reconciliation to the atoning work of Christ as High Priest. This was the tendency in the entire Protestant tradition, both Lutheran and Reformed. Roman Catholic theology, as set forth in the Decrees of the Council of Trent, described the work of Christ in terms of satis-faction and sacrifice. Christ merited justification for us, and by his death on the cross made satisfaction to God the Father.[8]

Nearly a century ago, Albrecht Ritschl suggested that, since the middle ages, reconciliation as a theological topic had most frequently been dis-cussed in terms of Jesus Christ's reconciling of God to man. The images used to express that view were those of satisfaction, expiation, ransom, mediation.[9] As we have seen, reconciliation is scarcely mentioned as one of the benefits of Christ in Lutheran, Reformed, or Roman Catholic ver-sions of the way of salvation *(ordo salutis)*.

Reconciliation in the theology of Albrecht Ritschl

But after long generations of neglect, the idea of reconciliation made a dramatic impact on both secular and theological thought in the nine-teenth century. The most massive presentation of the idea appeared in the great treatise of Albrecht Ritschl, *The Christian Doctrine of Justification and Reconciliation* (1870). Ritschl (1822-1889) was the most influential Protestant theologian of the late nineteenth century. As he looked back over three centuries of Protestant theology and churchmanship, he be-came convinced that the entire development had deviated from the evangelical insights of the Reformation. Luther, in his opinion, had re-covered the original apostolic gospel by declaring that love exhaustively expresses the Christian idea of God. Love is the essence of God in Christ and the redemptive activity of Jesus Christ is the concrete manifestation of the divine mercy. Luther had presented justification as a thoroughly practical and personal experience of forgiveness or restoration to fellow-ship with God. In the process of defending his new perspective, Luther attacked the inherited scholastic theology and "articulated a series of pro-found insights into the authentic religious meaning of the church's age-old teaching—insights which had the potential of completely transforming the received doctrinal tradition. Luther loosed the bonds of medieval intellectualism, sacramentalism, and clericalism. . . . He recalled men to a Christianity once more construed as a religion—a new relationship with God based on God's own faithfulness to his redemptive purpose—rather than a system of doctrine and morals handed down by a hierarchical institution." [10]

According to Ritschl, Luther's work fell into ruin, even among those who called themselves his loyal heirs. The distortions of genuine Protestant Christianity began quite soon. During the sixteenth century, Lutheran theology was shaped by the demands of internal controversy as well as by the need to respond to polemical attacks by Roman Catholics and by left-wing Protestant radicals. It was fateful for the future of Protestantism that the Reformers were forced to respond to Roman Catholic pressure by adopting, for polemical purposes, the Catholic ways of formulating the issues. Thus, as David Lotz puts it, "the decisive issue of justification became centered more on the problem of relating grace to good works (a moral issue) than on the believer's consciousness of reconciliation with God (a religious issue) " [11] The general spirit of contentiousness led all Christian groups to identify themselves in terms of doctrinal purity.

As the central religious reality of justification by grace through faith alone became converted by aggressive and ingenious minds into a series of dogmatic propositions, doctrine prevailed over life and the gospel of free grace became a form of objective knowledge. Thus Luther's reformatory ideas were never brought to complete expression. Instead they took the distorted forms found in the intellectualism of Protestant Orthodoxy, the rationalism of philosophical theology, the individualism and natural theology of the Enlightenment, the mysticism of the Romantic movement, and the sectarian inclination of Pietism. All these tendencies and schools of thought disfigured evangelical Protestantism, in Ritschl's opinion, and he set himself to repair the damage by recovering the practical and personal character of Luther's original viewpoint.

But Ritschl hoped to do more than purge theology of distortions by returning to Luther. As he looked about him, he saw a Protestantism weakened by ignorance and unable to give a coherent and positive response to the religious needs of persons in an age of mechanistic natural science. An immature Protestantism could scarcely vindicate the spiritual dimension of life in a time when material progress and intellectual doubts about revelation and dogma had caused many to wonder whether all religion had become obsolete. This was the crucial question behind nine-teenth-century theology. "How are we to understand the human situation, and what is the place of Christianity in relation to it? Have we sur-passed the religious stage of humanity?" [12]

In this ecclesiastical and cultural setting, Ritschl assumed the role of a reformer. It was his intention to recover the authentic theology of Luther and to defend the lasting significance and power of true Protestantism. Ritschl stated his thesis forthrightly when he asserted that the Christian doctrine of justification and reconciliation "constitutes the real center of the theological system." [13] More than once he describes justification or the forgiveness of sins as "the foundation-stone of the Christian religion" or as "the key to the whole domain of Christian life." [14]

It should be noticed that the idea of reconciliation, even in the sense of a synonym for justification, has a prominence in Ritschl's thought that it has never had before in Christian theology. But it is clear that he uses the language of reconciliation in order to say something his predecessors had not said. He underscores the deeply personal and experiential char-acter of reunion with God through forgiveness and faith by declaring that reconciliation is the *content* of justification or forgiveness. "In so far as justification is viewed as effective, it must be conceived as recon-ciliation." [15] Justification and reconciliation are bound inextricably to-gether, yet they are not simply synonymous. Ritschl complains that "in traditional dogmatics too narrow a scope is ascribed to reconciliation." [16] The fact is that "the conception of reconciliation has a wider range . . . than that of justification. For it expresses as an actual result the effect ever aimed at in justification or pardon, namely, that the person who is pardoned actually enters upon the relationship which is to be estab-lished. By the idea of justification sinners are merely passively deter-mined. . . . On the other hand, the idea of reconciliation is expressive of the fact that those who formerly were engaged in active contradiction to God have, by pardon, been brought into a harmonious direction toward God." [17]

Ritschl held that the idea of reconciliation has a more comprehensive range than forgiveness. It implies more than justification. Ritschl be-lieved he was in full agreement with Luther in suggesting that justifica-tion and reconciliation are the negative and positive poles of the saving interaction between God and man. It is as though justification clears away the guilt of sin, the impediment caused by the inviolability of God's holiness and justice, while reconciliation clears away the enmity of sin, the obstacle to reunion caused by man's mistrust, isolation, and ignorance of the gracious acceptance of sinners actualized by God's act in Christ. Reconciliation could be called the goal or practical result of justification. It is what God intended to accomplish. The awareness of living in a reconciled state, of being accepted by God and of being able to accept ourselves and others because of the redemptive life, death, and resurrection of Jesus, is the content of justification or forgiveness. This is the awareness of gracious reality, with all the consequences for thought, conduct, and hope, that God intends to give sinners.

Ritschl was sure that "theology must speak of both the living God who justifies and the living person who is reconciled." [18] The latter stress was fundamental to Luther's thought, for Luther was not afraid of the subjective pole of man's relationship to God. Implicit in his idea of justification was the practical and experiential dimension of personal response. Luther's followers, however, did not focus on the subjective pole of the religious relationship to God. Instead they soon turned justification into a dogmatic proposition to be accepted on the authority of Scripture. Once that happened, both the objective and subjective dimensions of grace in action were distorted in Protestant theology. Ritschl hoped to undo the damage by using the language of reconciliation to explicate the personal, existential aspect of justification.

But why did Ritschl use reconciliation imagery for this purpose? The Christian tradition offered little precedent for such a move. The idea is found in Paul, of course, but in only five passages. The major theologies of the Western church concentrated on justification, satisfaction, and forgiveness. There must have been something about Ritschl or about the nineteenth century that dictated his choice of imagery. It was a significant choice, for once Ritschl had done his work the idea of reconciliation came to play a part in Christian thought which far surpasses the place which it occupies in the New Testament or in subsequent theology.

It is clear that Ritschl, as a systematic and historical scholar, was sensitive to inadequacies and incoherencies in the inherited theological tradition. He believed that church-related theologies, as well as the more individualistic interpretations of Christianity that had appeared during the eighteenth and nineteenth centuries, had distorted the balance between the objective and subjective poles of redemption and had thus prevented Protestantism from reaching maturity and effectiveness. It is also clear that Ritschl intended to defend the essential themes of Protestant theology, especially the doctrine of justification by faith, against the assaults of certain nineteenth century historians and philosophers.[19]

But Ritschl was motivated by more than a desire to purge the Reformation heritage of distortions and an impulse to defend that heritage against its secular critics. He was driven to his program of reform not only by internal necessities and pressures of theology itself, but also by his awareness of the distinctive needs revealed through the impact of events and movements within the larger society. The theme of reconciliation was peculiarly appropriate to the conditions of life in the nineteenth century. As an era it was ripe for talk about the subjective and the personal, about the resolution of conflict and the cessation of hostility, about the restoration of relationships and the realization of integrity and wholeness. Judging by the subsequent prominence of reconciliation imagery in Christian thought, Ritschl had said the inevitable word.

Reconciliation and estrangement in the thought of G. W. F. Hegel

The nineteenth century cannot be characterized in any simple way. It was a time of complex and disturbing changes in political, economic, and cultural circumstances. Most areas of thought witnessed a great explosion of knowledge and the exuberant growth of new theories about man and his world. Although the revolutionary impulses of the nineteenth century tended to dislocate traditional structures, including the church, it was also a period of great religious awakening and produced the most active and original theological work within Protestantism since the sixteenth century.

If one can abstract from the sprawling process of change some of the factors which created a climate of readiness for the concept of reconciliation, the names of G. W. F. Hegel and Karl Marx immediately come to mind. For the combined force of these two thinkers had made the concepts of estrangement and reconciliation major tools for understanding the predicament of modern, post-industrial man. Few philosophers have had so pervasive an influence as Hegel (1770-1831). His reconstruction of philosophy and theology fascinated the nineteenth century whether by attraction or repulsion. Paul Tillich regards Hegel as "the center and turning-point of a world-historical movement which has directly or indirectly influenced our whole century." "Neither Marx, nor Nietzsche, nor Kierkegaard, nor existentialism, nor the revolutionary movements, are understandable apart from seeing their direct or indirect dependence on Hegel." [20]

It was Hegel's aim to bring the philosophical and theological positions of many predecessors into a whole which would be complete and satisfying. Despite the warning of Immanuel Kant (1724-1804) that it was impossible to produce a rational and comprehensive metaphysical system, Hegel proceeded to construct one in which he claimed that the substance of all previous philosophies was contained. He began his academic career as a student of theology and always considered himself a theologian. He had observed during the period of the Enlightenment the conflict between traditional Protestantism and the rationalistic criticism of it. Like Schleiermacher, he sought to defend and revalidate classic Christianity. But in his reconstruction of theology, he was not interested in a mere re-statement of traditional formulas. He aimed instead at a sweeping understanding of the nature of reality which would include Christian faith within its totality. It is generally agreed that he did, in fact, transform theology into philosophy and thereby invited the disintegration of his great synthesis.

The vital center of Hegel's thought lies in his conception of the *dynamic* character of reality. He was not interested in the unknowable abyss from which things are said to come, or that into which they go. Such speculative categories seemed to him static and useless. Everywhere he saw process, motion, unfolding. As an idealist, he took his stand upon consciousness and its contents and sought to interpret the universe in terms of the thinking individual. The laws of the movement of all things became clear to him as he considered the process of thinking.

Hegel thought that the method by which the mind proceeds is something like this. Some idea or concept is fastened upon, as though it were a complete account of any given matter. Then difficulties are seen in it, and somebody brings forth an exactly opposite suggestion as an improvement. Soon this proves to have the same difficulties in it as the original suggestion. It turns out that each idea or statement, when taken apart from the other, is false, but that, if each is taken as the complement of the other, it is true or part of a larger truth. First there is a thesis or affirmation. Then we discover the antithesis to this thesis or its contradiction. But the human mind will not rest content with contradictions. It will move on to find a way of reconciling opposites in a synthesis which includes both thesis and antithesis but on a higher level. This sort of process Hegel calls by the old Greek name of *dialectic*, because it naturally fell into the form of a controversy, whether between two combatants, or with a single thinker sustaining both parts. The highest function of the mind is that activity which enables one to see things whole, to see opposites unified. Thinking moves from the simple to the complex not by unrelated or random leaps but by a gradual development into syntheses which become theses for still higher syntheses.

Hegel saw what few philosophers had realized to his day. He recognized that thought is not a static thing, a mere receiving of impressions. Thought, for him, is a process, a progression, a moving from one point to another. The operation of the dialectical process shows that reason is dynamic. But Hegel went on to affirm that dynamic reason exists within or is the embodiment or expression of a dynamic reality. In thinking logically, in following out the law of its own nature, the mind is tracing out the actual structure of reality. Thus the mind finds in nature that which is akin to itself. The universe is like man and the processes in the universe are the same processes, on a larger scale, which we find in the mind of man. Man is the universe in miniature. The entire universe is a continuation of the dialectical process. It, too, has its thesis, antithesis, and eventual synthesis. Reality itself is a process of logical development, a process of thought, a thinking whole. Nature and man are one within this whole. In nature the dialectical movement proceeds unconsciously, whereas in man it becomes conscious.

For Hegel, then, the universe is a totality which is to be explained as the unfolding of a rational principle, namely Absolute Idea or Spirit. "God" is the Absolute Idea or creative reason of the universe. God actualizes his own potentialities in time, space, nature, history, and human personality. Everything in its essential nature is the self-expression of the divine life. As God reveals himself in the evolving process of nature, history, and personality, he becomes self-conscious. In man, and especially in his consciousness of God, the Absolute reaches the clearest self consciousness.

The central insight of the Hegelian scheme of thought is that the universal rational principle, in order to develop, differentiates itself in forms that inevitably conflict with each other, but are ultimately reconciled. The dialectical mode of thought must be the true method of philosophy because the world is really made up of reconciled opposites, and so can only be understood by contradiction followed by reconciliation. Hegel believed that the truth as an intricate conceptual theory could be understood only by philosophers. For the masses, the truth had to be translated into the pictorial forms of religion. All religions reveal the ultimate nature of reality. But the historical process of the unfolding of the Absolute Spirit culminates in Christianity. Hegel saw Christianity as the one absolutely true religion because the inner meaning of its figurative expressions was identical with the principles of true philosophy. In the doctrine of the incarnation, for example, one sees the religious expression of the reconciliation of God and humanity, which are no longer to be considered as contradictory or antithetical. The doctrine of the Trinity was for Hegel the central doctrine of Christianity. It exhibits in a supreme manner the reconciliation of opposites. In the Trinity we have God who wills to manifest himself, Jesus in whom he is manifest, and the spirit common to them both. God's existence is dynamic, not static. It is in motion, not at rest. God is revealer, recipient, and revelation all in one.

Hegel's intention in reinterpreting Christianity was to enable it to understand itself more perfectly. But it is a question, says Alec Vidler, whether he did not change it into something else. "God is subordinated to the Absolute, Christ is a logical construction and not a living person, evil is raw material on the way to becoming good or spirit, redemption is not an event in time but an eternal truth, the resurrection and ascension of Christ mean that the universal which became particular returns into itself." [21]

Our interest in Hegel centers, however, not on the exposition of his total system nor on its theological adequacy, but rather on the concepts of estrangement and reconciliation. These ideas had to wait until the nineteenth century to come into their own as major tools for understanding the human predicament and for articulating the Christian message of salvation. It is clear that Hegel played a principal role in giving these concepts a currency that made them available for the work of theological interpretation.

Within Hegel's marvellously intricate system, contradiction and resolution, estrangement and reconciliation are pervasively present. They are intrinsic to the logical mechanism of thesis, antithesis, synthesis. But they escape the realm of abstraction and prove to be powerful tools for the illumination of that movement or process which is observable in actual personal and historical experience. The concept of estrangement made contact with the nineteenth century's awareness of the divided self and the depersonalization of the urbanized industrial worker.

The attention Hegel gives to such empirical phenomena proceeds, of

course, from a rather abstract conception. His logic describes the structures of reality as they exist within the Absolute before anything has
happened in time and space. But how do they become actual? The
Absolute Spirit, or God, goes out of his inner life to achieve self-expression in nature and in human nature. Spirit is thus present in nature but
in terms of estrangement, since spirit has not yet reached its ultimate
goal or perfection. Paul Tillich points out that "Hegel unites the idea
of creation with the idea of the fall, and speaks of nature as the alienated
or estranged spirit. . . . So the whole world process is seen by Hegel as
a process of divine self-estrangement." [22]

In keeping with the radical centrality given to development and
thought in Hegel's perspective, he declares that the historical process of
God's self-realization is essentially a knowing process. That is, "God is
not fully God until he *knows* himself to be God." [23] In order for spirit,
reality, or the world-self to become conscious of itself, it must express
itself and assume various objective forms. The capacity for creative self-
expression on the part of the world-self is necessarily correlated with the
urge to self-knowledge. Nature is externalized spirit that is unconscious
of itself as spirit, while man is spirit in the act of becoming conscious of
itself as spirit. Thus man as conscious subject confronts the world as
external object and becomes aware of self-division. The subject experiences the object as something that stands opposed to itself, an alien and
hostile being. This awareness of confrontation Hegel calls "self-estrangement" or "self-alienation" *(Selbstentfremdung)*. But man as a knower
has a craving to pierce the objectivity of the world that confronts him
and through knowledge to divest it of its strangeness. Knowing activity
is, then, the overcoming of alienation. It is spirit's means of reintegration
or repossession of itself in consciousness.[24]

Hegel's concept of estrangement, of self-alienated spirit locked in conflict with itself, has obvious connections with the traditional Christian
doctrine of the fall and of sin as separation from God, nature, and other
persons. But there was also immediate precedent for Hegel's preoccupation with the human experience of contradiction and reintegration in
Immanuel Kant's picture of self-divided man. In his moral philosophy,
Kant had described the fundamental dilemma of human nature. On the
one side, there is a compulsion to achieve absolute moral perfection. But
on the other side, man is a merely finite and fallible creature who cannot
succeed in the effort to be absolutely good. Thus man is "a divided
being, a dual personality." [25] He is an ideally perfect person on the one

hand, and a practically imperfect creature of the senses on the other. Since he judges the actual self by the ideal self, he finds himself to be in a state of inner conflict. He is a stranger to himself. There is no possibility of overcoming the state of contradiction short of personal immortality.

There is a close analogy between the pictures of human self-alienation given by Kant and Hegel. The differences appear when it is seen that Kant thought in terms of volition and Hegel in terms of intellection. According to Hegel, the act of understanding strips the external world of its alien objectivity by seeing through the illusory otherness of the world to its essential subjectivity. Knowledge de-alienates the objective world by transcending the subject-object relation. When the world is encountered in a subject-subject relation, spirit is at home with itself.[26] Reintegration has occurred. Hegel is basically optimistic about the capacity of knowledge to cope with successive historical cycles of externalization, alienation, and transcendence of the alienation.

Hegel's system of thought took the form of a grand philosophy of reconciliation. By placing this idea in the forefront of European thought, Hegel was giving expression to the inarticulate, half-hidden longings and convictions of nineteenth century man. In this sense, he was a prophet in vital touch with the cultural life of the age. At the same time he refined the categories in terms of which the positive and negative ingredients of human experience could be analyzed and expressed. The comprehensiveness of his system, together with its thoroughly intellectualist bias, made Hegel's synthesis vulnerable to attack. His followers separated into opposing parties. A right wing regarded him as the champion of orthodox Christianity, while a left wing stripped his system of religious and ethical meaning and turned it into a thoroughgoing atheism. Between the right and left wings there were various mediating schools.

As Albrecht Ritschl contemplated his re-statement of authentic Christian theology, he reflected the impact of Hegel. At the beginning of his career, Ritschl was a promising Heglian recruit. But he soon reacted violently against the intrusion of Hegelianism, and of any metaphysics whatever, into Christian theology. Thus the idea of reconciliation seemed right and useful, but it had to be disengaged from its setting in the "theological rationalism" of Hegel's system.[27] Ritschl could not tolerate the idea that God and man could be reunited by means of a cognitive process. Christian faith is not a matter of intellectual penetration, but of a response of person to person, in which the will plays a larger part than the intellect. With both positive and negative impetus from Hegel, Ritschl went his own way.

Others before Ritschl had reacted to Hegel by accepting the principle of reconciliation as a dominant and inescapable mode of interpreting human existence, but disagreed with him in saying that there is no reconciliation to be found either in thought or in wider human experience. Still very much alive was the philosophy of Kant, which insisted that man must accept the principle of finitude and recognize his inability to reach the infinite, the transcendent reality beyond his grasp. Theologians dependent on Kant declared that not even Hegel's great attempt had broken through the prison of finitude. The world is still unreconciled.[28]

Soren Kierkegaard (1813-1855) drew a remarkably powerful picture of the world as unreconciled reality. We live, he said, not in a realm of logical essences but in the realm of existence where estrangement overpowers reconciliation. Man lives in the place of decision between good and evil. The dialectical process of which Hegel spoke is not a real process in time, but only a description of logical relations. Reconciliation is real in the realm of abstractions, or in the inner life of God, but it is not a reality in the external process of human existence. There the actual situation of man is one of anxiety and despair. There is nothing in man, nothing he can do, that will enable him to escape contradiction. Hope for the overcoming of estrangement lies not in logical mediation, education, or moral virtue. Reconciliation can only come as a gift of grace from the God who acts in Jesus Christ to invite the individual into a new and fulfilling relationship. By a decisive leap of faith, the individual encounters God in the conflicts of experience as both his judge and his savior, and thus his personal existence is realized. Kierkegaard set the primacy of personal existence and authentic subjectivity over against all abstract systems, timeless essences, and collective authorities. In doing so, he spoke to and for men who felt themselves caught in the toils of mass culture, industrialism, and superficial religiosity.

Alienation and the hope of reconciliation in the thought of Karl Marx

Karl Marx (1818-1883) stands alongside Hegel in his importance as a shaper of the ideas of estrangement and reconciliation. That these concepts should have become the dominant tools for understanding the predicament of man in the nineteenth and twentieth centuries is largely due to the combined force of Hegel and Marx. The awareness of estrangement or self-alienation is, of course, a theme of age-old and universal human interest. But Marx, in an even more convincing and effective manner than Hegel, recorded and shaped its emergence as one of the most prominent subjects of conscious concern to nineteenth century man.

Marx had studied Hegel carefully, but his interpretation of the master was decisively influenced by Ludwig Feuerbach (1804-1872). Feuerbach contended that the dialectical process of Hegel was not taking place in an ideal or imaginary world of Absolute Spirit but in the real world of men. Actual men in the real, material world do suffer estrangement. If one inverts Hegel's scheme and substitutes "man" for "God" or "spirit," then one gets from Hegel a true reading of human existence. In other words, Hegel's abstractions do correspond to something quite real.

Thus Marx followed Feuerbach in stripping Hegel's thought of its idealistic mystifications or in "turning it upside down," as they put it. Marx retained from Hegel the concept of development interpreted as dialectical movement, the notion of self-alienation, and reconciliation as the ultimate goal. But he added elements to Hegel's structure that gave his thought immense practical significance. Marx united a patient economic analysis of contemporary industrialized society with a passionate desire for a just distribution of material wealth. His sensitivity to the social context of life and thought led him to see estrangment not from the point of view of the individual but of society. He agreed with Hegel that estrangement is a hard, objective fact of life, but contended that in a world of class struggle reconciliation has not occurred, except perhaps in the philosopher's head.

Self-alienated man was the central subject of Marx's early writings. The tragic situation of man is that he is not fully human. He is an alienated, dehumanized being, aware of an internal split within himself and of separation from others, from his work, and from nature. His inward unity is broken. The ultimate evil is alienation and the loss of supportive and fulfilling ties with the sources of authentic personal existence. In this openly subjectivistic early period, Marx developed a phenomenology of man based on the model of Hegel's phenomenology of spirit. But at a later point in his life, he sees the alienated self-relation as a social relation of labor and capital. Alienation has become a social process, a massive fact of life throughout modern society. With this insight, the psychological bias of the early Marx has turned into the sociological thrust of the later Marx.

As Marx observed the social setting of nineteenth century man, he saw a predatory industrialism subject to the unregulated tyranny of the mill— or mine-owner, whose survival depended on the ruthless exploitation of wage-labor in the interest of mounting profit on a limitless market. Marx's famous descriptions of the dehumanizing effects of capitalist economy center around the proletariat, but they are meant for all groups of society. Everyone, insofar as he is drawn into the all-embracing mechanism of production and consumption, is enslaved to it, loses his character as a person and becomes a thing.

Within a society dominated by the acquisitive passion that sees money as the means of exercising power over everything, man finds that his very work, his self-externalization in productive effort, becomes the source of his alienation. The worker puts his life into the object he makes, yet through the wage system he loses something of himself since he does not retain control over or receive the full value of that which he has produced. The social relations of production become a form of bondage, for labor is monotonous, involuntary, and exhausting. The worker is alienated from other men since industrial capitalism involves the exploitation of man by his fellowmen. Man is dehumanized because he is treated as a commodity, like coal or iron ore, valued primarily in terms of his usefulness in the productive process. In a capitalist economy, men, women, and children can be made to work under inhuman conditions with no concern for dignity, health, or safety. When workers are no longer usable, they are thrown away.

A quite different understanding of the meaning and dignity of human work had been set forth in the Reformation doctrine of vocation. The doctrine was relatively constant from Luther through Calvin and Puritanism, with some degeneration as the Puritan pattern of life felt the corroding touch of industrialism. But the Industrial Revolution negated the received doctrine, and Marx provided the ideological account of this negation. Yet Marx was more than a destructive critic. He believed it was possible to humanize the technical process, although he did not believe that this could happen within the framework of a society organized along class lines. Therefore he became a political rebel against the social and economic structure of bourgeois society. He appealed to the proletariat, especially the vanguard which consists of proletarians and people from other groups who have joined them, to become engaged in a world revolution. The aim of the revolution will be to bring about a radical reversal in the condition of man by means of the abolition of private property. With the revolution, Marx foresaw the recovery of human freedom. Once the class structure has been destroyed, man will be released to a new nonacquisitive life. He would enjoy his productive activity and would develop in a spontaneous way the deeply human potentialities which had been stultified by the inhuman, soulless force of capitalist technology.

When Marx speaks of the future of mankind, he contrasts present dehumanization with the achievement of true or real humanism. These concepts imply both that man can be distorted by social conditions in such a way that his humanity is lost and that there will be an ultimate stage in which man is to be reintegrated with his human nature externally and internally. Robert Tucker comments that "human self-alienation and the overcoming of it remained always the supreme concern of Marx and the central theme of his thought." [29]

It was in the midst of a general preoccupation with the experience of estrangement and the hope of reconciliation that Ritschl proposed to restate the Christian message. He thought of himself both as a modern man, in touch with the currents of his age, and as one who was able to mediate the central themes of classical Protestantism. There is no reason to think that he selected the dominant ideas supplied by philosophical schools from Kant to Hegel and Marx, and then deliberately constructed an apologetic theology to fit these ideas. Yet it is a fact that he defined the fundamental predicament of sinful man as one of alienation and spoke of the overcoming of disharmony and separation in terms of reconciliation, which he saw as the concrete, subjective content of justification. The fruitfulness of Ritschl's approach to the reconstruction of theology can be seen in the impact he made on the line of thought developed by Adolf von Harnack, Ernest Troeltsch, Walter Rauschenbusch, and others.

The pervasive sense of estrangement in the nineteenth century

As we have seen, a readiness to interpret the human situation in terms of estrangement and reconciliation had been provided by nineteenth century philosophy, psychology, and economic theory. Yet there was a wider preparation for this mode of understanding in the pervasive sense of disorientation, disillusionment, and estrangement so characteristic of the age. It is said that when Arthur Schopenhauer (1788-1860) published his brilliantly pessimistic work, *The World as Will and Idea* in 1818, the book was given a poor reception partly because people were too "sick" to read of the misery which they felt all too keenly themselves. No one could fail to be aware of the misery of Europe. It was the end of the Napoleonic era. The rise of Napoleon had crushed the hopes of a new order glowingly portrayed by Rousseau. Napoleon's campaigns had involved the loss of millions of lives and the destruction of lands and cities, particularly in Germany. With the fall of Napoleon, the Bourbons had been restored in France, and the landed aristocracy had moved back to occupy the land. Consequently, there was much suffering and hardship on the part of the masses of people. There was famine even in England, which had been the victor in the struggle. Added to the military and political disturbances were the dreadful consequences of the replacement of the prevailing rural economy by rapidly growing mining and manufacturing towns. The effects of this development are described by Kenneth Latourette: "The Industrial Revolution gave rise to a ruthless exploitation of labour. Long working hours, poverty accentuated by low wages, wretched housing, periodic unemployment, the menace to health and physical safety, intolerable conditions in crowded jails and prisons, and the deterioration of morals in festering slums evoked angry assaults on the system of which they were a feature and on the failure of the Church to remedy them." [30] It is worth noting that Hegel's *Early Theological Writings* coincide almost exactly as to date with William Carey's initiation of the modern missionary enterprise. Hegel criticized the Reformation doctrine of vocation for its social quietism. He contended that "the subjection of the individual worker to the tyranny of industrialism and the expropriation of his labor-power by the mechanical processes of the market represent a deep offence against the very center of man's personality." [31] It is almost as though the churches had resigned their responsibility of interpreting the situation of industrial man, and had turned to foreign missions instead, only to find that the task was taken up by Hegel and by Marx. Thus the churches were seen as the representatives of the ideologies which kept the ruling classes in power over against the working masses, and a great gap developed between the churches and the labor movements in Europe.

The general sense of estrangement deepened at mid-century. The high hopes of a new era of popular freedom and universal peace which were abroad from 1848 to 1852 were dashed. War followed on war, and the free progress of commerce and industry seemed to be leading less to general happiness and harmony than to increasing misery in the great cities and to fiercer international competition for markets. The ensuing wave of pessimism caused people to be more interested in reading Schopenhauer's description of human stupidity and suffering.

The inclination toward pessimism about the human situation, and the associated sharpening of hope for some resolution of the contradictions of life, were actually strengthened by the series of scientific discoveries which lay at the base of industrial development and promised an era of plenty through technology. The natural sciences gave strong support to pessimism. The Darwinian theory provided somewhat of a scientific ground for belief in a cold, relentless, and indifferent nature in which man must struggle as best he can toward no particular goals other than those he himself is able to imagine. This scientific naturalism found expression in many quarters, among them notably the literature of the last half of the nineteenth century and the first part of the twentieth. A generation came into being which was impressed by the failure of philosophy to reveal the secret of the universe, and also of the natural sciences, despite the progress they had made during the first half of the nineteenth century, to solve what Tennyson called "the riddle of the painful earth." Paul Tillich points out that at the end of the nineteenth century people who were intensely sensitive to the multiple estrangements of man "all seemed to live on the boundary line of insanity." [32] He mentions Nietzsche, Baudelaire, Rimbaud, Strindberg, Van Gogh, and Munch. They were representatives and recorders, in an extreme sense, of the cleavages in the modern mind.

The age in which Ritschl chose to express his theology in the language of reconciliation was surely a time of ferment, confusion, revolution, and progress. Such an era exhibits many kinds of readiness, and there were many elements in Ritschl's theology to match a variety of nineteenth century interests. But there can be no doubt that in his use of the ideas of estrangement and reconciliation, Ritschl was thoroughly compatible with the mood of the time. As we have seen, he understood the fundamental human predicament to be one of alienation. David Lotz comments on Ritschl's central thrust: "Sinful man lives in a state of separation from God and hence, in terms Ritschl appropriated from the Augsburg Confession, he is 'without fear of God, without trust in God.' The inescapable reality of man's moral turpitude cannot be evaded by authentically Christian thinkers any more than the scrupulous Kant could gloss over the radical evil latent within the heart of 'enlightened' man. Christian theology must therefore accord pride of place to the question of the restoration of fellowship with God, the perennial question of divine pardon and faith's response to that pardon . . . whatever one's final evaluation of the adequacy of Ritschl's actual performance to his stated intentions, the fact of those intentions remains and demands full recognition." [33]

The growth of interest in the subjective pole of the divine-human relationship

Although Ritschl had an enormous influence on subsequent theology, not every school of thought seized upon the idea of reconciliation as the vital center or organizing principle of Christian doctrine. Many of Ritschl's distinctive themes were met with vigorous opposition. Yet the steady growth of interest during the late nineteenth century and the early years of the twentieth in the subjective, personal pole of the religious relationship between God and man clearly owes much to Ritschl's emphasis on reconciliation as the experienced content of God's saving work. A new concentration on the human response to God's grace could be seen in several classic studies of the mystical element in religion and in religious experience taken more broadly as the result of the presence of the divine within the soul. The tendency to replace authority with experience was naturally associated with a strong emphasis upon the doctrine of God's immanence. The same interest in the actuality of the personal dimension of the divine-human relationship was evident in the numerous efforts to recover and understand "the Jesus of history." Much theological controversy centered on the issue of the historical Jesus and the necessary recasting, if any, of the classic dogma of the incarnation. Even today the dust has not entirely settled on this topic, yet it may safely be said that practically all schools of theological thought take the full humanity of Jesus Christ more seriously than has ever been done before by Christian theologians. It is now seen to be entirely consistent with the decisions of the ecumenical creeds to insist that the human nature of Jesus Christ involved the fully subjective elements of human growth, struggle, temptation, ignorance, disappointment, and faith in God. He was not even spared the deep awareness of estrangement and reconciliation, unless one chooses to hold that his life was simply a divine life lived in a human body.

But it was in the seemingly inexhaustible flow of books on the doctrine of the atonement that a deep and sustained interest in the genuinely personal pole of the God-man relationship became most obvious. The subjective factor was never absent, of course, from Christian faith and life, but it usually found its place in mystical sentiments, in the emotional response to the liturgy, or in the moral response to the claims of piety. Over against those areas where the subjective element was acknowledged, there stood the classic theologies of the work of Christ which stressed the objectivity of salvation in the legal or governmental imagery of holiness, justice, punishment, satisfaction.

Several great theories of the atonement have dominated the thought of the church from time to time. Ransom theories, victory theories, bargain theories, satisfaction theories, penal substitution theories, governmental theories, all have had their day. Most of these theories have described the atoning Christ as acting on God *for* man, or as acting on God *as* man. The Godward theologies of the atonement have played a great and necessary part in Christian thought. They have insisted that the atonement is an essential, deliberate, and costly act of God, not a lucky chance, an afterthought, or kindly indulgence. The objectivity of the atonement was given a most thorough expression in the theologies of the seventeenth and eighteenth centuries. God's initiative was safeguarded, although by means of legalistic and impersonal categories of thought.

By the end of the nineteenth century, a new concern was abroad, as we have seen, for the personal and human element in religion. It was as though men were no longer content with any thought of God less than the thought that God is love. Theories of satisfaction and vicarious punishment were still being defended with impressive scholarship and assurance. But even the most conservative theologians were beginning to introduce new elements that were responsive to the mood of the nineteenth century. They continued to use forensic, penal, and substitutionary language, but in one way or another they supplied as the content of these forms an emphasis upon the personal relationship of love, and they often described this relationship as an experience of reconciliation.

While orthodox theologians were personalizing and ethicizing the judicial metaphors of the Godward theories, another classic theory was given remarkable development. Centuries earlier Abelard had given a distinctively manward quality to the doctrine of the atonement by saying that the atoning Christ acts on man *for* God. Christ died, neither because a ransom had to be paid to the devil, nor because the blood of an innocent victim was needed to appease the wrath of God, but in order that a supreme exhibition of divine love might kindle a corresponding love in men's hearts and inspire them with the true freedom of sonship to God. Abelard's view came to be known as the "moral theory," and there can be no doubt that the moral, or perhaps we should say the emotional, influence of the cross is his real interest. Abelard's thesis was needed as a counterweight to the forbidding and impersonal dialectics which fortify Anselm's satisfaction theory. J. K. Mozley comments: "Abelard did most valuable service in proclaiming love as the motive, method, and result of God's work of reconciliation." [34]

Of all the theories of the atonement, it was the moral theory that had to wait until the nineteenth century for fuller and more adequate treatment. When modern versions of the moral theory began to emphasize the subjective, personal, manward dimension of the divine-human relationship, the development was largely due to the impetus provided by theologians who were sensitive to the pervasive awareness of estrangement and hope of reconciliation so characteristic of the nineteenth century.

If the Godward and manward theories of the atonement are held in balance, it is seen that while God takes the costly and total initiative, man is no mere passive recipient of the benefits of Christ's passion. The saving encounter involves a real response of the human heart to the offer of the love of God. This response is directly dependent upon the Holy Spirit, yet it is the response of man himself and not of another. L. W. Grensted remarks: "We are left with an antinomy. Unless remission of sins is given the response is impossible. Until the response is given remission is meaningless. And both these propositions are true in the experience of man." [35]

The several modern versions of the Abelardian or moral theory have one clear point of contact. They are not afraid of the subjective. They are interested in human experience and want to express religion in terms of man's response to God's grace. They insist that the atonement must mean something for man, have an experienced content, and be explicated in terms of personal relationships. They wish to say that justification becomes an abstraction apart from reconciliation and sanctification.

Throughout the history of Christian thought, the idea of union or reunion between man and God has been expressed in mystical language. The language of mysticism has emphasized the essential unity of our life with that of Christ. In order to describe the deeply and truly personal dimension of religious experience, theologians have appealed to the phrases of Paul which tell of the self-identification of the believer with Christ (Galatians 2:20). Faith, as the pre-logical act of the undivided self, "puts on Christ," the very presence and actuality of the gracious God. Insofar as this personal, preconceptual identification or participation is an experienced power in the life of the believer, it has served again and again as the living center and connecting link in theological perspectives which are notable chiefly for their inconsistencies and ecclesiastical structures known chiefly for their pragmatism. L. W. Grensted argues that it was always this deeply personal and mystical ingredient "which made the Satisfaction theory comprehensible, the Penal theory endurable." [36] It is at the level of the preconceptual, predoctrinal experience of God's grace, that one can affirm the actual unity before God and under the heavens of Christian people who otherwise exhibit considerable theological diversity

The Theme of

6

Reconciliation in

20th Century Theology:

Some Case-Studies

James Denney

We have never been far from the idea of reconciliation as we have traced through the nineteenth century the cultural, philosophical, and theological insistence upon human experience as the subjective pole of the objective reality and grace of God. We have noted that the peculiar quality of nineteenth century subjectivity can be expressed in terms of estrangement and reconciliation. As we look forward from the nineteenth century into the twentieth, we can see the gradual emergence of reconciliation language as either an indispensable or a normative way of interpreting the religious reality of grace. The progress of this development can be observed in the work of four British theologians. James Denney, one of the most learned and incisive of Scottish New Testament scholars early in the twentieth century, expounded and passionately defended the substitutionary or penal conception of the atonement. He contended that Christ stood in our place and bore the just condemnation of our sins. In doing so, he fulfilled the will of God, who revealed his love for sinful men by sending his Son to die for them, and thereby to do for them what they could never do for themselves.[1] This is, in substance, the doctrine of penal substitution, as it was taught by Lutheran and Reformed theologians in the sixteenth and seventeenth centuries and by most of their successors.

174

But Denney's theology is a striking example of those interpretations in which the forms of a forensic, legal, or judicial doctrine of man's relation to God have been preserved, while personalistic or subjective elements have been introduced that are expressive of the new concern for the human experience of God's grace. Despite his insistence upon the word "substitution" and upon the necessity of external, objective propitiation for sins, Denney always made it plain that he did not view the atonement as a kind of legal transaction involving notions of quantitative comparison—so much sin, so much punishment, and of retributive justice as possessing the primacy among the divine attributes. Alongside the objective, judicial language, there is an emphasis upon the wonder and power of love. Denney at times approximates those versions of the moral theory which do dwell upon the law of God, but identify it with his love. The new concern for subjectivity shows itself in Denney's remark about the death of Jesus: 'Nothing else in the world demonstrates how real is God's love to the sinful, and how real the sin of the world is to God. And the love which comes to us through such an expression, bearing sin in all its reality, yet loving us through and beyond it, is the only love which at once forgives and regenerates the soul." [2] There is at least an anti-forensic sentiment in Denney's admission that "the relations of father and child are undoubtedly more adequate to the truth than those of judge and criminal," [3] and in his description of faith: "Faith fills the New Testament as completely as Christ does: it is the correlative of Christ wherever Christ really touches the life of men. . . . It is just as truly the whole of Christianity subjectively as Christ is the whole of it objectively." [4] In his final work, *The Christian Doctrine of Reconciliation* (1917), Denney deals explicitly with the theme which, as we have seen, had come to play so important a part in the mind and spirit of the nineteenth century. Denney wrote: "Just because the experience of reconciliation is the central and fundamental experience of the Christian religion, the doctrine of reconciliation is not so much one doctrine as the inspiration and focus of all. . . . In the experience of reconciliation to God through Christ is to be found the principle and the touchstone of all genuine Christian doctrine." [5]

P. T. Forsyth

P. T. Forsyth, the English nonconformist divine, was close to Denney in his advocacy of the penal substitutionary theory of the atonement.

He is also like Denney in the fact that he modified the objective and judicial language of orthodoxy by putting into its forms a moral, emotional, and subjective content. The twin themes of estrangement and reconciliation, however, assume a greater prominence in his work than in Denney's. Forsyth's thought was deeply grounded in biblical studies and in the Calvinist tradition. Philosophically he stood with the voluntarists' who traced themselves ultimately back to Kant. The stress laid on the moral sense by Kant and Butler, together with the growing insistence of psychology on the primacy of will among the faculties, combined to give Forsyth the formula by means of which he envisaged the nature of reality.

The centrality of grace is the theme of every paragraph written by Forsyth. "The first feature of a positive gospel is that it is a gospel of pure, free grace to human sin. . . . The initiative rests entirely with God. . . . On this article of grace the whole of Christianity turns." [6] But the grace which is the center of the Christian revelation is not a substance or special form of supernatural aid given to sinners. It is simply the content and action of God's will. "Grace is not a force. It is not among natural causes, quantities or infusions, nor is it due to natural effects. It is nothing corporeal or emanative. It is a person's will. . . . It aims, therefore, at the production of a certain type of free personal life in those to whom it comes. It aims at their will and its re-creation to a new freedom. It is the action of will on will, of soul on soul." [7]

Forsyth's voluntarist perspective led him to see personal relationships as the heart of religion. Accordingly, he combined his emphasis upon the objective reality of the act of God with a rejection of many forensic or judicial notions which have fastened on to the idea of atonement. [8] Although he did not write a book on the doctrine of reconciliation as such, Forsyth uses this idea as the master image of his entire presentation of Christian theology.

Forsyth's thought is biblical in orientation, but within the Bible he finds the message most clearly in the Pauline epistles. He writes: "In connection with the work of Christ the great expositor in the Bible is St. Paul. And Paul has a word of his own to describe Christ's work—the word 'reconciliation.' . . . On this interpretation of the work of Christ the whole church rests. . . . By reconciliation Paul meant the total result of Christ's life-work in the fundamental, permanent, final changing of the relation between man and God, altering it from a relation of hostility to one of confidence and peace. . . . This reconciliation, this atonement, means change of relation between God and man—man, mind you, not two or three men, not several groups of men, but man, the human race as one whole. And it is a change of relation from alienation to communion—not simply to our peace and confidence, but to reciprocal communion. The grand end of reconciliation is communion." [9]

The compatibility between Forsyth's interpretation of God's gracious deed in Christ and the themes of estrangement and reconciliation so pervasive in the philosophy, culture, and spiritual aspirations of the preceding generation, is quite obvious. Forsyth had found in biblical and Reformation theology a message to deliver that differed from the objectivism of conventional orthodoxy as well as from the subjectivism of a more recent "liberal Protestantism."

John W. Oman

John W. Oman's book *Grace and Personality* (1917) placed its writer among the most penetrating religious thinkers of his generation. Oman gave his attention chiefly to the philosophy of religion, and, in particular, to man's response to the divine initiative. He was greatly concerned to repudiate all notions of an impersonal order, where the relations of God and man were being considered. In his treatment of disputed questions, such as the Pelagian controversy, he tried to show how impossible it was to arrive at any true understanding of grace and freedom, so long as conceptions which implied that God operated in ways which viewed men as less than personal, were dominant. It was fundamentally wrong, Oman thought, for Augustine as well as Pelagius to say that God stood over against man in such a way that the divine action excluded the human and the human action the divine. The divine initiative in salvation could be affirmed and protected without using categories so false to the nature of personal and moral reality.

The subjective element is intrinsic to every definition of grace or reconciliation. Oman often asks why the entrance of divine grace into our lives should go by the roundabout method of experience and historical revelation. He answers: "Only as we see how this necessity arises from the personal nature of the grace which would manifest itself, can we discover the complete statement of revelation to be that God was in Christ reconciling the world to himself." [10] "Precisely because a gracious relation is personal and ethical, God's dealings with us must take this circuitous route, this way of immediate conflicts but ultimate harmonies.

It is the essence of its personal nature to proceed by seeming opposites, which, mechanically considered, are irreconcilable, but which it is the nature of a right relation to reconcile. . . . The doctrine of grace which operates directly with love to God commits itself, from the start, to the conception of grace as a mysterious influx of God into the soul."[11]

Grace is both prior and ultimate and because this is true, "Christ's whole manifestation of the Father depends on putting reconciliation first in our thoughts."[12] That which is both prior and ultimate is known by us "in a free, truly personal acceptance of God's gracious relation to us."[13] Grace as reconciliation is simply "present fellowship with our Father in his Kingdom."[14] What distinguishes Christianity from all other religions is the kind of redemption it offers. In contrast to all ways of renunciation, its way of being redeemed from the world is reconciliation."[15] The "actual, working meaning of reconciliation in the language of the market-place" has to do directly with the experience of estrangement. "Reality is not one thing and God another; and if we are at enmity with God, we are at enmity with reality, past and present, as well as to come. To be at enmity against God is neither more nor less than to be in bitter hostility to reality, with the sense that it is all against us. We think reality ought to go the way of pleasure and possession, and when it goes quite another way . . . it not merely appears to be, but actually is against us. Nor can its enmity fail to cause fierce antagonism; for, in a quarrel between us and reality, the strife is unequal, and we cannot escape a resentment which is fierce in proportion as it is futile."[16] But it is of the nature of grace to resolve contradictions, to overcome estrangement, to unify persons in relationship. "While grace as the action of omnipotence is a straight line undeflected by any conscious experience, a gracious relation is a curve which encircles our whole world, and all our dealings with our fellow-men, and our complete victory in the Kingdom of God."[17]

Throughout our survey of theologians who were sensitive early in the twentieth century to the awareness of estrangement and hope of reconciliation so characteristic of the nineteenth century, we have noted a shift in the manner of coping with the objective and subjective elements in religion. Because they have seen grace as exclusively personal, and have explicated it in terms of reconciliation, the objective and subjective elements remain, but they are no longer set against each other as though they were mutually exclusive.

Donald Baillie

Donald Baillie, another Scottish theologian, was almost contemporary with Oman and a generation removed from Denney and Forsyth. His principal work, *God Was in Christ* (1948), is by common consent one of the most important British theological writings of mid-century. By the time Baillie wrote, he could draw on a long heritage of reflection about grace as the reconciler of personal and theological contradictions. He asks whether the atonement is an "objective" reality, something done by Christ, quite apart from our knowledge of it and its effect on us, or is it a "subjective" process, a reconciling of us to God through a realization of his eternal love? He answers: "Surely these two aspects cannot be separated at all. . . . In theological argument on this subject we are apt to forget that we are dealing with a realm of personal relationships and nothing else." [18] Since the atonement "is neither a 'material' nor a 'legal' victory, neither a battle conducted outside human life altogether nor a transaction completed as it were behind our backs or before we were born, but a spiritual process in the realm of personal relationships, the objective work cannot be separated from its subjective aspect by which it becomes a reality in the hearts and lives of men. And this happens above all through the story of the Cross of Christ, the point in human history where we find the actual outcropping of the divine Atonement. That is what brings us individually back to God. 'God was in Christ, reconciling the world unto himself; . . . we beseech you on behalf of Christ, be ye reconciled to God.' " [19]

Our survey of the use of the term "reconciliation" from St. Paul to Donald Baillie cannot pretend to be a complete history of the word or of the idea which it expresses. Eccentric though it may be, however, the record we have sketched does raise a question and suggest an answer. Paul used the concept of reconciliation to describe the grace of God and thus introduced into the Christian vocabulary an image of great richness and power. Yet the idea lay almost dormant for nineteen centuries except as an infrequently used synonym for justification, satisfaction, expiation. Why? It was suggested at an earlier point that every age reads the Bible with a special sensitivity to certain aspects of its message and a special insensitivity to others. The norm of interest is determined by man's understanding of his own predicament. For many centuries the church interpreted the relation between God and man in categories that were largely legalistic, objective, and impersonal. Of course human experience in all its imperious subjectivity was there. But it was not integrated into the structure of theological interpretation. Eventually the conditions of life, both social and personal, stimulated certain creative thinkers to acknowledge the existence of human selfhood and to recognize the importance of regarding subjectivity, with all its moods of insecurity, anxiety, aspiration, and hope, as a trustworthy index to reality. Kant, Hegel, and Marx incorporated the heightened sense of estrangement and desire for reconciliation into their philosophical systems. Ritschl incorporated these themes into his theology. Theologians who followed Ritschl, even though they disagreed with him in many respects, showed the same concern for integrating into the structure of theology the subjectivity of the human response to God. For this purpose they found that reconciliation was an indispensable or normative way of explicating the truly personal character of grace and the relationship it creates.

It is very difficult to establish causal connections between ideas or schools of thought, even though one may know something about the influence of teachers and books on a given thinker. On the one hand, we may suppose that there was "something in the air," a pervasive experience of alienation and insecurity, which made the idea of reconciliation an appropriate or inevitable tool for understanding the human predicament. On the other hand, it is certain that thinker stimulated thinker and a tradition arose in which new concepts clarified experience and experience, in turn, enlarged and verified the concepts.

Karl Barth

In any case, reconciliation language has become firmly settled in the vocabulary of present-day theology. A rather small-scale sampling of significant theological writing reveals the presence of reconciliation as a central motif of Christian thought. For high visibility, the treatment of reconciliation in Karl Barth's *Church Dogmatics* is in a class by itself. The doctrine of reconciliation occupies twenty-five hundred pages within the twelve volumes of this massive work. The five main divisions of Barth's *Dogmatics* consist of the doctrines of: the Word of God, God, creation, reconciliation, redemption. The main structure of Barth's system is quite simple, but the actual elaboration of these themes results in a theology of vast scope and complexity. Moreover, Barth's reinterpretation of Christian faith involves some highly individualistic conceptions. Consequently no simple or accurate summaries can be given. Yet it is significant that he has chosen the idea of reconciliation as the comprehensive heading under which to describe our present faith-relationship. Reconciliation is "the fulfillment of the covenant of grace." [20] It is the resumption, restoration, and upholding of the fellowship with God which was the original purpose of creation. In Christ, God has acted as a wholly free subject to heal the breach caused by sin. But he has not treated man as a mere object. Man as subject is fully involved.[21] Barth does not conceive of reconciliation as the fulfillment of man's destiny. He uses the term "redemption" for that ultimate consummation. In reconciliation we are forgiven and justified. The justified man now lives a life of faith and love and hope and looks forward in confidence to becoming the child of God in fulness.

Emil Brunner

Emil Brunner, like Karl Barth, preserves much of the format and terminology of classical Calvinism. But he pours into those forms a thoroughly personalistic content derived from the philosophy, psychology, and theology of the recent past. Thus in the second volume of his *Dogmatics, The Christian Doctrine of Creation and Redemption,* he locates the topic of reconciliation under the heading of the three "offices" of Christ: prophet, priest, and king. Reconciliation is the "priestly work" of Christ. But unlike the traditional view which followed the penal substitutionary theory of Anselm in saying that Christ reconciles God to man, Brunner insists again and again that God is not the object of the atonement. "It is men who are reconciled, not God; God alone is the Reconciler, the One who makes peace, who restores man to communion with Himself." [22] Reconciliation means essentially the bridging of a gulf, "the restoration of fellowship between man and God." [23] Brunner explains that his entire manner of understanding the Christian message is dominated by the presentation of the "I-Thou" perspective in the writings of Ebner and Buber.[24] In the light of "I-Thou" thinking, Brunner consistently sees faith as "encounter," rather than as the acceptance of "revealed truths." "The truth which broke through at the Reformation (though later it was again obscured) of the personal character of faith, . . . means liberation from the rigidity and ethical sterility of orthodoxy, and sets us free to have a faith which is based on nothing save the Love of God revealed in Jesus Christ." [25] The exclusively personal character of faith and love in the interaction or encounter between man and God means that Anselm and Abelard are both right, yet both wrong. We are concerned with Anselm about the objective character of God's act, but we are also concerned with Abelard about the subjective reaction of man. "We are not dealing with a purely subjective or a purely objective process, but with an Event which is both objective and subjective at the same time, a truth of 'encounter'." [26] Throughout his writings, Brunner uses the language of reconciliation to describe the subjective apprehension of God's gracious act in overcoming estrangement.[27]

Rudolf Bultmann

Rudolf Bultmann did not produce a systematic theology in which reconciliation might function as the unifying idea. In his exegetical and historical studies, however, the themes of estrangement and reconciliation, under one form of language or another, are constantly used as tools for understanding God's grace in relation to the human predicament. The whole aim of Bultmann's theology is to spotlight the essential message of the New Testament for men and women of our time. Stripped of unnecessary and misleading elements, that gospel is the only relevant possibility for a bewildered world. There is, however, no unitary theology of the New Testament, but a number of theologies, each with its own terminology and distinctive emphasis. Among these, Bultmnan favors the theology of the Pauline epistles.

Bultmann finds that Paul's exposition of the gospel falls into two parts —the life of man apart from faith in Christ, and the life of man in the Christian faith. Man apart from or "prior to the revelation of faith" is a being who has a relationship to himself and is responsible for his own existence. But this existence is never to be found in the present as a fulfilled reality. It always lies ahead of him, as a quest, and in it he may find himself or fail to do so. Paul is of the opinion that man has always "missed the existence that at heart he seeks." [28] The failure to find his true existence, or the good, is "rebellion against God." [29] The state of rebellion or sin is experienced as an inner dividedness, a warfare within the self.[30] "Everyone exists in a world in which each looks out for himself, each insists upon his rights, each fights for his existence, and life becomes a struggle of all against all even when the battle is involuntarily fought." [31] In *Primitive Christianity,* Bultmann sums up the situation of man without Christ: "Man is the lonely victim of a dreadful fear—fear of infinite space and time, fear of the turmoil and hostility of the world, or rather, fear of the demonic powers at work in it, seeking to lead him astray and alienate him from his true self. . . . He is no longer his own master. . . . He is estranged from his own spiritual life." [32]

Man lives in a state of alienation and slavery until he has appropriated the grace of God manifested in the event of redemption accomplished in Christ. It is fair to say that "the forgiving grace of God" is at the heart of Bultmann's entire scheme of thought. "If pre-faith man is man fallen into the power of death, man under faith is man who receives life." [33] Paul expresses God's gracious gift of life in terms of "justification" or "righteousness." After a lengthy discussion of righteousness, Bultmann remarks: "Another term can be substituted for the term 'righteousness' as the designation of the new situation which God Himself has opened up to man: 'reconciliation.' Examination of Paul's statements on 'righteousness' and of those on 'reconciliation' results in mutual corroboration." [34] But the use of the word "reconciliation" makes some things especially clear. Since it is directly related to the experiences of enmity and peace, it conveys in a more vivid way that "a complete reversal of the relation between God and men has taken place." Moreover, the term "reconciliation" has the special advantage of showing man's radical dependence upon the grace of God, since it indicates that before there is any effort or response on man's part, God has made an end of enmity.[35] In a quantitative sense, the term "reconciliation" occupies one specific section in Bultmann's *Theology of the New Testament*. This reflects the fact that the term is limited within the New Testament to five passages in Paul. But the content, in both Paul and Bultmann, of all the salvation-words is controlled by the deeply personal and experiential imagery of reconciliation, of being reunited, of having peace, of knowing that one is accepted by God's generous grace.

Paul Tillich

Paul Tillich, more than any other theologian, has worked systematically and explicitly with the themes of estrangement and reconciliation. Grace is clearly at the center of Tillich's theological system. Whether it be considered as creative, saving, or providential, "grace *(gratia, charis)* qualifies all relations between God and man." [36] Grace is ultimate as well as inclusive. To participate in the infinite, in the unconditional, "means living in the reality of grace or . . . in a 'Gestalt of grace,' in a sacred structure of reality." [37] Yet within the context of grace, distortions, contradictions, and cleavages are to be found. "Christianity has emphasized the split between the created goodness of things and their distorted existence." [38] Of this split or alienation, Tillich writes: "It is not an exaggeration to say that today man experiences his present situation in terms of disruption, conflict, self-destruction, meaninglessness, and despair in all realms of life. This experience is expressed in the arts and in literature, conceptualized in existential philosophy, actualized in political cleavages of all kinds, and analyzed in the psychology of the unconscious. . . . The question arising out of this experience . . . is the question of a reality in which the self-estrangement of our existence is overcome, a reality of reconciliation and reunion, of creativity, meaning, and hope. We shall call such a reality the 'New Being.' " [39]

In the second volume of his *Systematic Theology*, entitled "Existence and the Christ," Tillich deals extensively first with estrangement and then with the conquest of estrangement through the New Being in Jesus as the Christ. The New Being or Jesus as the Christ is equated with the meaning of grace and the form or effect of grace is reconciliation.[40] Tillich writes: "Sin is estrangement; grace is reconciliation" [41] The original meaning of "salvation" is healing. It corresponds to the state of estrangement as the main characteristic of existence. "In this sense, healing means reuniting that which is estranged, giving a center to what is split, overcoming the split between God and man, man and his world, man and himself." [42] In Jesus as the Christ "we experience the reconciling will of God." [43]

Christian thought has always been concerned to safeguard both the independent and gracious initiative of God and the reality and genuineness of man's response to grace. As we have seen, the theological tradition has emphasized the objectivity of God's act and subordinated the subjectivity of man's response in the belief that active participation by man would infringe upon the free and sovereign grace of God. Tillich's thought is so thoroughly qualitative and personalistic that he can show an unrestricted concern for the human and experiential element in the divine-human encounter. He writes: "Grace does not create a being who is unconnected with the one who receives grace. Grace does not destroy essential freedom; but it does what freedom under the conditions of existence cannot do, namely, it reunites the estranged." [44] Tillich's comment on the atonement is consistent with a personalistic alternative to the quantitative, impersonal, judicial language of conventional orthodoxy. "The atonement is always both a divine act and a human reaction.

. . . In atonement, human guilt is removed as a factor which separates man from God. But this divine act is effective only if man reacts and accepts the removal of guilt between God and man, namely, the divine offer of reconciliation in spite of guilt. Atonement therefore necessarily has an objective and a subjective element." [45]

In one of his sermons, Tillich writes about grace, estrangement, and reconciliation with a most remarkable emotional power and systematic coherence. " 'Where sin abounded, grace did much more abound,' says Paul in the same letter in which he describes the unimaginable power of separation and self-destruction within society and the individual soul. . . . In the picture of Jesus as the Christ, which appeared to him at the time of his greatest separation from other men, from himself, and from God, he found himself accepted in spite of his being rejected. And when he found that he was accepted, he was able to accept himself and to be reconciled to others. In the moment in which grace struck him and overwhelmed him, he was reunited with that to which he belonged, and from which he was estranged. . . . Do we know what it means to be struck by grace? It does *not* mean that we suddenly believe that God exists, or that Jesus is the Saviour, or that the Bible contains the truth. . . . It strikes us when we walk through the dark valley of a meaningless and empty life. It strikes us when we feel that our separation is deeper than usual. . . . It strikes us when our disgust for our own being, our indifference, our weakness, our hostility, and our lack of direction and composure have become intolerable to us, . . . when despair destroys all joy and courage . . . a wave of light breaks into our darkness, and it is as though a voice were saying: 'You are accepted. *You are accepted,* accepted by that which is greater than you. . . . Do not try to do anything now; perhaps later you will do much. Do not seek for anything; do not perform anything; do not intend anything. *Simply accept the fact that you are accepted.'* If that happens to us, we experience grace. After such an experience we may not be better than before, and we may not believe more than before. But everything is transformed. In that moment, grace conquers sin, and reconciliation bridges the gulf of estrangement." [46]

Gustaf Aulen

Further evidence that the idea of reconciliation, enunciated by Paul and rediscovered in the nineteenth century, has come to play a major role as an appropriate and even indispensable mode of interpreting the doctrine of grace can be found in the writings of several theologians who have undertaken to present the whole compass of Christian beliefs in one-volume systematic theologies. Gustaf Aulen's *The Faith of the Christian Church* divides the content of theology into three parts: "The Living God," "The Act of God in Christ," and "The Church of God." Within the second division, the doctrines of the incarnation and atonement are placed under the heading, "The Victorious Act of Reconciliation." Aulen chooses the term "salvation" as the most comprehensive description of the divine activity.[47] Yet he explains the work of Christ as "an act of reconciliation, as a deed accomplished by divine love through which God effects reconciliation between himself and the world." [48] The term "reconciliation" is indispensable because it indicates the nature of salvation. "The essential character of salvation is a reconciliation, the re-establishment of a broken fellowship between God and the world." [49] Since the divine will carries out its purpose through a bitter struggle with hostile forces, the image of redemption is also essential. But God's victory over the hostile powers is for the sake of reconciliation. Thus "the triumph of Christ is at once a victorious and reconciling act which involves a transformation of man's estate and a new situation for the 'world'. . . . The victory of Christ through his self-giving is the means whereby God reconciles the world to himself and is at the same time reconciled. . . . The act of reconciliation appears with crystal clarity as the victory of divine love itself. But it remains nevertheless a mystery, the mystery of divine love." [50] In common with others who have chosen to interpret the divine activity of grace in terms of the love, experience, and personal relationship that are involved in reconciliation language, Aulen rejects the traditional distinction between objective and subjective theories of the atonement.[51]

John Macquarrie

The capacity of reconciliation language to express the inclusiveness of grace is brought out most clearly in John Macquarrie's *Principles of Christian Theology*. The term "reconciliation" is used primarily in connection with the person and work of Christ. But Macquarrie sets it in the widest possible framework by relating it directly to the creative work of God the Father and the on-going presence of God the Holy Spirit. Three terms—creation, reconciliation, consummation—are usually com-

bined to describe the "whole activity of God."[52] The systematic unity of
the three terms can be seen by observing that "by 'creation' is not meant
simply that God set things going in the beginning. Creation, involving
risk, passes without interruption into providence, whereby the threat of dissolution is continually being overcome. Providence, in turn, is continuous
with reconciliation; or, to express it in another way, reconciliation is the
highest providential activity of God. By 'reconciliation' is meant the activity whereby the disorders of existence are healed, its imbalances re-
dressed, its alienations bridged over. Reconciliation in turn is continuous
with consummation, the bringing of creation to its perfection. . . . They
must be seen as three moments in God's great unitary action. Creation,
reconciliation, and consummation are not separate acts but only distinguishable aspects of one awe-inspiring movement of God."[53]

Within this inclusive context, the life and death of Christ are seen as
effecting a reconciliation or atonement which is at once the high-water
mark of God's providential activity and equiprimordial with creation.
Christ's own parable of the prodigal warns us against constructing too
elaborate a theory of atonement. There is no special machinery required
to make possible a reconciliation. The first step is taken when the son
becomes aware of the disorder of his existence. The father does not need
to be placated. He is waiting for his son, sees him at a distance, and is
already on his way to meet him and bring him home. "This parable
stresses the unchanging character of God's attitude and work, which is
always one of reconciliation."[54] Consequently, it is sub-Christian to hold
that some particular historical event is required to change God's attitude,
to make him from a wrathful into a gracious God, to allow his reconciling work to get started. Such misleading notions apparently have some
biblical roots, but the mischief is caused by the use of objective and
legalistic images to express realities that are exclusively personal.

The language of reconciliation is also appropriate for the description
of the nature and function of the church. Since sin is more than individual disobedience, and has a social character, "reconciliation must aim at
the human race as a whole, and at the overcoming of sin in its communal dimensions."[55] The utter self-giving of the Christ who overcame
sin in human existence was the founding of the Christian community.
"This new community which itself began with the incarnation and with
Christ's victory over the powers of sin and evil is the ever-expanding
center in which Christ's reconciling work continues." Reconciliation is as
wide as creation, and potentially all men are embraced within its out-

reach. "Without in any way taking away from the historical and eschatological work of Christ, we can recognize its continuity and kinship with
that universal reconciling work of God in all creation, a work that has
as its goal the gathering of all creaturely beings into a commonwealth of
love." [56]

Gordon Kaufman

Gordon Kaufman, in his *Systematic Theology: A Historicist Perspective*, does not use reconciliation as a comprehensive heading under which
to discuss the whole activity of God. The ideas of estrangement and
reconciliation are located within his exposition of "The Christ-Event."
But throughout the volume there is an insistence upon the genuineness
of man's historically-formed selfhood. Neither in Christ nor in the sinner does the omnipotent God overpower or manipulate the freedom of
response so essential to authentic human nature. Thus Kaufman can say
that if man "is to be saved, it will be necessary to work in and through
history itself, turning it from the sinful process it is to one increasingly
responsive to God's will. Moreover, since human history and human
creativity have themselves become corrupted, this transformation cannot
be effected by purely immanent historical powers, that is, man cannot
himself overcome his alienation from the origin and ground of his being; there must be a movement from God's side through which reconciliation and renewal are brought into history." [57]

Reunion between God and man was accomplished in Jesus Christ.
Kaufman points out that many of the most central theological terms
have as their root meaning an experienced at-one-ness between God and
man. This is of course true of "reconciliation," which signifies the bringing together of parties who had become alienated and reuniting them.
Distorted relations are brought back to the peace and fulfilment of
friendship and love. This is also true of "atonement," which has been
identified by the tradition with a kind of propitiation of God the Father
by the Son. Actually the word means literally at-one-ment, a bringing
together of parties divided against one another. They remain two parties,
but are now at-one with each other, in communication. Thus, atonement
and reconciliation have the same meaning. The word "salvation" is similar. It means a making well or whole. That which had been distorted
and wounded is now healed and brought to its proper fulfilment. "Thus
man's salvation is his reconciliation, his atonement, with God." [58]

It would be inconsistent with this line of thought to distinguish sharply between the objective and subjective elements in the atonement. Reconciliation cannot be confined to an act by God accompanied by a change in his disposition toward man, nor to a transformation in man. "On the one hand, since man's estrangement from the ground of his being is the problem, genuine reconciliation with God will necessarily change man: a kind of personal and communal fulfilment, unknown before, will become possible. Unless we can speak of such empirical historical consequences, the atonement will be abstract and ultimately meaningless. On the other hand, . . . God must act decisively to restore man, breaking into the circle of human existence from beyond it." [59] As reconciliation occurs, there is an experienced healing for man, and for God also. "If the relation between God and man is in fact personal-historical and living, no event that occurs between them can fail to have its effects on both." [60]

Daniel Day Williams

The Spirit and the Forms of Love, by Daniel Day Williams, concentrates on the theme of reconciliation and regards it as the normative way of speaking about the nature and inclusiveness of grace. He announces at the outset that "the concepts of evolution, development, growth, and becoming have become indispensable terms for conceiving what things are. Process theologians believe that this revolution in our world view must be incorporated in Christian doctrine and that it brings us closer to the biblical view of the creative and redemptive working of God than theology has been since the first century." [61]

The love of God is defined as "the gracious love which God gives to man and which takes on the special character of forgiveness and reconciliation. . . . Mercy, forgiveness, and reconciliation are not simply formal ideas of what love ideally is. They are the rendering in human terms of what the love of God is doing in human life." [62] Although the meaning of love in the New Testament is identified with God's gift of his son to the world that all things might be reconciled to him, the traditional doctrines of the incarnation and atonement have rarely given love its central importance. Instead "the traditional doctrines of atonement, except Abelard's, are shot through with metaphors from law court, battlefield, and penitential office which express the theme of love only indirectly, if at all." [63] There has never been an orthodox doctrine of the atonement, perhaps because the multiple images and metaphors found in the New Testament make the theme itself too great for any single interpretation. Each of the major theories of the atonement "has its existential aspect, that is, its way of expressing the concrete human situation and what redeems us from futility." [64] It is a remarkable fact, however, that no traditional theory has taken as its point of departure and its key an experiential analysis of the work of love. At this point, Williams chooses reconciliation language as the normative mode of describing the actual nature and inclusiveness of God's loving grace. He writes: "If God's work is reconciliation, that is, personal restoration of his people to the community of love . . . , one would suppose that the profoundest insight into the 'how' of reconciliation would come from the experience of reconciliation between persons. Yet this has rarely been given full scope in theology. . . . What we seek is a personal, experiential interpretation of atonement through analysis of reconciliation in human life. Love takes a new form in the work of reconciliation." [65]

The theological works we have examined show the gradual emergence of the image of reconciliation, with its associated conceptions of sin as estrangement and of grace as a loving and fulfilling personal relationship, to a dominant position in much of modern theology. We can also conclude from our survey that the conditions of life which led philosophers, psychologists, and theologians of the nineteenth century to interpret the predicament of man in terms of a dividedness, estrangement, and emptiness which must be met by an authentically personal reintegration, reconciliation, and fulfillment, have not changed. In the twentieth century, the twin themes of estrangement and reconciliation are still the appropriate and effective tools for understanding the human situation and God's answering grace.

Further confirmation of this claim could be found in numerous theological studies which are either organized around the idea of reconciliation or introduce the idea at the crucial point of defining the essential nature of love, grace, or the gospel. Preeminent among such works are *Reconciliation in Christ* (1959) and *I Believe* (1960) by G. W. H. Lampe, *The Reality of the Church* (1958) by Claude Welch, *Victor and Victim* (1960) by John S. Whale, *The New Creation as Metropolis* (1963) by Gibson Winter, *Agents of Reconciliation* (1964) by Arnold B. Come, *Reconciliation: The Function of the Church* (1969) by Eugene C. Bianchi, *Man Becoming* (1971) by Gregory Baum, *The Apostles' Creed* (1972) by Wolfhart Pannenberg, and *Theology in Reconciliation* (1975) by T. F. Torrance.

The Confession of 1967

The most dramatic and explicit focus on the idea of reconciliation in recent Christian thought is found not in a theological book, but in a church confession. In 1958 The General Assembly of the United Presbyterian Church, U.S.A., appointed a Special Committee on a Brief Contemporary Statement of Faith. After much deliberation, the Committee presented what has come to be called *The Confession of 1967*. The document was not intended to revise or replace the historic confessions of the Reformed tradition, but was to be included with them in a "Book of Confessions" as a fresh effort to bring the Reformed heritage to bear on modern life.

The Confession of 1967 did not attempt to touch upon all the traditional topics of theology, but aimed rather to express the heart of the gospel for a specific time and situation. In its Report to the General Assembly, the Committee asked: "What, then, out of the Christian past needs most to be said and most to be reformulated for the sake of the church's confession in our day? The church preaches, teaches, and celebrates above all else God's gift of salvation to men. This is the main theme of the Bible and the main theme of Christian theology and worship, faith and life. In the ancient church, salvation needed creedal definition in terms of the deity of the Redeemer. Later, the work of the Redeemer came to the fore, then the means of redemption. What do the 1960s especially call forth from the teaching of the Scriptures?"[66] The Committee answered that Paul's declaration in 2 Corinthians 5:18-20 had imposed itself irresistibly as "the touchstone for the meaning of salvation expressed especially for the conditions of our day: the reconciliation of the world by God to himself in Christ together with the resulting mission of the church."[67]

The text of the *Confession* states: "God's reconciling work in Jesus Christ and the mission of reconciliation to which he has called his church are the heart of the gospel in any age. Our generation stands in peculiar need of reconciliation in Christ. Accordingly this Confession of 1967 is built upon that theme."[68] This stated perspective controls the entire text. The meaning of reconciliation is unpacked and affirmed in three major parts: "God's Work of Reconciliation," "The Ministry of Reconciliation," and "The Fulfillment of Reconciliation." Each part of the *Confession* elucidates a particular facet of the unifying motif.

The Confession of 1967 epitomizes a long and rich process of theological development. Our concern has been with reconciliation as a means of expressing the religious reality of grace-in-action. We have observed that although Paul introduced this word, with its deeply personal and experiential content, into the Christian vocabulary, it was not until the nineteenth century that its importance was recognized and a proposal was made to incorporate it, with all its implications, into the structure of theology.

It was Ritschl who suggested that alongside the conventional description of Christ's reconciling of God to man in terms of satisfaction, expiation, ransom, etc., there was a second persistent and valid strain of thought. This position understood reconciliation as what Christ did for man, overcoming his enmity and restoring him to fellowship with God, to his true being and vocation. God's love made the restoration possible, but the focus of reconciliation language was properly on what it meant for men to be reconciled to God, to themselves, to their neighbors and the world. The term "reconciliation" had the advantage of expressing the personal and existential depth of grace as well as its comprehensiveness.

One cannot say that Ritschl produced or was the fountainhead of the development we have traced. There were forces at work in the nineteenth century larger than any one thinker. Yet when Ritschl offered an alternative to a non-existential orthodoxy on the one hand, and to an unevangelical romanticism on the other, he sounded an alarm. The steady growth of interest in the subjective pole of the divine-human relationship, with the consequent revision of traditional doctrines, has continued into our own century. It is quite clear that amid the diversity of present-day theology, the note of reconciliation is repeatedly sounded as the dominant theme of the Christian message.

7

Paul's Theology of Reconciliation: Its Roots in the First Century

To inquire at this point into Paul's reasons for using reconciliation as a salvation word might seem a rather eccentric way of fulfilling the prediction that "the first will be last, and the last first" (Matthew 19:30). Usually the biblical roots of a theological conception are examined first, and the history of the term follows. Yet there is something to be said for an effort to sketch out the shape and content of a biblical theology of reconciliation against the background of a growing awareness that our generation has a specific and peculiar need for a healing word of grace, a word that speaks of God's reconciling presence and action in the lives of alienated men living in a disrupted world. F. W. Dillistone asserts that reconciliation "is perhaps the most comprehensive single word of the New Testament for it tries to gather within its embrace the original creation, the estrangement caused by evil in all its forms, and the restoration brought about through the work of God in Christ." [1] If the word has both the existential timeliness and the comprehensive range claimed for it, we may well look to Paul for resources that will help us to understand the fullness of grace-in-action.

Paul's introduction of "reconciliation" into the New Testament vocabulary

We have observed more than once the curious fact that the large part reconciliation language has played in recent Christian thought far surpasses the place which it occupies in the New Testament itself. The Greek word which is translated into English by the term "reconciliation," is found only in the Pauline epistles and there only in five passages.

Romans 5:10-11. For if while we were enemies we were reconciled to God by the death of his Son, much more, now that we are reconciled, shall we be saved by his life. Not only so, but we also rejoice in God through our Lord Jesus Christ, through whom we have now received our reconciliation.

Romans 11:13-15. Now I am speaking to you Gentiles. Inasmuch then as I am an apostle to the Gentiles, I magnify my ministry in order to make my fellow Jews jealous, and thus save some of them. For if their rejection means the reconciliation of the world, what will their acceptance mean but life from the dead?

2 Corinthians 5:17-21. Therefore, if any one is in Christ, he is a new creation; the old has passed away, behold, the new has come. All this is from God, who through Christ reconciled us to himself and gave us the ministry of reconciliation; that is, God was in Christ reconciling the world to himself, not counting their trespasses against them, and entrusting to us the message of reconciliation. So we are embassadors for Christ, God making his appeal through us. We beseech you on behalf of Christ, be reconciled to God. For our sake he made him to be sin who knew no sin, so that in him we might become the righteousness of God.

Ephesians 2:13-16. But now in Christ Jesus you who once were far off have been brought near in the blood of Christ. For he is our peace, who has made us both one, and has broken down the dividing wall of hostility, by abolishing in his flesh the law of commandments and ordinances, that he might create in himself one new man in place of the two, so making peace, and might reconcile us both to God in one body through the cross, thereby bringing the hostility to an end.

Colossians 1:19-22. For in him all the fullness of God was pleased to dwell, and through him to reconcile to himself all things, whether on earth or in heaven, making peace by the blood of his cross. And you, who once were estranged and hostile in mind, doing evil deeds, he has now reconciled in his body of flesh by his death, in order to present you holy and blameless and irreproachable before him.

The noun *katallage* (Romans 5:11, 11:15, 2 Corinthians 5:18f) and its corresponding verbs, *katallasso* (Romans 5:10, 2 Corinthians 5:18-20) and *apokattallasso* (Ephesians 2:16, Colossians 1:20, 22) are distinguished by the peculiarity that they derive from no word in the Old Testament nor in Hellenistic religious language. The root of the Greek term is *allos,* which means other or different. By the addition of the prefix, the word meant to change or exchange. It was used originally to mean changing money from one currency to another. In classical Greek the word came to have a wider meaning in which it denoted a change from a state of enmity to one of friendship, the healing of a quarrel. Through the exchange of sympathy and mutual understanding, a radical change occurs in which an intimate and personal relationship is renewed. There is the suggestion of real friendship, first existing, then broken, and finally restored. Thus by derivation arose the ordinary secular meaning "reconcile." *Katallasso* signified the change or transformation of a person into an *allos,* another person or another stage in personal relationships in which hostility or estrangement between those who had previously been on terms of close friendship has been put away in some decisive act. Paul uses the word in its ordinary secular meaning in 1 Corinthians 7:11, where he speaks of the possibility that a Christian wife who has departed from her pagan husband might be "reconciled" to him. In all other cases, Paul uses the word in a strictly religious context.[2] It is as though the event of redemption brought about so radical a change in the situation of man that a new and original word was needed to describe it.

What, in fact, did Paul accomplish by introducing the word "reconciliation"? The answer to this question becomes clear if we examine the context of the term in one of the principal Pauline passages, Romans 5:10-11. In chapter 5 Paul begins to consider some of the consequences of the new life into which we enter through Christ. Three and a half chapters earlier he had introduced as his major theme the "gospel." "It is the power of God for salvation to every one who has faith. . . . 'He who through faith is righteous shall live'" (Romans 1:16-17). In chapters 1, 2, 3, and 4 Paul has dealt with righteousness, judgment, and justification. Now he wants to describe the nature of the new life which is to be lived by one who is righteous through faith.

The first consequence of justification is peace with God (v. 1). To live in Christ is to be free from the "wrath" of God. The concept of peace speaks of the mutual relationship between man and God. If one stands in right relation with God, it follows that his inner condition is one of calm and rest. The subjective feeling of peace and security is a consequence or reflection of an objective status created by God through his justifying action.

To have peace with God also means that we have access to his grace (v. 2), for grace and peace are inseparable (1:7). To "stand in grace" is to share "in the glory of God." Christ has made us sharers in God's own eternal life. The completeness of the sharing or communion is ours only "in hope," yet even this present life is made new by God's act in Christ and we can accept and use suffering as a positive reality within God's providence (vv. 3-5).

How is it possible for God to give grace, peace, and confidence to those who have been his enemies? The basis of God's action is love. But what is the basis for God's love? There can be no answer to this question. "God's love has its basis only in God himself. It cannot be referred to something still more ultimate. . . . There is no help in rationalizing and seeking to make God's love more understandable by referring to human parallels."[3] If God's grace, or love-in-action, is ultimate, how can we know about it, speak about it, be certain that our hope will not be disappointed? We can know, speak about, and depend on God's love because he has revealed it in Christ who "died for us" while "we were yet sinners" (v. 8). Moreover, this love has already "been poured into our hearts through the Holy Spirit" (v. 5). The gift of the Spirit now is the pledge or guarantee that our salvation will eventually be complete. Since God has already done so much for us in the past and in the present, we can have a good hope for the future and be confident of final reunion with God (v. 9).

Thus far Paul has been speaking about justification, which he has presupposed as an event from which conclusions may be drawn (v. 1). In vv. 10-11 he repeats and summarizes his theme. Again he affirms that Christians stand between two decisive moments in God's work of redemption. Because God has revealed his righteousness, to faith, in Christ crucified, believers have been justified. Because they have been justified, they will finally be saved when God brings history to a close.[4] The believer looks to the past in gratitude, to the future in hope, and sees the present, even though it be a time of tribulation, as a time to exult in God (v. 11).

The pattern of thought in vv. 10-11 is clearly that of justification. But it is important to note that when Paul repeats his thought, he chooses to introduce a new word—"reconciliation." In one sense, justification and reconciliation are synonymous. Rudolf Bultmann says that "reconciliation" can be substituted for the term "righteousness" as "the designation of the new situation which God Himself has opened up to man." Examination of several Pauline passages in which the two terms are used "results in mutual corroboration." [5] Victor Furnish, after comparing the relevant passages, concludes that " 'reconcilation' is but an alternate way of expressing the reality of what has occurred in 'justification.' " [6] C. K. Barrett, in commenting on Romans 5:10-11, writes: "The same truth is now differently expressed in an illuminating parallel." The almost exact parallel between verses 9 and 10 show that "justification and reconciliation are different metaphors describing the same fact." [7]

The special characteristics of the reconciliation image

But if the new word is simply "an alternate way" of saying something, we have no idea why Paul chose it, even though we do know what he said. What does Paul's new word add to the exposition of his theme? We can begin to see what the reconciliation metaphor adds to justification language when we observe that the meaning of the verb "to reconcile" in Romans 5:10-11 is determined by the noun "enemies." "To reconcile" puts an end to enmity, just as "to justify" puts an end to legal contention. The two metaphors evoke rather different images of the human situation. "Justification" gives a picture of men who have offended against the law and are therefore arraigned before God their judge. "Reconciliation" represents men acting as rebels against God their king, and making war upon him.[8] The king, who could have annihilated his enemies, did not do so, but actually reconciled them by the death of his son (5:10). The rebels were obviously in no position to effect the reconciliation, but the king took unilateral action to make peace after war. The rebels have been readmitted to the presence and favor of their rightful sovereign as a precious gift made possible by the conquering death of Christ. God's initiative is demanded by the enmity and hostility presupposed by the metaphor. "While we were enemies," "while we were still helpless," "While we were still sinners" are parallel phrases heaped up by Paul to characterize the nature of man's estrangement and the absolute priority of God in overcoming it. If "justification" triumphs over law and guilt, "reconciliation" triumphs over hostility, separation, and chaos.

In Romans 5:10-11, the state previous to reconciliation had been "enmity," a state of warfare. But in other Pauline passages the verb "to reconcile" is also controlled by nouns that suggest enmtiy and separation. In Ephesians 2:13-16 the reconciling work of Christ is said to have resulted in the abolition of "the hostility," the cross having actually been the means whereby the hostility was destroyed. The phrase in verse 13, "you who once were far off," points back to verse 12 in which there is a reference to those who were once "alienated" from the commonwealth of Israel and "strangers" from the covenant of promise. In Colossians 1:19-22 the idea of enmity involves two levels of meaning when it is said that those who had been "estranged" and "hostile" in their mind had been reconciled by God.

The pictures of men evoked by the "enmity" idea in the Ephesians and Colossians passages do not suggest conflict or scenes of battle. "The whole stress is on feelings of hostility between those who should be bound together by the closest ties of friendship." [9] In Ephesians 2, the "hostility" and "alienation" concern the Jew and the Gentile, and the "claim is made that by his cross Christ had destroyed this old racial antagonism and at the same time had broken down the hostility which both Jew and Gentile felt towards God." The picture is one of estrangement of feeling within the family relationship. Those who should be brothers are separated from one another as aliens. In Colossians 1, the focus is on man's hostility towards God. God intends friendship, but man remains stubbornly resentful and hostile. Thus, according to F. W. Dillistone, nouns which control the meaning of the verb "to reconcile" represent men "as separated from their true home, hostile to the Father who loves them and alienated from their brethren with whom they should be living on terms of closest relationship within the same family. The essence of the work of reconciliation was thus the restoring of men to their true relationship as sons and friends of the Heavenly Father and as brothers and friends of one another. Although parental and family relationships are not explicitly mentioned, it seems fair to say that behind the word *katallage,* there lies a system of relationships best symbolized and represented by those of a human home." [10]

Starting with the assumption that "justification" and "reconciliation" are different metaphors describing the same fact, we have asked what Paul added to his exposition of God's grace by introducing reconciliation language. We observed that "justification" evokes a picture of men who have offended against the law, have been arraigned before God their judge, and have been put in the right by Christ's triumph over law and guilt. The "reconciliation" metaphor, however, brings to mind pictures of men engaged in conflict or suffering the distress of hostility and alienation from those with whom they should be living in the closest and most fulfilling relationship.

It is clear that "reconciliation" involves an important dimension of the total interaction between God and man. It speaks more directly and suggestively about the subjective, the emotional, the personal, about what it means to the sinner who is on the receiving end of God's grace. Exegetes who see "justification" and "reconciliation" as parallel metaphors do tend to allow a difference between them at the point of subjectivity. For example, Barrett implies such a difference when he describes the rather different picture of the human situation evoked by the two metaphors. Other examples could be cited of scholars who hold that "reconciliation" emphasizes or unfolds the personal dimension of the "peace" which is the consequence of being made "righteous." It is only fair to observe that a case can be made out against the tendency of some interpreters to reduce Paul's idea of "justification" to the level of a formal verdict, "Not guilty," as though this metaphor is a more or less formal one, devoid of the richly personal content of the concept of "reconciliation."

It can be pointed out that God's "righteousness" must be understood in terms of relationships. It is true that *dikaiosis* (righteousness or justification) is a forensic category and may be described as receipt of the verdict of "acquittal" (Romans 5:18). But since Paul uses this term in a way that differs from its use in Judaism, namely, to express the conviction that God's future judgment is already breaking in and that righteousness is already given to those who belong to the crucified and risen Christ, he adds to the forensic meaning of the word a specific content that includes the effects of God's victory over the "powers" that alienate man and hold him in bondage. Thus "righteousness," which brings to the helpless sinner "salvation," "peace," and "life," has to do with the restoration of man to a proper relationship with God.[11] Paul's forensic imagery therefore does point to the subjective experience that accompanies a declaration of acquittal or amnesty with its decisive release from fear of ultimate authority and power.

Yet even if it is granted that "justification" should mean more than a legal declaration, one may be inclined to maintain that on the whole and for the most part, as Aristotle liked to say, "reconciliation" does offer a surplus of meaning over "justification." Amos Wilder makes out a strong case for regarding "reconciliation" as something more than a substitute for "righteousness" or an alternate way of saying the same thing that is said by "justification." He argues that the reconciliation image has a special significance in the New Testament and warns against any attempt to merge or equate the image with others. The particular force of *katallage* led Paul to choose it for a description of the work of Christ. The basic image is a very simple one. "It represents a perennially moving and a very human occurrence: that of two alienated persons finding each other again, opening their hearts to each other again, and sharing each other's confidence again, after a period of alienation and reproach or even bitterness and incrimination. The image is a very personal one as compared, for example, with the forensic character of justification or the transactional character of ransom or victory. The image, when it is vital, means more than just reestablishment of a previous relationship. There is a dramatic moment of interpersonal acknowledgment involving poignancy, relief, and joy, all deriving a special pathos from the previous separation, as in the meeting of Joseph with his brethren." [12]

Wilder underlines the special significance of the image of reconciliation and contends that none of the main images for the work of Christ have the deeply personal character that reconciliation has. But the specific quality of reconciliation appears when we note that the image is associated with the love of God or of Christ and a positive emphasis is placed on the outcome in terms of joy. This is especially true of 2 Corinthians 5:17-21 and Romans 5:10-11. Neither justification nor expiation has this richly human core, the "subjective experience that accompanies a declaration of love with its dispelling of the burden and anxiety of hostility." [13] It is "this feature of rejoicing in personal fellowship with God which identifies the surplus of reconciliation over justification." [14]

Wolfhart Pannenberg strikes a mediating position somewhere between the view that reconcilation is a synonym for justification and the view that reconciliation has a distinctive and independent meaning that does not allow it to be merged with other salvation words. He describes the forgiveness of sins as "the negative expression for faith's communion with God, mediated through Jesus. . . . Forgiveness of sins means liberation from everything which divides us from God and therefore from a fulfilled and free life." He goes on to say that "in the positive sense, the real riches of salvation owned by Christians are participation through the Spirit of love in the life of God revealed in Jesus Christ." [15] In all fairness, it must be granted that Pannenberg does not want to make the point quite so simply as to say that forgiveness or justification is the negative side and participation or reconciliation the positive side of God's saving action. Yet the suggestion is there.

F. W. Dillistone comes very close to designating forgiveness and reconciliation as the negative and positive aspects of God's grace-in-action. He points out that Paul's word for forgiveness, *charizomai,* is intimately associated with his word for grace, *charis.* The verb *charizomai* generally meant "to give." But Paul's consciousness of the divine grace in pardon was so strong that the thought "God gives" easily became "God forgives." *Charis* and *charizomai* share the same underlying meaning. "For Paul they expressed . . . the great act of divine self-giving whereby God had given the Son of his love to a world of unlovely and sinful men." [16] An examination of Paul's use of *charizomai* shows that he used the word to describe "that free forgiveness which is an essential preliminary to the restoration of full fellowship." [17] There is no case in which Paul uses *charizomai* to mean the full restoration of broken relationships. The word means action leading to this goal. The term Paul chooses to describe full restoration to the family relationship is reconciliation. [18]

It would be too much to say that "forgiveness" is negative and "reconciliation" positive. Nor can it be said that "reconciliation" is the only image which describes the positive content of God's saving action. Images tend to resist propositional abstraction. But if we hold in combination the overcoming of estrangement and hostility, the specific association with the love of God or of Christ, the full restoration of relationship, and the stress on rejoicing, then we have in reconciliation an image of peculiar intensity and of great positive force. We see in Paul's metaphor that element of subjectivity which Abelard had missed in medieval theology. Anselm and others had properly emphasized the objective reality of the divine substance as it is given through revelation, tradition, and authority. But little was said about taking this reality into the personal life. In another age, Albrecht Ritschl called attention to the missing or displaced element of subjectivity and used the Pauline concepts of estrangement and reconciliation to make his point. A century later, Paul Tillich and Daniel Williams reasserted the claim of reconciliation to be regarded as a necessary and strategic manner of proclaiming God's love for sinners. As Williams puts it, "Love takes a new form in the work of reconciliation." [19]

The biblical testimony to God's reconciling action

We have asked about Paul's reasons for choosing to amplify his exposition of God's "righteousness" by the use of reconciliation language, and have seen that the special characteristics of the image make it peculiarly suitable for expressing the subjective dimensions of salvation. Before going on to specify some reasons that might have motivated Paul, it would be well to consider whether the idea of reconciliation, granted its special qualities, is actually a valid and appropriate method of describing God's grace. That is to say, does it "fit" with the whole of Scripture, or is it, in view of its restriction to five Pauline passages, a minor theme or even a foreign element introduced into the simple teaching about forgiveness?

There can be no doubt that the term, although new and unusual, is in fact harmonious with the general biblical testimony to God's redeeming purpose and action. In 2 Corinthians 5:19, Paul wrote: "God was in Christ reconciling the world to himself." An alternative translation, noted in the RSV margin, reads: "In Christ God was reconciling the world to himself." The latter translation of the passage expresses its strong "imperfect" sense, indicating that what was being undertaken in Christ was open-ended. That is, God's redemptive purpose was not inaugurated at the incarnation, nor was it completed during the lifetime of Jesus or even with his resurrection. On the one side, reconciliation is the story of the Old Testament, and on the other, the ministry of reconciliation has been entrusted to the church.

We have already emphasized the fact that the word "reconciliation" has no exact equivalent in Hebrew. Yet a whole body of Old Testament texts or ideas might be assembled which more or less precisely foreshadow its use. Something about the theology of reconciliation can be learned by observing that the idea had a history of its own within the Old Testament. During the early centuries of Israel's existence, the concept of reconciliation did not play a dominant role. The religions of the nations surrounding Israel saw their gods and goddesses as representatives of the powers of nature. But nature is unpredictable. It can smile one day and bring disaster the next. When calamity strikes it is seen as a sign of divine anger. So reconciliation between man and the gods is needed again and again. Through prayers, vows, rituals, and sacrifices man takes the initiative to expel hostile powers and to encourage friendly ones. The disturbed balance is restored by means of magic.

Israel could have nothing to do with such religion. The God of the covenant could not be manipulated by magical incantations. He does not work primarily through the cycles and powers of nature, but through persons and events. He makes agreements and is faithful. He calls Israel to an obedience which would bring prosperity and security as its reward. Consequently the idea of repeated reconciliation did not play a part in Israel's faith, even though it took centuries for Israel to grow accustomed to such a strange God, and here and there one finds traces of attempts to imitate the religious practices of their neighbors (1 Samuel 26:19).

The life-situation of Israel changed when the Babylonians captured Jerusalem in 586 B.C. The people found themselves in exile not because God was capricious or unfaithful but because they had broken the covenant. Jeremiah, Ezekiel, and other prophets told them they had good reason to feel guilty and frustrated, and made it clear that if God were to maintain the covenant, it could only be by an act of reconciling grace. It is from the period of the exile and a span of time following the return that we have much testimony to God's gracious restoration of the people to his favor. In Isaiah 11 the reign of the Messiah brings about a sort of cosmic reconciliation of the creatures. The Suffering Servant of Isaiah 53 healed the people by his vicarious passion. Hosea (2:23) spoke of aliens brought by love into a family relationship. The appendix to Ezekiel (40:1-48:35) provides detailed instructions for the making of atonement. Nehemiah 9 preserves a moving prayer of repentance after the return from exile.

The high point of the literature of repentance and reconciliation is the Priestly writing to which belong the laws about sacrifice in the book of Leviticus. The ritual of the Day of Atonement (chapter 16) indicated how the people might enter anew into fellowship with the God of grace. The cult and sacrifices are understood not as magical procedures but as a gracious gift of the covenant God. "The Priestly writer was fully aware of the unique God of the covenant with whom reconciliation had to be established. He knew that reconciliation can come only from God's side by an act of sovereign grace. . . . God himself gives the means for the daily restoration of the covenant relation. . . . Now the archaic magical elements are demythologized and they acquire a new and even opposite function. Now they symbolize the fact that man himself cannot establish reconciliation. It must come from outside, by an act of substitution. . . . It is by his grace that the gulf is bridged." [20] To these passages one could add all the prophecies and prayers which predict the great intervention of God on behalf of his people at the end of time, that restoration of Jerusalem which often seems like the signal for a universal reconciliation.

Other antecedents could be multiplied to show that Paul found the reality of reconciling grace in his own Scriptures. Not only could he find the broad conception there, but also the roots of its constituent elements. When Paul tells us that the proper condition of man rests upon a relationship to God and that at the heart of human misery is our alienation from him, he could think back to the transition from primitive innocence to rebellion and estrangement set forth so picturesquely in Genesis 2-3. In Job (12:10, 27:8ff.), in Psalms (88, 143:12), and in Deuteronomy (30:15), the difference between relationship and alienation is described as one of life and death. Under the dominion of death we experience internal anxiety, fear, and guilt, as well as external aggression and disturbance (Ecclesiastes 2-8, Job 2:4, 7:7-10, 14:7-12). But the gracious offer of life is the theme of Paul's Bible. The range of life offered "varies from the prolongation of days (Deuteronomy 4:40) and escape from physical annihilation (Amos 5:4, 6, 14f.) to a more qualitative distinction characterized by the covenant relationship (Deuteronomy 30:6, 15-20, Isaiah 55:1-3, Habakkuk 2:2)." [21]

But the life that is offered cannot be grasped by any human efforts, whether of a psychological, social, legal, or religious sort. Man's self-sufficiency is negated in the classic story of the Fall (Genesis 3) and throughout the Old Testament. The only authentic life available to men takes the form of a restored relationship (Exodus 6:6-8, Deuteronomy 29:12 f., Jeremiah 31:31-34). When Paul used the word which signifies the reunion of estranged marriage partners to describe the restoration of the relationship between God and man, he had ample precedent for doing so in Hosea (2:16-23), Ezekiel (16), Isaiah (54:5-8, 62:4-5), and Jeremiah (31:32). And Paul could use the word *katallage, katallassein* without apprehension because against the background of his own Bible there was now no danger that the word would be misunderstood in a magical way. "Now it is no longer man who reconciles God by magical rites or by his merits, but the faithful God who reconciles the estranged partner to himself." [22]

The fact that Paul found so solidly embedded in his own Scriptures the reality of God's reconciling action must have been at least one reason why reconciliation imagery seemed to him a valid and appropriate mode of speaking about the ultimacy and scope of grace. The linkage between reconciliation and grace is obvious. Paul makes the interconnection very explicit in all his reconciliation passages. Grace, that is to say, the loving divine initiative, was fundamental in his thinking. Everything in religion that matters starts from God's side. Even the human attitudes that constitute the response to God are his creation, his gifts. Of ourselves we can do nothing. "It is all the doing of the God who has reconciled me to Himself through Christ" (2 Corinthians 5:18, Moffat translation). This is the meaning of grace. It is the free and undeserved good will of God, extended without any conditions except the condition that it be accepted. Reconciliation expresses not only the inmost secret of grace, but it also possesses a breadth and profundity which enables it to embrace the whole of Scripture.

Reconcilation and the sense of estrangement in Paul's world

But reconciliation also expresses the intimacy of grace. The force of *katallage* and its cognates has an intensely personal character since the word describes the deeply moving human experience of two alienated persons finding each other again after a period of estrangement or even bitterness. Surely there were special factors in Paul's personality which made him unusually sensitive to the tensions and divisions which bring ruin to the individual and society. It may perhaps be said that organic unity and disruptive conflict provide many of the essential interpretative categories of Paul's thought. If there is a root metaphor to be found in Paul it is that of the reintegration of a broken organism. He saw the need and the well-being of man in terms of such a metaphor. God created the world as a unity: man dis-created the world and plunged it into discord; God exerts steady pressure against all the forces that ruin life and thus re-creates the world. "If anyone is in Christ, he is a new creation; the old has passed away; behold, the new has come" (2 Corinthians 5:18).

The special quality of reconciliation imagery lies in the fact that it matches and meets the human experience of dividedness, isolation, and hostility. It implies that the new situation is a state of peace, a restoration of fellowship and communication. Paul was surely aware of the match between the message of reconciliation and the mood of estrangement that pervaded his world. It is hazardous to characterize the many-sided spirit of an age, yet it is done and sound conclusions can be drawn. Paul's century has been worked over in detail and much is known about the ideas and feelings not only of literary spokesmen but also the masses.

Our concern at this point is not with the full range of attitudes toward life expressed in the wide variety of myths, religions, and philosophies of the time, but only with the sense of dislocation, estrangement, and isolation which could have encouraged Paul to emphasize the theme of reconciliation. The sentiment of alienation is strong in the *Meditations* of Marcus Aurelius, even though, as a Stoic, he never wavered in his conviction of the providential guidance of the world and spent his days administering an empire. "All that is of the body is as coursing waters, all that is of the soul as dreams and vapours; life a warfare, a brief sojourning in an alien land; and after repute, oblivion." [23] That the earth is physically tiny in comparison with the vastness of space had been noted by astronomers. Cicero, Seneca, Lucian, and others had concluded that the magnitude of the universe reduces human wishes to mere vanity. But Marcus Aurelius develops the idea with a new intensity. Just as "the entire earth is but a point, and the place of our own habitation but a minute corner in it," [24] so "the vastness of time is a pinpoint in eternity." [25] "How small a fraction," he writes, "of all the measureless infinity of time is allotted to each one of us; an instant and it vanishes into eternity. How puny, too, is your portion of all the world's substance; . . . on how minute a speck of the whole earth do you creep." [26] Amid the ceaseless sweep of time, "what is there for a man to value among the many things that are racing past him? It would be like setting the affections on some sparrow flitting by." One should "grow accustomed to looking on all that is mortal as vapour and nothingness." [27] Marcus Aurelius jots down a series of images for human life: "An empty pageant; a stage play; flocks of sheep, herds of cattle; a tussle of spearmen; a bone flung among a pack of curs; a crumb tossed into a pond of fish; ants, loaded and labouring; mice, scared and scampering; puppets, jerking on their strings—that is life." [28] In such a world, the emperor reminds himself to "withdraw into the little field of self. Above all, never struggle or strain; but be master of yourself, and view life as a man, as a human being, as a citizen, and as a mortal." [29]

Despite his sombre and disenchanted reading of man's place in the world, Marcus Aurelius was a responsible administrator, the most loyal and loving of men to his family and friends, among the noblest of those who have achieved goodness without the support of any religious faith. Granted that he was an unusual man and that in his diary he was writing to himself. Yet, the thoughts he expressed were the thoughts of his time, and he could not escape them. It is probable that he both reflected and formulated a widespread sense of the nothingness and futility of all earthly things.

There was precedent for his outlook in the Stoic tradition which he had learned from his teachers. A century earlier, Seneca, statesman, philosopher, man of letters, Nero's tutor, and Paul's contemporary, had set forth a version of Stoicism that took account of the frailty of man's nature and humanized the austere creed of the early Stoics. The ideal of self-sufficiency remains, but is much modified. The wise man can have friends and can grieve, within limits, at the loss of one. It is his duty to be kind and forgiving towards others, indeed to "live for the other person." [30] His belief in the Stoic "brotherhood of man" which broke down barriers of class and state led him to insist upon human rights and fair treatment for slaves. His attitudes are religious beyond anything in Roman state religion, in his day little more than a withered survival of formal worship paid to a host of ancient gods and goddesses.

His whole philosophy is practical and directed to the reformation of morals. But life is filled with hazards and is in its entirety subject to the tyranny of Fate and Fortune. Only the exercise of reason can confer the power to endure the assaults of ill fortune. The study of philosophy provides the armor to withstand the force of adversity. It is doubtful whether Seneca thought that many men were capable of the requisite mental and moral discipline.[31] And, in any case, the sense of futility and nothingness we have seen in Marcus Aurelius also hangs over Seneca's philosophy. He too was impressed by the astronomers' account of the vastness of space. As the earth is a pinpoint in infinite space, so the life of man is a pinpoint in infinite time. Despite his frequent references to an immanent, pantheistic deity, Seneca sees man as lost somewhere between the immensities and eternities of the universe. It is man's duty to make the best of even a very minor part. But he must do so as a segment of "the mighty and eternal train of destiny. . . . There is no means of altering the irresistible succession of events which carries all things along in its binding grip." [32]

These convictions of an immovable Fate, or of a blind chance, created a widespread feeling of pointlessness and tedium, a feeling which Seneca describes as characteristic of his time. Seneca fought against the sense of pointlessness, but in the long run he advises a spirit of resignation in the face of omnipresent and omnipotent death. We are, he writes, like a lamp in that "we, too, are lit and put out. We suffer somewhat in the intervening period, but at either end of it there is a deep tranquility. . . . Death follows after. . . . Death is all that was before us. What does it matter, after all, whether you cease to be or never begin, when the result of either is that you do not exist?"[33] Human cooperation is important. Some good things can be accomplished. But finally, or at any time, we will be "thrown out." The wise man, however, escapes the indignity of a reluctant expulsion "because he wills what necessity is going to force on him."[34] In the last resort, there is the "open door" of suicide. "A person who has learned how to die has unlearned how to be a slave. . . . He is . . . beyond the reach of all political powers. What are prisons, wardens, bars to him? He has an open door. There is but one chain holding us in fetters, and that is our love of life."[35]

Reflective men in the Roman world were preoccupied with the picture of the individual heroically at grips with the universe. In their quest for self-sufficiency they found guidance in the Stoic philosophy as it had been adapted to the Roman scene by Cicero and Seneca. A shift from the sense of public responsibility stressed by Seneca to the more individualistic concept of virtue characteristic of the original Greek Stoics, who had sought to arm the individual so that he might meet bravely all the buffets of Fortune and Fate, can be seen in Epictetus. This freed slave and cripple was probably a child in the household of Epaphroditus, one of Nero's courtiers, at the time of Paul's death and Seneca's tenure as Nero's unofficial chief minister. Upon gaining his freedom, he turned to Stoic philosophy and gained the largest audiences of any contemporary moral and religious teacher.

Epictetus wrote nothing himself and we owe the survival of what he said to the lecture notes of pupils. He excoriated the stupidity and immorality he saw about him and urged an austere and disciplined morality. Among the many virtues he recommended, the most important were a realistic way of thinking about what can and cannot be done, and courage to face with good cheer and self-respect the worst that unhappy circumstances may bring. According to Stoic theory, the world was well ordered, but in actual fact it was experienced as so complex and incoherent as to appear meaningless. Thus one must cope with the world by narrowing one's contact with it to a small and controllable point.

Despite his wit, cheerfulness, and frequent references to Divine Providence, the message of Epictetus is a grim one. "Everyone's life is a warfare, and that long and various." [36] In order to stand against the encroachments of the world and maintain integrity, self-respect, and some measure of contentment, we must learn to renounce everything except the one thing which it is within our power to control, namely, the operation of our own will, and that we must direct with all the strength we can muster. If we can manage this, nothing can really hurt us, we are absolutely safe, there is no final threat to us in reality itself.[37]

A proper distinction between what is "mine" and what is "not-mine" is the foundation of the wise man's imperturbability. It is well to practice resignation with respect to all forms of loss, especially those brought about by the inevitability of death. "All things made are perishable." It is simply "not possible that man and man will always live together," for men "were born to die . . . a fever will get the better of one, a highwayman of another, a tyrant of a third. For such is the world we live in; such they who live in it with us." [38] Death is not to be feared. It is simply a return to the elements of which we were made.[39] It is the "safe harbor," the "refuge for all," and for that reason "there is nothing difficult in life." [40] We can even face the loss of the possessions and persons that mean the most to us if we remind ourselves that we love what is mortal, what is not ours. "It is allowed you for the present, . . . not forever, but as a fig or a bunch of grapes in the appointed season. If you long for these in the winter, you are a fool. So, if you long for your son or your friend when he is not allowed you, know that you wish for figs in winter. For as winter is to a fig, so is every accident in the universe to those things which are taken away by it. . . . What harm is there while you are kissing your child to say softly, 'Tomorrow you will die'; and so to your friend, 'Tomorrow either you or I shall go away, and we shall see each other no more?' " [41]

But we can let them go, and ourselves as well, bravely and without complaint if we consider that the deity brought each of us into the world as "a mortal. Was it not as one to live, with a little portion of flesh, upon earth, and to see his administration; to behold the spectacle with him?" But when the solemnity is over, "Go away. Depart like a grateful and modest person; make room for others. Others too must be born, as you were, and when they are born must have a place . . . and necessaries." [42]

Since all things are determined, Epictetus advises: "First say to yourself what you would be, and then do what you have to do." [43] Each day should be devoted to the practice of such resignation. It is well to begin with a broken jug or cup, then on a coat, a puppy, or a piece of land, and so on up to one's body, children, wife, brothers.[44] Thus one "may be unconquerable," by wishing for nothing but to be free, and "the only way to this is a contempt of things not in our power." [45]

Epictetus has been admired by many for his clear-headed and courageous discipline of the mind and heart. Others have seen in him a pathetic, weary longing for a passive kind of happiness. But he was a man whom Trajan listened to, Hadrian befriended, and Marcus Aurelius studied. They responded to the Stoic tradition as it had been filtered through the genius of his own practical and indomitable spirit. Yet much that is in his thought must be taken as the impressions left by the city of Rome and the household of Epaphroditus upon a slave's mind. There is a special pathos, then, in his description of the dreadful loneliness that can beset a man in the midst of his fellows. "We often say we are left solitary even in the midst of Rome, where such a crowd is continually meeting us, where we live among so many. . . . We ought, however, to be prepared in some manner for this also, to be self-sufficient and able to bear our own company." [46] E. R. Dodds, in his book *Pagan and Christian in an Age of Anxiety,* comments that the loneliness described by Epictetus "must have been felt by millions—the urbanized tribesman, the peasant come to town in search of work, the demobilized soldier, the rentier ruined by inflation, and the manumitted slave." [47]

Our concern is with the state of mind of the world in which Paul lived. There can be no doubt that he was thoroughly familiar with Stoicism. In his native Tarsus, he breathed a Hellenistic atmosphere. It was all around him. Tarsus itself was a prominent center of Stoic culture, and Strabo mentions by name five distinguished Stoic teachers who resided there. Wandering scholars and orators carried the message far and wide. Paul must have found much to admire in the heroic creed that filled the gap left by the decline of earlier philosophies and religions. But it is probable too that he saw Stoicism as a counsel of despair which could never lead to the peace and freedom he had found in Christ. "Across the pages of Seneca, Epictetus, and Marcus Aurelius the shadow lies. Beneath their bravest words the feeling of futility lurks. What is God, after all, but just fate? And what can man do, caught in the toils of a harsh determinism, but bow his head and submit? . . . This was the direction in which Stoicism had its face; and the road led—as Paul saw—straight out towards unyielding despair." [48] A. H. Armstrong suggests that it is instructive to read the letters of St. Ignatius, Bishop of Antioch and Martyr, alongside the writings of Epictetus and Marcus Aurelius, and especially to contrast their attitude to death. One sees clearly "the difference between the temper of the two religions, the new fire breaking out on the earth which is Christianity and the gray light of the end of Stoicism." [49]

Futility, despair, and estrangement, in combination with courage, were all present in Stoicism, and Paul had seen them there. Yet it would be a mistake to think that Stoicism was the only or the most widespread belief-system of Paul's time. Many Romans, especially emperors and administrators, found in Stoicism some foundation for life, a means of linking the individual to something that could not be shaken. But by A.D. 180 Stoicism, as well as nearly every distinctive mark of classical antiquity, had run its course and was gone. Marcus Aurelius was the last of the line. [50] In any case, the philosophers' path of the intellect had never satisfied more than a small minority. The mass of the people had reacted from the hopeless prospect which a cruel and pointless life presented by "turning to a picturesque variety of more or less sensational superstitions." [51]

The feeling of homelessness and futility which led both scholars and common folk to demand philosophies and religions of salvation in Paul's time was not unlike the mood of intellectual and spiritual unrest which called forth a variety of cults and moral philosophies in fourth century Greece. The conquering sweep of Alexander the Great out of Macedonia to the east finally destroyed the old intense, narrow, concentrated life of the independent, self-contained Greek city-states. Old ties and associations were broken, old gods and goddesses were displaced, the intimacy and comfort of hearth and home no longer provided a secure habitation. Alexander established political controls which made it impossible for the city states to determine policy. They no longer had autonomy. Their foreign affairs were controlled from the imperial capitol. Gilbert Murray points out that the collapse of the traditional religion of Greece might not have mattered so much if the form of Greek social life had remained. "If a good Greek had his Polis he had an adequate substitute in most respects for any mythological gods. But the Polis too . . . fell with the rise of Macedon. It fell . . . because there now existed another social whole, which . . . was utterly superior in brute force and money. Devotion to the Polis lost its reality when the Polis . . . lay at the mercy of a military despot." [52]

More important than the political demoralization was the expansion of Greek ethnic life to include those outside the realm of Greek speech. The barbarians—"babblers"—are now made fellows in the Greek-speaking world. They move in with their mercenary soldiers, their merchants, their scholars and priests. The strange cults of Isis, Osiris, and Adonis flourish in Greek cities. The Greek was no longer a member of a small intimate community in which his language, his moral code, his religious practices, and the details of his life were determined by custom and environment. The individual now feels himself distressingly small in a world that has become increasingly large. The Greek once had security in his old city-state. Now there are millions of people swarming about the Greek world. The individual is driven in upon himself and becomes self-critical, self-distrustful. Murray's phrase, "a failure of nerve," is as applicable to fourth-century Greeec as to the rise of Christianity. There is a sense of "pessimism; a loss of self-confidence, of hope in this life and of faith in normal human effort; a despair of patient inquiry, a cry for infallible revelation. . . . It is an atmosphere in which the aim of the good man is not so much to live justly . . . but rather . . . by contempt for the world and its standards . . . to be granted pardon for his . . . immeasurable sins. There is an intensifying of certain spiritual emotions; an increase of sensitiveness, a failure of nerve." [53]

Alongside the sense of inadequacy, there is also a sense of expansion. The horizons of the individual Greek were greatly enlarged. He is now not merely a citizen of Athens but of the greater cosmos which gives him a sense of the magnitude of human life. He has become both an individualist and a cosmopolitan man, and in both respects felt more isolated in the world and more uncertain about the foundations of belief and conduct than ever before. The Hellenistic man reacted to this new situation by responding to the philosophies and religions that promise security in a time of vast uncertainty. The schools of thought which arise offer themselves not as ways of knowledge, but as practical ways of life. There were mysterious cults in abundance but the most worshipped of Hellenistic goddesses, Tyche or Fortune, is "a different and very much less alarming Power than the astrological Fate which terrorized the peoples of the later Roman Empire and in which they imaged the unreasoning cruelty of their lot." [54]

Is it too much to say that the Romans were "terrorized" by Fate and by the mythologies they devised, or accepted, to cope with its implacability? It would not be wide of the mark to say that the thousand years of Rome are still the most impressive single chapter in human history. But alongside the magnificent achievements of Rome, there were other and less pleasing dimensions. The world was even larger than in the days of Alexander. The individual had even more reason to feel inadequate and lost. Within the stable framework of Roman law, government, and commerce life could be very harsh. Millions of subjugated people lived under the rule of a foreign race. They were always discontented and frequently rebellious. Economic and political problems became so severe that only by means of a rigorous, dictatorial regimentation could Roman supremacy be maintained. Class hatred, the humiliation of the poor, unspeakable cruelty to slaves, and the bloodthirsty sports of the amphitheater point to the dark side of the Roman character.

In commenting on "the ever-recurrent horrors and brutalities" which were the daily experience of citizens and slaves, Michael Grant writes: "The Roman age was a time not only of uncontrolled blood lust but of pessimism and nerve failure regarding the powers of man to work out his own future." [55] The peoples of the empire had good reason to believe that every man was adrift, and everything hazardous. Economic and political causes were bringing the empire to ruin even in Republican times. The reforms of Augustus gave the empire a strong central government, secured the provinces against random aggression, and paved the way for a kind of partnership between Rome and its dominions. But the system of farming out taxation and public services to the great financial corporations hastened the process of concentrating the world's wealth in the hands of a few plutocrats who somewhat precariously made and unmade governments. The squandering of money upon luxury, buildings, and entertainments laid an intolerable burden upon the middle classes. With the creation of a vast urban proletariat, the depopulation of the countryside, and the consequent shortage of food, decline was inevitable and rapid. Land went out of cultivation. Tax-payers were too precious to be allowed to serve in the armies, and the frontiers could be guarded only by enlisting barbarians.

A succession of capable rulers maintained public order until the close of the second century. But after Commodus the task became too great. Economic exhaustion produced civil disturbance. Pressure on the frontiers demanded continuous military activity. In the eighty years between Pertinax and Diocletian there were some twenty-five emperors, and few of them died in their beds. Civil war threatened to become endemic. There seemed to be no power which could check the total disintegration of society. Cyprian, bishop of Carthage in the third century, wrote: "The world today speaks for itself: by the evidence of its decay it announces its dissolution. The farmers are vanishing from the countryside, commerce from the sea, soldiers from the camps; all honesty in business, all justice in the courts, all solidarity in friendship, all skill in the arts, all standards in morals—all are disappearing." [56] To take such a world seriously as a place to live and labor in must have demanded more courage than the average man possessed. Plotinus, Cyprian's contemporary, would have agreed with Albert Camus, of our century, that man's activity in the world is less than serious, less than fully real, "absurd." [57]

To many who watched the course of events in the third and fourth centuries it must have seemed that the fate of ancient Egypt might well be theirs. It is small wonder that a sense of despair was widespread. Pliny the elder had written in Paul's own century: "We are so much at the mercy of chance that Chance is our god." [58] The cult of Fortune, widespread before Paul's birth, symbolized the conviction of millions that all human affairs were governed by sheer luck. At some point Fate was added to Fortune and both were presiding deities of nerve failure. It did not matter much whether one was the victim of blind chance or ineluctable Fate. Both conceptions undermined the significance of human effort. People found many ways of coping with the tyranny of an external and incomprehensible power that moved them without regard to their wills. By far the most predominant religion of the time was astrology, which fell upon the Greeks and Romans "as a new disease falls upon some remote island people." [59] The planets and stars were seen as powers of evil, predestining all that will happen. Some relief from this unendurable predestination lay in the technique of determining what heaven had in store, and then to time one's activities so as to escape its hostile influence. Michael Grant describes this governing creed of the Romans as "one of the most terrible doctrines which has ever oppressed humanity." [60]

Not everyone sought relief in the casting of horoscopes which would enable them to outwit the heavens. There were also millions of inhabitants of the Roman empire, of all cultural levels, who sought to avoid the terrifying weight of chance or destiny by the more primitive means of magic. The omnipresence of magical practices gives a picture of a fear-ridden world.

Still another avenue of escape from the decrees of Fate was found in the mystery religions. No remedy for the hopeless feeling of isolation and defeat could be found in this world, so faith must focus on the next world instead. The cults of Dionysus, Asclepius, Cybele, Isis, and Mithras provided "saviors" who would give believers purity and strength and a happy immortality beyond the reach of luck, destiny, or death. The profound myths, exciting pageantry, and community spirit of these cults gave estranged people the sense that life, after all, had some meaning.

Our course of thought began with Paul, jumped to the nineteenth and twentieth centuries, then moved back to Paul, and finally settled in the Graeco-Roman world in which Paul lived. Our purpose in all this traveling between centuries has been to review the history and meaning of reconciliation language. Our approach was developed in three stages. First, we observed that the idea of reconciliation did not play a significant part in theology until it was put forward in the nineteenth century as an address to the widespread experience of estrangement. Our survey of several leading theologians of the twentieth century indicated that the idea of reconciliation proved its value as a mode of proclaiming grace and has become a central motif of Christian thought. Second, it was necessary to determine whether the use of reconciliation in recent theology was true to Paul's meaning and intention. We found that Paul chose a word that had the special quality of emphasizing and opening up the subjective dimensions of salvation—the freely-given love of God, the full restoration of fellowship, the experience of peace, confidence, and joy. We also saw that Paul's word was not only expressive of his own experience of reconciling grace in Christ, but was harmonious with Israel's testimony to God's redeeming action. Third, assuming that there were special factors in Paul's personality which made him unusually sensitive to the dehumanizing power of hostility, isolation, and despair, we inquired into the beliefs and attitudes of his age and found that he had good reason to speak of reconciliation. For it was an "age of anxiety" in which men were oppressed with a sense of the nothingness and futility of all earthly things. Dislocation, loneliness, fear, and estrangement were the stuff of life. We may conclude that Paul saw in the idea of reconciliation a religiously appropriate and strategically important way of proclaiming the grace of God.

Reconciliation and the anxiety of twentieth century man

It is now time to ask, however briefly, whether the idea of reconciliation matches the experience of life in the twentieth century as it matched that of the first. If it does, then we have the same reasons Paul had for addressing this special image to special circumstances. One need not pose as an expert on every aspect of life in the twentieth century in order to record a growing agreement among thoughtful observers of the human condition that man today is expressing a mood of profound alienation. If the church is to speak to its particular age in the face of realities which emerge from current experiences and interpretations of life, then it must speak of God's grace in the key or mode of reconciliation.

An ancient king, weary of the world and especially of reading, once complained that of the making of many books there was no end (Ecclesiastes 12:12). This is surely the impression of the modern reader as he greets, or deplores, the endless flow of literature about the meaning of the twentieth century. It would be impossible, and probably superfluous, to attempt to summarize even the most important cultural diagnoses of our time. But the theme of estrangement or alienation deserves some attention, especially in view of the claim of *The Confession of 1967* that "our generation stands in peculiar need of reconciliation in Christ." [61]

W. H. Auden's poem, "The Age of Anxiety," gives a proper name to our century, and Paul Tillich's *The Courage to Be* epitomizes the nature and content of that anxiety. Rollo May contends that "our middle of the twentieth century is more anxiety-ridden than any period since the breakdown of the Middle Ages." [62] But the items in any morning newspaper that show how the foundations of our world are shaken, are not all that different from the testimony in Paul's time about the transformation of the Roman world. Paul himself had witnessed the destruction of ancient communities and had seen individuals and groups perilously isolated. The predicament of man in Paul's world was spelled out in Ephesians 2:11-16. "Remember that you were at that time separated from Christ, alienated from the commonwealth of Israel, and strangers to the covenant of promise, having no hope and without God in the world." Separation, alienation, and estrangement all imply a prior state of concord which has been disrupted. The self can only exist in relation to supporting realities that are other than self. When these relations are sound, one lives. When they are broken, one dies. Paul said those supporting realities had been broken in his day, and in the fourteenth and fifteenth centuries, when Europe was inundated with anxiety in the form of fears of death and devils and agonies of doubt about the meaning and values of life, they were broken again.

What has happened to those supporting realities in our century? It is a truism to say that we are intimidated by the vastness and the silence of the universe. Some, of course, enjoy astronomy, others revel in the exploration of space, and still others want to use a neutral and objective world for moral and social purposes. The religious man sees the heavens as God's speech and handiwork. But it must be a rare believer, servant of a cause, or watcher of the skies who has not felt at times the irrationality and unmanageability of the given, the lack of a sense of final order, harmony, purpose and goodness in the world. We are not the first to feel that our powers of intelligence and goodwill are eroded by our encounter with the faceless mystery of the cosmos.

Nature in its more available form has been controlled to an amazing degree and its resources have been used for our health, comfort, and safety. But human progress has always been at nature's expense. During the last two centuries, science and technology have combined to give mankind powers which, ecologically speaking, are out of control. So long as we think of nature as a vast warehouse of materials to be used up or as a great workshop within which goods might be produced for human consumption, we are estranged from our physical environment.

Our inventions are equally ambivalent. Scientists and engineers have given a new face to existence and we would not cheerfully do without the benefits of technology. But we have reason to fear not only the side-effects of automation, urbanization, electronic media, mobility, and bio-medical experimentation. For our inventions also include weapons of an incalculable destructive potency which have proved that the twentieth-century mind is as full of cruelty and depravity as was any period in the past. Elation over technological advance is considerably qualified by the anxiety men feel when they see themselves as the helpless victims of forces which are beyond human control.

We are estranged from one another. Our relations with the social order are out of joint. The fabric of ancient custom and authority has been shattered by the social and economic convulsions of our century. Prejudices of race, class, and nation, ideological hatreds between communist and capitalist countries, between rich nations and poor, the alienation of millions from the sources of political and social decision-making, war and hunger are so common as to be taken for granted. It is, of course, platitudinous to mention these things. Somehow our hopes have been reduced and our indignation muted by the very impossibility of coping in any coherent way with the forces of malice and misfortune that ruin the relationships we need to be truly human. We have become resigned to estrangement.

What happens to persons in all this? For we cannot avoid internalizing the dislocations we see all about us. The information given us by sociologists, psychologists, philosophers, and historians about the emptiness, loneliness, apathy, alienation, and anxiety of "modern man" is staggering in its bulk. If to this evidence we add the analysis of the modern sensibility as reported by contemporary poets, novelists, dramatists, and artists, then the conclusion that man is alone and alien in a meaningless cosmos, an erratic history, and a disrupted society is overwhelming. Man's context is constituted by blind nature, a universe with neither a transcendent source nor an inherent or ultimate order. Thus the meaning, security, and value of his life cannot come from outside himself. He is utterly dependent on his own resources to forge what meaning he can in his brief span of life. Since the supporting realities have no cosmic ground and are marked, on the social and interpersonal level, by irrationality, aggression, and greed, the individual senses a distance between himself and the sources of authentic life. This distance is known as estrangement, alienation, anomie, apathy, anxiety. One feels trapped in a world in which one cannot be intimately personal, in which there can be no permanent gains, and from which there is no exit except into nothingness. The language sounds "existentialist." But the claim is that all of us—atheist and believer, humanitarian and rebel, dreamer and executive—have felt the cold wind of despair, if we will but admit it.

There can be little doubt that *The Confession of 1967* is right in saying that "our generation stands in peculiar need of reconciliation in Christ." It is often said that modern men find the religious symbols of sin, atonement, and justification meaningless because there is in the modern consciousness no experience of sin and no felt need of "being made right" with God or with anyone else. Langdon Gilkey claims that if the religious symbols seem irrelevant, it is because their meaning as answers to our very common experiences of alienation, isolation, and guilt has not been spelled out. "For modern life is as much qualified and shaped by the search for personal reintegration and innocence, and for the healing of our broken communities, as has been that of any other age. What else explains the almost universal response to the healing arts of psychoanalysis; our frantic claims of moral innocence in almost all aspects of our communal existence; and our continual flight into racial and political communities which, on the one hand, absorb and subvert our hostilities and at the same time give to them a cleansing moral justification? The need for *religious* justification and reconciliation is surely not explicitly felt among us; but much of our lives and our wealth is spent in the search for psychological, moral, and social forms of the same necessary blessings." [63]

The biblical word for today is "reconciliation." The advantages of using this mode of expression are clear. Reconciliation puts the whole message of grace in the language of personal relations, it refers discipleship to the community of God's people and to individual and corporate obedience in the world, and it meets the most radical need and profound longing of man.

8

Paul's Theology

of Reconciliation:

Its Meaning Today

Our purpose has been to recommend that the religious reality of grace-in-action be understood in terms of the idea of reconciliation. One point remains to be explored. Should this metaphor be restricted to the description of the subjective aspect, the feeling-tone, of actualized redemption, or is it capable of serving as a coordinating doctrine, one that can express and interpret the whole range of meanings associated with God's saving action?

At first glance, there is nothing startling about the shape or content of a "theology of reconciliation." It has a familiar ring in that it covers the essential points of the biblical testimony as well as the central features of Catholic and Protestant schemes of salvation. Yet the image of reconciliation is able both to clarify and underscore certain facets of Christian belief and to personalize and universalize the doctrine of grace.

God—the subject of reconciliation

Reconciliation makes it crystal clear that the movement of grace is the one-sided initiative of God's love. The doctrine of sin is by no means the essence of the gospel, yet the gospel can hardly be set forth apart from the understanding that man can do nothing to save himself. He cannot change himself from a self-centered to a God-centered and neighbor-centered person. He cannot remove himself from the state of estrangement or deserve personal reconciliation with God. God in his power and goodness must take the decisive step to bridge the gulf and enter into man's situation so as to remedy it from within. It is the essence of the gospel that God has done precisely this. He has acted in such a way as to reconcile man to himself (Romans 5:10-11).

Paul's reconciliation passages are in complete agreement that it is God alone who is the sole initiator of the movement of reconciliation. "All this is from God" (2 Corinthians 5:18). The church fathers of the first five centuries were more insistent than many of their successors on the principle that God does his own work. Only God can redeem. He does not ask any third party to do his work for him. If he did, both the unity of God's nature and the validity of the work would be called in question. When Paul says that God is himself the prime mover, that the initiative and the whole course of the saving work are God's, he is reflecting the steady teaching of the Old Testament, in which God is never the object of the verb "to atone." He is always its subject. The objectivity of the atonement does not lie in the fact that an effective gift was offered to God, but that it was offered by God. All the expiatory praxis whereby men were to be reconciled to their Lord was of God's own initiation. God gave the sacrifice to make atonement (Leviticus 17:11).

It is very important to be clear on this point. Reconciliation in our day is a word from the newspapers. It generally signifies the intervention of a third party who patches up a marriage on the verge of divorce, mediates a dispute between antagonistic factions, or effects a cease-fire between warring nations. But God can never be regarded as the object of some third party's intervention to reconcile. In such a case, there could be no grace since grace is free and that which is bought or procured is not free. Paul knew there were other religions which strive to make peace between God and man. But the pagan creeds declare that man must take steps to reconcile his God, and so restore himself to favor. Paul wants to say that Christianity declares the exact opposite: it is God who reconciles, man who is reconciled. A God who stands over against offending man and waits until satisfaction is made and his anger placated, is not the God of grace whom Paul had come to know in Jesus Christ.

There is not a trace in Paul's language of the notion that God requires to be reconciled. His concept of the divine initiative stands in opposition not only to paganism but also to the sub-Christian idea that Christ acted to placate God's anger. Paul says very plainly that the problem is man's hostility, not God's (Colossians 1:21; Romans 5:8, 10). While we are yet sinners, "God shows his love for us." Antagonism could never motivate God's act in Christ. But does not Paul's talk about the "wrath of God" (Romans 1:18; Ephesians 5:6; Colossians 3:6) imply that God cherishes resentment against the wrongdoer and must be pacified before fellowship can be restored? This might be the case if there were a close analogy between God and a man who has lost his temper. But there is no such parallel between human anger and the divine wrath. Paul uses anthropomorphic language, to be sure, but there is some ground for discrimination within that mode of discourse. When Paul speaks of God's love, grace, or faithfulness, God is always the subject of the verb. But God is never made the subject of the verb "to be angry." This suggests that we are not meant to understand "love" and "wrath" as being parallel terms, as having equal force. It is not as though "love" and "wrath" both describe "emotional" attitudes of God, who is like us in that wrath alternates with love and where the one begins the other ends. We should understand rather that love, grace, faithfulness, and all other terms that express the unlimited self-giving of God, should be taken as describing the personal attitude of God to men, while wrath, judgment, and retribution should be taken as describing, not God's personal attitude, but the objective consequences of human wrongdoing.[1] James Stewart asserts that the wrath of God means "the totality of the divine reaction to sin. Everything that man's rebellion against the moral order brings upon him—suffering for his body, hardening for his heart, blinding for his faculty of inward vision—is included in that reaction. Is this punishment? Yes, certainly; but it is not God's outraged dignity retaliating by a direct, penal act." [2] Rather it is the sinner who punishes himself by going against the grain of things, by trying to get out of life what God has not put into it, by having to live with the consequences of his actions. "This is the judgment, that the light has come into the world, and men loved darkness rather than light" (John 3:19). Paul is saying that wrath must be understood as the obverse of grace. It is, as Gustaf Aulen puts it, God's love keeping itself pure by refusing to condone the evil that ruins life and makes us into "enemies." [3]

We have seen that the idea of God's wrath cannot be taken to mean that God is resentful and needs to be pacified before fellowship can be restored. To think that God needs to be pacified is to lose the idea of grace, and therefore the gospel, because God would no longer be the prime mover. The pacification would be the result of a negotiated grace, which is a contradiction in terms. The biblical word "propitiation" (*hilasterion*) can also be understood in such a way as to open the door to sub-Christian conceptions of grace and the divine initiative. In classical Greek the verb means primarily to placate or appease an angry person or god, with the object of averting vengeance. It can also mean to atone or expiate for some offence by offering sacrifice or making reparation. But the idea of placating an angry deity is foreign to biblical usage, although it forms a large part of pagan religion and cultus.

Although the word "propitiation" occurs four times in the New Testament (Romans 3:25; Hebrews 2:17; 1 John 2:2; 4:10), it never bears the usual meaning of a human act of reparation. Yet the dominant view of the atonement throughout the history of Christian thought has been that man's sin has offended God's holiness and dignity and merits infinite punishment. The notions of "merit" and "satisfaction" found their way into Christian theology as early as the time of Tertullian and Augustine. Anselm gave this line of thought enormous prestige. Even though some reformers in the sixteenth century proclaimed again the gospel of free grace, medieval notions of "merit" and "satisfaction" continued to distort the New Testament teaching. The idea that Christ bore a penalty or punishment instead of us, in order that God might forgive us and yet remain just, has no basis in biblical teaching. Alan Richardson says flatly: "The New Testament does not say that God demands satisfaction (in terms either of honour or debt) or that man (even the God-man) renders it to him. It does not say that God needs to be reconciled to man; St. Paul speaks only of man's having to be reconciled to God." [4] James Stewart says of the conventional theory of the atonement: "It's greatest merit was the serious view it took of sin. Its greatest defect was its disastrous view of God." [5]

A disastrous view of God surely results when any theory of the atonement suggests a difference of attitude towards men on the part of the Father and the Son. As we have seen in an earlier chapter, the unity of God implies the unity of grace. In the saving work of Jesus, the initiative is with God. It is man who needs to be won over and reconciled to God, not God who needs to be persuaded to change his attitude to man. The attitude of God is pure love and it is a single, unchanging atttiude. Thus, God's love and judgment, wrath and mercy are not opposed as though different forms of the divine activity could be in conflict or the divine attributes be at variance with each other. Both the unity of God's being and the transcendent grace of his initiative are undermined when it is suggested that the part played by God the Father is in some way different from, or even opposed to, that of Christ. G. W. H. Lampe reacts vigorously to such well-meaning but misleading notions: "What Christians believe about God's reconciliation of the world is sometimes caricatured so as to suggest that the Father's attitude represents God's justice whereas that of Christ represents God's love, as though the divine justice and love could be set in opposition to each other instead of being recognized as but two ways of describing the same attitude of one and the same personal God." The caricature of Christian belief sometimes goes so far as to teach that the Father was bent upon destroying rebellious humanity, but was persuaded to let man escape doom by the Son, who loved sinners and offered himself as a substitute to take man's punishment upon himself, thus satisfying the Father. Lampe comments: "Such a travesty of Christian belief refutes itself. There is one God, and the will and action of the Father and the Son are one and the same." [6] In saying that God is the subject of reconciliation, we are rejecting any doctrinal formulation that by implication divides God into a being whose offended righteousness demands satisfaction and a being whose sinlessness enables him to meet this demand on the part of the sinner. Instead we must say that the atonement is the saving act of God in Christ and that the death and resurrection of Christ are the sphere of the Father's own activity.

Jesus Christ—the mediator of reconciliation

The New Testament proclamation that Jesus Christ "is the mediator of a new covenant" (Hebrews 9:15) is inseparable from the principle that reconciliation is a one-sided act of God. The reconciliation passages are unanimous in affirming that the reconciling act of God was accomplished in Christ and especially through his death and resurrection. The work of reconciliation was done by Christ as "the Son" of God (Romans 5:10), as "the first-born of all creation" (Colossians 1:15), and still more precisely as the one who died on the cross (Ephesians 2:16; Colossians 1:19); Romans 5:10). He died for us (Romans 5:6) and for all (2 Corinthians 5:18-21). In his death he abolished all enmity and hostility (Ephesians 2:15-16) and has reconciled us, together with "all things," by making peace through the blood of his cross (Colossians 1:19-22). The wonder of it is that he in whom "all the fulness of God was pleased to dwell" (Colossians 1:19) was "made sin for us" (2 Corinthians 5:21).

These passages present a mixture of images. It is most instructive to note the simplicity, yet the profundity, of Paul's address to the Corinthian congregation. When God was reconciling the world in Christ, what did he do? He simply came to men just as they were, "not counting their trespasses against them" (2 Corinthians 5:19; "no longer holding men's misdeeds against them," NEB). And in coming to men, he established a relationship with them. A sense of astonishment that God would thus relate to sinful men is found not only in Paul but throughout the entire Bible. If there is any way at all of accounting for such a happening between persons, it can only be said that God comes, accepts, and incorporates sinners because he loves them (Romans 5:8; Ephesians 2:4; cf. Deuteronomy 4:32-40; Hosea 11:1).

It is clear that the reconciliation was effected by the exercise of divine forgiveness. To the amazed recipients of this love, the reconciling presence of God was at the same time the sign, or evidence, or actualization of their forgiveness. This is especially noteworthy in the poignant story about "a woman of the city, who was a sinner." Jesus related to her, included her, in his generous, spontaneous, and unstereotyped way, and said to his respectable and somewhat shocked host, "Do you see this woman?" Do you *see* her? Then he said to her, "Your sins are forgiven. . . . Go in peace" (Luke 7:36-50). At times Jesus forgave sins explicitly, but more often forgiveness was inherent in his behavior (Matthew 26:26-28). The classic instance of reconciliation as forgiveness—acted-out is found in the story of Zacchaeus, the rich tax-collector who climbed a tree to see Jesus pass by. Jesus simply looked at the man and announced that he was coming to his house for lunch. Jesus did not wait for Zacchaeus to repent of his misdeeds and pledge to become a decent tax-collector. Instead, he made the first approach, taking the initiative himself, and offering his friendship. There was nothing Zacchaeus needed to do but accept the offer. It was at a later point that he was moved to repent and make amends (Luke 19:1-10).

The attitude of free and undeserved love in which Jesus approached Zacchaeus is called "grace" in the Bible. It is the generously given personal relatedness to God, extended without any conditions except the condition that it be accepted. Thus it would be a mistake to understand the "repent and believe" of Jesus' earliest preaching (Mark 1:15) as laying down a hard and fast sequence. To think that the Kingdom was offered only to repentant sinners is to distort the gospel and the apostolic record. Man's repentance is not a condition of God's loving, but of man's believing. John does not even mention repentance as a separate step because he sees it as integral to faith or the move to accept and live in the proferred relationship. It is certain that the earliest Christian tradition understands the reconciling work as a whole to be one of forgiveness (Matthew 26:26-28).

This interpretation is consistent with what has been said about grace in an earlier chapter. If theology is to be developed in dialogue with the New Testament, then we must reject any suggestion that grace is an impersonal force or supernatural power instilled into us, like an injection of medicine. We cannot even think of grace as an influence from God given to assist us in our progress along the road to readiness or perfection. Grace can only be seen as the active and loving presence of Christ himself mediated through the Holy Spirit to be the new center of our life in God.

It is not our purpose to provide an extensive discussion of the work of Christ. Thus far we have stayed close to 2 Corinthians 5:17-21 where the focus is on the free and unconditional offer of a personal relationship which presupposes and actualizes forgiveness. There is, of course, much more to be said about atonement or reconciliation. But most of the images found in other passages coalesce into a coherent pattern if we use the Corinthians passage as a rather general control.[7]

It is of the utmost importance that forensic images of the atonement be delegalized and our interpretation of Christ's work be expressed in personal categories. It is difficult to see in Paul any tendency to connect the justification of the sinner with an imputation to him of the superabundant merits of Christ. On the contrary, his mind moves within the sphere of the altogether different set of concepts involved in the idea of personal relationships. Even his forensic imagery is controlled by the personalistic implications of the idea of being "in Christ." Man escapes condemnation not because merit is transferred to his account, nor because Christ has endured his punishment or paid his debt, but because "there is no condemnation for those who are in Christ Jesus" (Romans 8:1). It is *in Christ* that the sinner is justified. He is placed in a right relationship. "For our sake he made him to be sin who knew no sin, so that in him we might become the righteousness of God" (2 Corinthians 5:21). There is no way in which the message of Paul can be properly expressed in terms of impersonal quantities or transactions. He was indignant when some Christians in Galatia regressed to a legalistic perspective. If he had lived a century later, he would have found even greater cause for dismay in the general use of legalistic concepts by the sub-apostolic and patristic authors.

It is not easy to understand the reasons for the failure of these early theologians to conceive grace as the personal activity of God in Christ through the Spirit. G. W. H. Lampe suggests that "the religion of the ordinary man, . . . even in the apostolic age itself, tended to be legalistic and formal. . . . The spiritual insight of St. Paul or St. John was certainly quite exceptional then, as similar perception is in every age. . . . Side by side with these great peaks of spiritual understanding there was a lower level of piety which also called itself Christian." [8]

It is probable that patristic and medieval theologians spoke in terms of abstract and impersonal justice in order to safeguard the divine initiative against the Pelagian notion that man can stand before God and be regarded as righteous by virtue of his own spiritual and moral performance. It is ironic that it is precisely Pelagianism that fails to see the sinner's relationship to God as truly personal, involving love, trust, and rejoicing rather than reward and punishment. When Anselm said that man's lack of merit is compensated for by Christ's superabundant merits, he meant to protect the divine initiative. But he did not by any means safeguard the doctrine of grace. God still justifies on the basis of merit since he has received payment of the debt owed him and a free gift besides. Free, unmerited grace is hard to find in Anselm's scheme of thought. There is much of Anselm in subsequent theology, both Catholic and Protestant. Even the Reformers spoke often of "the merits of Christ," although the main thrust of their message was determined by their recovery of Paul's teaching about the free, undeserved, personal character of grace. As we have seen, the nineteenth century initiated a vigorous reaction against the impersonal and legalistic categories of the Anselmic type of atonement theology.

Man—the object of reconciliation

Reconciliation, as presented by Paul is a one-sided act but a two-sided event.[9] We have seen that God is the subject and Jesus Christ the mediator of reconciliation. Now we must observe that man is the object of reconciliation and that the event has far-reaching consequences. The target of God's reconciling action is variously described. In Romans 5:10-

11, it is ourselves, as enemies of God, who are reconciled. According to Romans 11:15, the object of reconciliation is the world, in the sense of the heathen peoples who are not participants in the covenant community of Israel. 2 Corinthians 5:17-21 speaks of the world in the sense of mankind as a whole. In Ephesians 2:16, reconciliation aims at the two segments of the covenant people, separated by the wall of partition and mutually estranged from each other. For Colossians 1:19-22, God reconciles to himself "all things, whether on earth or in heaven." The scope of reconciliation is clearly universal. God's grace is all-inclusive.

Paul speaks always of man, not God, being reconciled. The term "world" has a variety of meanings in the New Testament. But in the reconciliation passages, "world" has an existential meaning and refers to a quality of existence that is characterized by darkness, falsehood, dividedness, and death as opposed to man's true, authentic existence, which is characterized by light, truth, unity, and life. Thus the world that God seeks to reconcile to himself is the fallen world—human life in its disobedience, emptiness, lostness, and estrangement.

The need of reconciliation is spelled out at great length in the biblical testimony, as well as in the data and interpretations provided by psychology and sociology. We have come to understand that those who project hostility toward their neighbors "are likely to be harboring a large reservoir of hatred and resentment toward themselves." [10] Theology interprets self-hatred and animosity toward neighbors and the natural world as being rooted in alienation from God, the very ground of our existence. The contradiction between man and God is the root of all other contradictions (Genesis 2-3). Because of a pervasive sense of grievance or guilt in relation to whatever power determines our life, we reject ourselves and others and question the whole scheme of things. Although Soren Kierkegaard was not lashing out against God, himself, or his neighbors, he did pose a question which expresses the deep perplexity and the potential resentment we all feel when we ponder the bearing of happenings in which we find ourselves involved: "Who am I? How came I here? What is this thing called the world? . . . Why was I not consulted? . . . How did I obtain an interest in this big enterprise they call reality? . . . And if I am to be compelled to take part in it, where is the director? I should like to make a remark to him." [11]

The aim of God's reconciling action is to heal wounds, overcome barriers, arrest disintegration, neutralize hostility, restore harmony between God and man, man and himself, man and his world. Reconciliation is ultimately affirmative. In Christ God had shown that the world is loved, accepted, and affirmed despite its disobedience, estrangement, and guilt. It is the will and purpose of God to bring the fallen world, sinful mankind, and "all things" to the fulfillment for which they had been created.

For Paul the transformation involved in such fulfillment was so radical that he called it a "new creation." But the "new creation" did not imply the destruction of the old creation or the substtiution of an entirely different person for the old self. On the contrary, the gospel proclaimed God's endless love for fallen humanity and the reconciliation of this estranged mankind to community and fellowship with him who had called it into being. In Jesus Christ God affirms man unqualifiedly, and he who so affirms man is the one to whom man belongs. No root element of human existence is alien or forbidding to Jesus Christ. "In the community God has created in Jesus Christ man is not rebuked because he is always and necessarily less than God. He is rebuked because he is less than an adopted son of the Kingdom ought to be." [12] The purpose of reconciliation is to establish fallen man in his true humanity.

The personal dimension of reconciliation

The initiative of God and the work of Christ belong to the one-sidedness of the act of reconciliation. To say that man is the object of God's love and that reconciliation has rich and far-reaching consequences is to explicate the two-sidedness of the event. The reconciliation passages are unanimous in declaring that because of God's gracious intervention everything is now different. So radical is the cancellation of the past that Paul says, "if any one is in Christ, he is a new creation" (2 Corinthians 5:17). We have become the righteousness of God, have access to the Father, and are brought into his presence, holy and blameless (2 Corinthians 5:21; Ephesians 2:18; Colossians 1:22). The new creation is rooted in the Body of Christ, in which are incorporated without distinction Jews and Gentiles (Ephesians 2:16). God has entrusted to us the message of reconciliation, has appointed us ambassadors for Christ, and makes his appeal through us (2 Corinthians 5:19-20). Reconciliation gives us an assurance of our ultimate redemption and we can go forward to the end with confidence (Romans 5 and 11). God's reconciling love is intended for all mankind (Romans 11:13-15) and his peace extends to the entire cosmos (Colossians 1:20).

The scope of the reconciliation and the richness of its benefits are illimitable and mysterious. At the risk of oversimplification, we may group the consequences that pertain to the individual, the church, human society, and the whole world under three headings: the personal, the corporate, and the cosmic dimensions. We speak with some diffidence about the personal or individual dimension of anything nowadays, for we have been persuaded that personality is inherently mutual and that there is no such thing as a private sphere of life. Yet alongside the polarity of self and society, we must place the core conviction that life is indefeasibly personal. Perhaps the sphere of the primarily personal is rather small, but it is there. John S. Whale contends: "In one sense... the part is prior to the whole: but in another sense the whole is prior to the part. In short, human life demands to be understood in terms of its two complementary aspects, the individual and the corporate, the part and the whole. Each has to be interpreted in terms of the other." [13]

With the understanding that the wall between the individual and the group is rather porous, we note Paul's appeal: "Be reconciled to God" (2 Corinthians 5:20). Scripture and theology have much to say about the inwardness of man's response to the gospel. The response is both inward and essential, for reconciliation, though realized in the life, death, and resurrection of Jesus Christ, does not become complete and effectual until man responds to it in faith. Repentance is linked to faith, although not necessarily as the first step in a time sequence. In such an intensely personal phenomenon, chronology and sharp distinctions hardly apply. Repentance and faith together describe a change, a reorientation of the personality. Since the change involves a turning from sin and a turning to God, negative and positive aspects can at least be distinguished. Thus it can be said that repentance means a realization of an abnormal state of affairs, a wrong direction, a failure to be what one ought to be. A sense of regret or even despair is accompanied by an acknowledgement that God's judgment is just. Repentance is a movement of self-criticism stimulated by the divine criticism of the quality of our lives. But God is never present only as critic or judge. He is always present as affirmer and redeemer. Thus faith, the other side of repentance, is a positive move to accept the way out which God makes available. Just as God is gracious both as critic and savior, so repentance and faith are responses to grace that are made possible by grace. They are not human achievements (Acts 5:31; 11:18; Romans 2:4; 2 Timothy 2:25).

To be aware of God is to be aware of grace and to know that grace affirms, supports, heals, and includes. Awareness of the forgiveness of sins is the most immediate effect of the nearness of God mediated through Jesus Christ. Through the free grace of God the sinner is "adopted" (Galatians 4:4-5) or incorporated into Christ. He is placed in a right relationship and given the status of a son because he is *in* Christ and stands within the scope of the reconciliation that Christ effected (2 Corinthians 5:21). Although in himself the believer remains a sinner and continues to live by forgiveness, he is at the same time a son of God, in a right relationship to him through Christ.

Through repentance and faith, as responses to God's restoring grace, the believer is reconciled, adopted, incorporated, and comes to enjoy the "peace of God." The redeeming work of Christ is entirely contained in the word "peace." The whole preaching mission of Jesus is described in Ephesians 2:17 as a preaching of peace to all men, near and far. The term *eirene* (peace) in classical Greek is primarily negative, denoting the absence or end of war. But the biblical sense of "peace" in general is determined by the Hebrew word *shalom,* a much more positive and comprehensive word. It derives from a root which signifies totality, wholeness, harmony, integrity, well being. The essence of the word signifies productive and fulfilling community with others. If one were to trace the word "peace" through the Bible, one would see that the whole unfolding drama of redemption represents God's struggle to establish the reconciling peace, the *shalom,* among men and with himself. "Thus *shalom* describes the state of men who live on earth in reconciliation with nature, themselves, their neighbors, and God. This peace is seen as the gift of God's presence (Judges 6:24)." [14]

Both the nature and the content of God's action in Christ are described as love, grace, reconciliation, peace. But the tranquility and wholeness which accompany faith cannot coexist with illusions or pretensions of any kind. Thus the self-criticism known as repentance is indispensable. There can be no peace without realism. If we say that the man who is reconciled to God accepts himself as a sinner, the connection between realism and peace becomes clear. To be genuinely repentant, to accept oneself as a sinner, means that one at least begins to be objectively realistic about himself. He sees himself as he really is, has no illusions about the extent and culpability of his own shortcoming. When, under the explicit or anonymous pressures of God, one comes to a moment of disillusionment, he gets back into the world of realities. There is no longer the need or effort to offer extenuating excuses, to play roles, to pretend to be someone of superior knowledge or untainted virtue, above the ignorance, mistakes, and malice of ordinary folk. In short, one is through with self-justification and all the frantic dishonesties involved in maintaining one's own worth. And in that frame of mind one finds he is received without reservation and without condition. Somehow through contact with the crucified Christ one is brought into a new attitude of realistic judgment about himself and yet is at peace about it. He is at peace because the tension and struggle to prove himself worthy is over. It is unnecessary. Herbert Farmer puts it: "The forgiven man is content to stand before God just as he is and to be accepted of Him not because of his own deserving, not because he can urge a claim or make a convincing excuse, but simply because of the divine mercy. He is at peace about his sins in the presence of God." [15] It is the honest and hard-headed realism which makes the peace possible. Yet one could hardly bear to be so vulnerably realistic were it not for the prospect of the unconditionally given peace. Faith as trust mediates between repentance and peace and takes the forms of courage and gratitude as it faces the demand and the gift of God.

The personal dimension of reconciliation is not exhausted by the inward experiences of repentance, faith, and peace. It is somewhat misleading to describe these interpersonal realities as "inward experiences." They are not to be understood merely as subjective feelings. God does not accept us on the basis of the depth of our repentance, the strength of our faith, or the fullness of the peace we enjoy. Moreover, these experiences are never merely private, since membership in the Christian community is inseparable from the status of sonship which is conferred by the grace of God in justification. Yet repentance, faith, and peace are surely the interior experiences of individuals. They have their place in human self-consciousness. They are not God's own feelings, credited to our account, nor are they the actions of a committee, although, as Paul might put it, "there is no law" against the participation by a committee in the sobering, yet uplifting, realities of repentance, faith, and peace.

But the outgoing or exterior aspect of the ingoing or interior encounter with God on the personal level becomes quite clear when Paul tells us that God has reconciled us in order to present us "holy and blameless and irreproachable before him" (Colossians 1:21). When men are set free by forgiveness from their natural self-centeredness and accept the reconciling love of God in Christ, they are given a new relationship towards God and begin to live in a new spirit. They begin to experience the indwelling of the Spirit of Jesus. The work of the Spirit is to mediate Christ to them and to "conform" them "to the image" of Christ (Romans

8:29). Thus the holiness (or whole-ness) at which reconciliation aims is not a part of the inherent character of the believer, a possession or achievement of his own, but is the self-expression of the indwelling Christ. The Spirit of Christ becomes the principle of the new life. Though the believer can never become totally directed by or expressive of the Spirit of Christ, he is made fit for Christ's service. To be holy is not to be perfectly virtuous but to be an active and useful member of the holy community and to be capable of growth in knowledge and love.

G. W. H. Lampe rightly points out that the Christian "virtues" are not really virtues in the ordinary sense of the term. That is, they are not the natural or peculiar excellencies of individuals. They are rather modes of operation of the Holy Spirit who operates in those who are united with Christ by faith. The self-expression of the Spirit of Christ through the believer takes the form of many and various qualities of character (Galatians 5:22-23). But the chief "virtue" of the Christian life is love because this is the supreme and most inclusive mode of operation of the Spirit. "This will mean that the moral conduct of the Christian will be an expression of the reconciling love of God in Christ, going out to draw all men to himself." [16]

It is very clear that the new holiness which is associated with repentance, faith, and peace on the level of the personal encounter with the God of grace, is not a mere indwelling quality nor is it intended for the believer's private enjoyment. It is a new attitude towards the world around us. The outward-looking character of holiness is underscored by Paul when he uses two phrases to describe the manner in which God accomplishes reconciliation. First, God does not count our trespasses against us and, second, he has entrusted to us "the message of reconciliation" (2 Corinthians 5:19). Thus the exercise of divine forgiveness is accompanied by a summons to proclaim the message of the gospel in order to elicit a response of faith on the part of the hearers. A sense of urgency pervades the passage in 2 Corinthians 5, indicating the great importance which he attached to this message and his profound conviction that he had been divinely commissioned to declare it. Once Paul knew himself to be right with God, he saw that if the estranging barriers had fallen for him, there was no reason why they should not fall for everyone. So Paul called himself an "ambassador for Christ, God making his appeal through us" (2 Corinthians 5:20). If God chose "ambassadors," it must be because the reconciliation inaugurated by Christ is not completed simply by divine action. God has not only invited men to respond in faith but has also assigned to men the "ministry of reconciliation" (2 Corinthians 5:18). In this ministry, men are God's agents, and through his "ambassadors" God actualizes reconciliation. Not only must reconciliation become effectual through the response of faith, but the ministry of witness must be continued on the earth until the grand consummation of God's purposes.

When we say that the new standing in grace carries an obligation to express or represent God's action through ministry, it becomes quite obvious that the personal dimension merges with the corporate. The individual is a member of the Body of Christ and is never involved in the cultivation of solitary spiritual and moral perfection. Yet, even though the whole is not merely an aggregate of parts, the response and action of the individual are real and indispensable. So we may focus for a moment longer on personal responsibility within the context of the community.

Paul tells us that holiness, the new attitude to the world around us, includes the witness to reconciliation by words and deeds. The ministry of words in public preaching and in personal conversation cannot be looked at in detail. It can be observed, however, that for Paul the ministry entrusted to Christians, as individuals and as a society, is defined by "the message of reconciliation" (2 Corinthians 5:19). In Colossians 1:23 he moves beyond the message of reconciliation to the mission, speaking of "the gospel which you heard, . . . of which I Paul became a minister." In the reconciliation passages Paul affirms that the mission of the church, although distinct from the work of Christ, is nevertheless a vital link in the same work of God. The interrelationship between proclamation and the Holy Spirit is such that the gospel is not only a message about reconciliation, but an instrument of God's achieving it. By the grace of God, those who are at once reconciled and reconciling can bridge the gap between the work of Christ and the world by preaching (Ephesians 3:8-11). In those who hear their message and believe, the work of reconciliation is realized (Romans 10:13-77). It is surely a cause for wonderment that in some extraordinary manner the announcement that Jesus had lived, died, and risen again led to a change in the lives of ordinary men and women from the time of the apostles to the present day. They experienced through the Holy Spirit reconciliation and peace with God.

But the ministry of words is not confined to the pulpit. There is also a ministry of conversation. We talk to each other for many reasons and our conversation is as varied as life itself. Much conversation is unhappily a form of disservice because it divides and depersonalizes. When speech between persons creates or maintains distance, ignores or trivializes needs, and falsifies or confuses meanings, it has become an instrument of self-assertion. But when conversation affirms the reality and worth of the other, keeps open the lines of communication, and makes the speaker immediately available to the other, it becomes a vehicle of reconciling personal presence, a means of grace. Since human hostility and alienation involve a break in personal trust, it is only through the deeply personal word that reconciliation can take place. Language does not mean any one form of speech and much of our most important communication, helpful or harmful, finds spoken words unnecessary. Yet in the context of personal existence, the direct word is unavoidable and only that word, spoken from one free subject to another in honesty and compassion, can be adequate for the restoration of relationship. Since the message of reconciliation clothes itself in human speech, we are "ministers" in the words we say to each other.

But reconciliation is actualized in deeds as much as in words. We cannot survey the mass of biblical injunctions, legal codes, and social customs that make up our composite moral tradition. There do seem, however, to be some basic laws of cooperative enterprise which in one form or another are acknowledged and professed wherever men live and work together. In most societies the phases of life which are the subject of regulation tend to be the same. The laws of distributive justice, the temperate discipline of various physical appetites, prescriptions relative to the ownership and transfer of property, and the definition of crimes all tend to work for the preservation of human life and the promotion of social stability and effectiveness. It is interesting to note that when Paul identifies a great number of vices and virtues in Ephesians 4-6, he sees vices as actions that tear down community and virtues as actions that build up community.

Our analysis must focus more closely, however, on the manner in which the experience of reconciliation affects conduct. Wherever the primary experience of reconciliation to God is realized, the secondary experience of reconciliation to the neighbor immediately follows. Paul's magnificent witness to reconciliation in 2 Corinthians 5:18-20 is followed by a reference to his own estrangement from the believers in Corinth. The message of reconciliation entrusted to him, "Be reconciled to God," is applied by the missionary pastor to his own congregation: "Our mouth is open to you, Corinthians; our heart is wide. You are not restricted by us, but you are restricted in your own affections. In return . . . widen your hearts also. . . . Open your hearts to us. . . . You are in our hearts, to die together and to live together. I have great confidence in you . . . I am overjoyed" (2 Corinthians 6:11-13; 7:2-4).

This loving appeal to his people for a renewal of their earlier one-ness with him is a concrete example of Paul's conviction that a person who has experienced the unrestricted affection of God *cannot* restrict his own affections towards his neighbors. A man who accepts the gospel, yet harbors resentment, bears grudges, indulges in habitual fault-finding, and closes the doors between himself and his neighbor is giving a clear signal that his sense of alienation on the human level reflects an alienation, at some point, between himself and God. Reconciliation, when it is real, changes all this. One sees all mankind with new eyes. To be in Christ is to feel towards others as Christ would feel towards them. It is to be raised above divisions and pettiness to the point where one can see that "there is neither Jew nor Greek, there is neither slave nor free, there is neither male nor female; for you are all one in Christ Jesus" (Galatians 3:28). This insight dominates Paul's appeal to his friend Philemon the slave owner, to be reconciled with Onesimus, the runaway slave. Paul asks not merely for acquittal of the offender but for fully personal restoration. He writes: "Perhaps this is why he was parted from you for a while, that you might have him back forever, no longer as a slave but more than a slave, as a beloved brother. . . . So if you consider me your partner, receive him as you would receive me. . . . Refresh my heart in Christ" (Philemon 15, 16 17, 20).

Behind Paul's conviction that being reconciled to God has its immediate effect in reconciliation to one's neighbor lies the preaching of Jesus. In the parable of the two debtors (Matthew 18:23-35) it is said that if we really believe that God overcame the immense barrier of our guilt, we must overcome the smaller barrier of our neighbor's debt to us. In the Sermon on the Mount it is clear that vengeance and retribution are to be put aside in human relationships. "You have heard that it was said, 'An eye for an eye and a tooth for a tooth.' But I say to you . . ." "You have heard that it was said, 'You shall love your neighbor and hate your enemy.' But I say to you . . ." (Matthew 5:38-45). The one who spoke these words bore in his own body all the consequences of the law of retaliation. To believe this is to know that bitterness, vengeance, and estrangement are ruled out.

The witness to reconciliation through deeds involves not only the effort to patch up differences between those who have become separated by bitterness, injustice, or custom, but also a steady and consistent person-to-person ministry. Jesus both recommended and demonstrated a way of treating others as persons and not as things. Persons are to be respected and loved, not used or manipulated as though they were instruments to any end other than their own inherent reality and worth. In Jesus Christ, God discloses himself as an active, outgoing love which seeks men, holds them, and calls them into personal fellowship with himself here and now in the very midst of the transiencies, frustrations, and suffering of life. Neither divine nor human love can deny the incompleteness of personal experience in this world. Yet the need for fulfillment is met by that peculiar finality of personal relationship which we call love. It is characteristic of love that it confers an immediate sense of worth and satisfaction apart from any other advantages that might be gained. Love is an end-point in personal relationship which is complete and beyond which there is nothing further to be desired, and this is true even though human love is imperfect and subject to many frustrations.

Psychologists insist today that the need to love and to be aware of being loved is absolutely fundamental to human personality. We must be supportively involved with other people, one at the very minimum, but hopefully many more than one. William Glasser asserts: "At all times in our lives we must have at least one person who cares about us and whom we care for ourselves. If we do not have this essential person, we will not be able to fulfill our basic needs. Although the person usually is in some direct relationship with us as a mother is to a child or a teacher is to a pupil, he need not be that close as long as we have a strong feeling of his existence and he, no matter how distant, has an equally strong feeling of our existence." [17] Glasser identifies two basic psychological needs: "the need to love and be loved and the need to feel that we are worthwhile to ourselves and others." [18]

In the light of the centrality of love to authentic personhood, it would seem clear that the finest thing we can do for another is build up his sense of being a person. James Pike suggests three ways in which this can be done, ways which correspond to the trinitarian pattern of the "image of God." We should evoke the creative possibilities in the other, responding to his special gifts so as to draw out of him by our interest the particular talents which may not have received adequate expression. We should redemptively accept the other person and relate to him in the very midst of his imperfections, even though he be rejected by others and, perhaps, by himself. "We should help bring him into community with others so that he may flower as a person, relating his special characteristics to a wider circle of other personalities to the mutual enrichment and fulfillment of all." [19] In all of this, Christian behavior will be the expression of one's personal relationship to Christ and it will therefore be concerned with the love of persons rather than with principles. Abstract formulations of principle divorced from personal relationship are as untrue to a morality of grace as to a theology of grace.

The corporate dimension of reconciliation

In setting forth the constituent elements of the personal dimension of reconciliation, we have been aware all along of the co-presence of the corporate dimension, for the personal center of life is never solitary or isolated from its social context. Private and public, self and society, part and whole, member and community are all polar realities. But the relation of reconciliation to the ministry of words and deeds leads us to a direct consideration of the corporate dimension. We cannot be *in* Christ simply as individuals, for to be in him is to be in his Body and his Body is the church. Grace aims at inclusion and relationship. Thus God does not justify or sanctify individual people in isolation. Union with Christ by faith responding to grace necessarily involves incorporation into the people of God, the Body of Christ, the church. It is the church collectively which is "in Christ," clothed with "his righteousness" and called to "grow up" into "mature manhood, to the measure of the stature of the fullness of Christ" (Ephesians 4:13).

The church of *Acts* exhibits the common experience of the early Christians. They had been made into a new community. The inner life of this community was permeated with a sense of the continuing presence of Jesus, the source and reality of the new peace. They also shared in the gift of the Spirit and from the day of Pentecost onwards there began the Christian experience, both for the individual and for the community, of the Spirit of God as the principle and guide of Christian life. Christians have never denied that the Spirit of God also operates outside the boundaries of the church. The Spirit is the giver of all life and works in ways beyond all human understanding and control. But the creative Spirit who gives life to all things also re-creates men's lives in the community of Christian people. There is a distinctively Christian experience of the Spirit and the church is the sphere of the Spirit's operation as the link between believers and Christ and the bond between fellow-Christians.

The Spirit communicates the presence of Christ to his people through the Word and Sacraments. Thus the church is enabled to be a worshipping community, a sphere within which men can honor God by offering their praise and prayer, as well as a compassionate and self-giving community, a sphere within which men embody reconciling love. Because the church is the Body of Christ and the fellowship of the Spirit, it is the privileged area where growth and reconciliation take place.

To describe the church in this manner as the sphere of reconciliation, peace, love, service, and praise is to say a great deal. It is easy for critics and friends alike to think that such pacific and productive excellencies are scarcely visible to the naked eye. But our conviction that the church is the sphere of reconciliation has always been an article of faith. The reality of the church is no more visible or capable of being demonstrated than is the incarnation, the authority of Scripture, the providence of God, the real presence in the sacrament, and so on. It is significant that in the ancient creeds it is not said, "I *see* the holy Christian church," but "I *believe* the holy Christian church." The very existence of the church is a matter of faith, not evidence or proof. One affirms that behind, above, beyond the visible institution that can be described exhaustively in sociological terms there is more than meets the eye. Faith apprehends a divine reconciling reality incarnate within the human institution. The Christian cannot affirm the doctrines of creation, providence, incarnation, and atonement without at the same time regarding the church as the primary sphere of reconciliation.

The church is, then, the sphere or privileged area in which the reconciliation is given and accepted. But it is more, because peace, love, joy, and service are expansive realities. It is impossible to think of such forms of grace as available for private or solitary enjoyment. Therefore the church is the instrument or agency by means of which the reconciling work of Christ is applied to all mankind. In the corporate as in the personal dimension, Christian behavior is, or ought to be, Christ's self-expression and its outreach should be as wide as the whole of humanity.

In saying that the church is summoned to go into the world as an agent of reconciliation and that each Christian is called to take a share in the task for which the church exists, we are coming very close to saying that the church does not exist separately and for its own sake. The peace which Christ brought is not given exclusively for the inner comfort of the church, nor was it his primary mission to establish an institutional church, but to initiate the universal reconciliation of all men into a final community of peace. Despite the rich, valid, and necessary inner life of the church, it must be said that the church is not an end in itself nor does it exist for the improvement of its members. The church, in fact, exists for the benefit of the world outside its present membership. When we have set the individual firmly within the wider context of the church, we have not finished with the factor of corporateness. Just as the individual does not exist by or for himself, so the church does not exist by or for itself. The church has been set by God within the corporate context of the human race, with which the people of God is ideally co-extensive.

Most Christians know that reconciliation means to have peace with God as an individual. A smaller group knows that reconciliation is relevant for the relation to one's neighbors. But, complains Hendrikus Berkhof, "it is only a very tiny minority which is aware of the fact that reconciliation is a movement of the Spirit on a world-wide scale. Colossians 1 testifies to that forgotten fact." [20] Dietrich Bonhoeffer, under the most extreme circumstances, warned that the church was more concerned about religion than it was about faith, more concerned about its own self-preservation than it was about the world. It had staked out a corner of life, withdrawn into it as a fortress, and forsaken the rest of the world to its alienation from God. In his later writings, Bonhoeffer summoned the church to be faithful to its mission of going out into the world. "The church is her true self only when she exists for humanity." [21] The church is true to its own nature only when it is busy taking risks and spending itself in the service of humanity. The church is the society of forgiven sinners through whom the Spirit of Christ extends reconciliation to the world at large. Wolfhart Pannenberg argues that "the universality of the church urges the existing churches to look towards the whole of mankind, beyond the limitations of a narrow ecclesiasticism but also beyond the bounds of nation, race and class, and to live for peace and justice among all men." "The church," he says, "needs the universal gaze outwards, to the whole of mankind, for whom God's will of reconciliation holds good; it needs it as the standard for its self-understanding today at least as much as at any earlier time, even beyond the ecumenical unity of Christians." [22]

In Jesus Christ the power and goodness of God are focused upon man's being so that he may recover health and creativity. Since the Lord so conceived and enacted his own ministry (Luke 4:18-22), the church created by the Holy Spirit is called to minister to the world for its restoration rather than for its rejection. From this point we could well launch into a detailed examination of the scope of the church's reconciling responsibility as well as the policies and programs by which the restoring grace of God is extended to all of life. But we must be content with sketching broad and suggestive outlines.

The scope of reconciliation is well-described by G. W. H. Lampe. "Reconciliation is to be effected everywhere: between races, nations, and classes; between individuals, within the minds and hearts of individuals who cannot easily come to terms with themselves or their environment. It is bound up, in one direction, with healing—a sphere in which the Church joins hands, or should join hands, with medicine. In countless other departments of human life reconciliation has to be effected. . . . The 'extension of God's kingdom' throughout the world, for which Christians work and pray, is not merely the numerical increase of the Church as a result of missionary enterprise. It is the extension of the sphere in which men regard themselves, their personal relationships, their homes and families, their work and their social environment as under the rule of God, governed by the Spirit of Christ and dedicated to his service." [23]

This reconciling work of establishing peace amid human divisions and alienations cannot be restricted to interpersonal relations but must also extend to the less personal structures of life. In Colossians 1:20, Paul says that God through Christ reconciled to himself "all things whether on earth or in heaven." These obscure words are open to more than one interpretation. Hendrikus Berkhof makes the interesting suggestion that the phrase refers back to the "principalities and powers" mentioned in verse 16. He finds that, according to Colossians 2:14-15, 20-22, the "principalities and powers" are identical with precepts, traditions, regulations, legal demands, with what Paul calls the "elemental powers of the world." This phrase, in turn, is Paul's name for the social and political structures of human life. "Not only do men have to be reconciled, but so also do these structures which tend to become ideologies and to absolutize themselves so that they estrange men from the dominion of God in Christ." [24]

Whether or not this interpretation of Colossians 1:20 is correct, it has now become generally accepted in the church that Christians as a corporate body have a ministry to the world of public affairs. This insight rests on a host of biblical passages, on systematic inferences from fundamental beliefs, and on the impulses of Christian conscience. As the church carries out its "ministry of reconciliation," it must co-exist and interact with the social and political structures of life. There was a time when the church was the arbiter of culture, with major responsibility for encouraging humane and reconciling behavior among men. But that time is gone. Today, as we have seen in a previous chapter, the church must fulfill its ministry in partnership with many other agencies in the community which aim at reconciliation in one form or another. As a member of such a coalition, the church has a unique role to play. The church is indeed sent to collaborate in the reconciliation of mankind, but what is specific about its mission is the proclamation of Christ. If the church will embody or enact God's gracious self-communication, it can serve as a divine catalyst of spiritual and social transformation.

Although we have urged that the dynamics of personality and the structures of society are penetrated by grace, it must be obvious that the penetration is not of such a nature as to eliminate the need of reconciliation. Christ did not remake the world by dethroning its rulers or reorganizing its structures. They are as influential for good or evil as they ever were. Nor did Christ put the church in charge of the world. Rulers, engineers, farmers, doctors, scholars are equipped with resources adequate for their responsibilities. They can perform their duties apart from faith in Christ. On the other hand, what churchmen know about the way the world works in its complex and concrete everyday operations, they have learned from the world, not from Christ. But the church has a positive responsibility to the world. Its mission is to speak and enact the reconciling word and to bring those who have responded to the gospel to the level of maturity in Christ (Colossians 1:28).

There is much discussion among Christians today about the church's mission, about the renewal of ministries, and about the important changes of thought, structure, and style that need to be made for the sake of a world-oriented ministry of reconciliation. The church can never be simply identified with the world. A certain tension must be maintained between church and world for the sake of both. Yet, as we have seen, the church must come very close to the world indeed. Eugene Bianchi asserts that "the risk of nearness must be run both for the sake of a more just human order and for the sake of a more mature community of reconciliation. The nearness-distance balance requires a true assessment of ourselves and

genuine confidence in God's presence at the heart of the universal transformation of all things." [25] In its three-fold task of strengthening its own
inner life, of preaching the gospel to every creature, and of witnessing to
God's righteousness and reconciliation in every sphere of human life,
the church has more than enough to occupy it until the end of the age.

The cosmic dimension of reconciliation

Paul pushes the thought of reconciliation beyond the personal and
corporate dimensions of the human response to God's action. He says
quite explicitly that the reconciliation accomplished by Christ's death has
a cosmic dimension. At first glance, it is surprising that imagery of so
personal a character should be extended to a realm so vast and mysterious
as that designated by the terms "world" (*kosmos*) and "all things" (*ta
panta*). But if we go back for a moment to consider the nature of grace
and its relation to reconciliation, the elements of surprise and mystery,
if not eliminated, are at least reduced and put in context.

The constant theme, emphasized or implied, of our entire study has
been the claim that grace goes out, gives, affirms, includes, enables. Grace
builds up wholes out of fragments. Grace unifies. Wherever that which
has become isolated is incorporated into a larger whole grace is at work.
To say that "God is love" (1 John 4:8) is to say that "the creative power
of the universe is also a reconciling power, seeking to bring all creatures
into ever fuller being." [26] The power of reconciling grace is experienced
in the lives of individuals when conflicting elements are integrated into
a larger pattern, enabling them to move towards authentic existence, and
in the careers of groups when the vision of a common purpose and the
impulse to cooperate enables them to achieve productive and humane
goals. In a specifically Christian sense, reconciling grace, mediated
through the sacraments, incorporates individuals into the believing community, and through the proclamation of forgiveness liberates sinners
for a new life of trust and holiness. Since grace *is* the personal presence
and power of God, it always unifies, integrates, incorporates in personal
terms.

It is sheer disaster when grace takes on the aspect of a technical or
abstract term. We have often complained that theologians themselves
have been much to blame when this has happened, for they have frequently spoken and written of grace as though it were a kind of substance existing independently, some mysterious essence that is "infused"

into the human soul; whereas it is, in fact, a quality of relationships between persons. There is nothing in all the universe more purely personal than grace.

Grace, reconciliation, the cosmos. If grace is so purely personal, how can these be linked together? Yet Paul does link them. In 2 Corinthians 5:19 Paul says that God was in Christ reconciling the *kosmos* to himself. In this passage, as in others (Acts 17:24, 1 Corinthians 3:22), the term "world" means the universe. In Colossians 1:19-20 Paul explicitly says that in the death of Christ God intended to reconcile to himself "all things, whether on earth or in heaven." Paul frequently uses the expression "all" or "all things *(pantes* or *ta panta)*. In Ephesians 1:10 he affirms that it is God's purpose, set forth in Christ, "to unite all things in him, things in heaven and things on earth." In 1 Corinthians 15:28 Paul uses the expression *ta panta* three times to set forth his supreme hope that at the conclusion of Christ's mission God "will be all in all," "everything to everyone," or "present in a total manner in the universe."

It is clear that Paul frequently uses the terms "world" *(kosmos)* and "all things" *(ta panta)* as technical terms for God's ultimate goal. Since scholars seem to have been endowed by their Creator with an appetite for disagreement, it is not surprising that some understand Paul to mean the universe, including persons, subhuman nature, the planets and galaxies, while others, holding that Paul had no conception of such a modern world-view, take him to mean by "world" the whole of mankind, including the structures of man's social, political, and ideological life. But in any case Paul is drawing a very wide circle indeed. To say, as we think he does, that reconciliation extends beyond the individual to embrace human society as a whole, and even beyond that again to include the universe, is to establish as wide a circumference as the mind can grasp.

In giving reconciliation such unrestricted scope, Paul reveals an extraordinary passion for completeness. It is impossible for Paul to think that God could leave the great enterprise of grace unfinished, on either the human or the cosmic scale. He tells his friends at Philippi: "I am sure that he who began a good work in you will bring it to completion at the day of Jesus Christ" (Philippians 1:6). With God there are no loose ends, no unfinished business. But while Paul's interest in the unification of being and the fulfillment of purpose is powerful and exciting, it is not unique.

The impulse towards completeness is deeply and generically human.

That the world is a unity of some kind, and that its unity transcends and yet is deeply involved in particular, everyday things, seems to be presupposed by the act of thinking itself. Thinking is the search for unity in the world. Thought proceeds by discovering patches of intelligibility, coherent patterns, "laws." Where there are no patterns, there is no thought. The mind is restless and unhappy in the presence of the non-related or the contradictory. It reaches out for unified apprehensions and if it can bring things together into a single perspective it experiences great satisfaction. The impulse to build up a sense of completeness by finding meaningful unities in life involves all the powers of man's nature. Herbert Farmer writes: "Reason demands that there should be an adequate reason for things, that they should be leading on to something worthwhile. Feeling insists that the worthwhileness should be such that the human heart can in the end rejoice in it. The will insists that its own activity should be a significant factor in the ongoing process." [27]

The very possession of such impulses and equipment exposes man to painful disappointments and frustrations. For life is no more than mildly interested in satisfying our needs. All human activity is characterized by incompleteness, impermanence, unsatisfactoriness. Even the goals we reach are not final for in the very quest new problems and goals open up. We can solve some problems in life, but they are usually the less significant ones. Those that are more significant we do not solve, but at best we only cope with them.

The human spirit has come up with various ways of adjusting to the perpetual inconclusiveness of human activity. Philosophers ancient and modern have recommended that one simply take life as it comes, in all its incompleteness, and make the most of it. Through indifference towards things one cannot control or self-sufficiency in the face of sustained bad luck, one can rise above the ambiguity and incompleteness of life and maintain a posture of dignity. Both philosophy and religion have sometimes presented belief in immortality as the answer to human incompleteness, for the fuller life in the hereafter cancels out the disappointments of our present existence.

Thus Paul is not unique in his passion for completeness and fulfillment. But, in speaking for the Christian community, he does offer a unique ground for hope and confidence when he says that the reconciling love of God in Christ reaches out to hold and affirm men in personal fellowship with himself here and now and promises a fully realized kingdom of God beyond the limitations of earthly existence. The doctrine that God is love says that persons are not cast aside but are held in being and valued in their unrepeatable individuality, that human history and the whole cosmic process move, however painfully, towards a consummation, and that "all things" will finally be unified. All other values are in principle secure in the eternal love of God. To say that the ultimate reality with which we have to deal intends through love to actualize our highest welfare is to give an all-inclusive answer to the human problem of incompleteness and impermanence.

Paul is saying all this, although much more concretely and personally, when he describes grace in the language of reconciliation. It is not our intention to discuss the general topic of eschatology, but only to focus on the special quality given by the idea of reconciliation to Christian thought about the "end of the world." Paul's reconciliation passages look back in time to the decisive event in which God in Christ reconciled the world to himself. It is a finished work. Yet these passages bear a future reference and when they are placed alongside other Pauline statements, as well as the entire range of eschatological elements in the Gospels and the non-Pauline writings, it is clear that the death of Christ did not usher in the time of fulfillment in the sense that what was done has been appropriated and accepted by all for whom it was done. The end lies ahead when all the results of Christ's work will have been achieved and God's reconciling purpose will have been realized in the universal restoration of mankind and of the whole cosmos.

Thus Christian experience points forward. The barrier of man's sinfulness was overcome and the way was opened to fellowship with God. Yet sin is still active and its estranging consequences are very real. Christ is rejected or ignored in the world at large at least as often as he is accepted in faith and obedience. The individual and the church cannot enjoy full and perfect union with Christ in the natural, historical, and social world as we know it. The fulfillment of reconciled existence is an object of hope, not of sight. In all its aspects, Christian faith is a matter of hope. We could as well say it is a matter of faith. The two ideas coalesce if we regard hope as faith directed towards the future. In any case, when Paul said "we walk by faith, not by sight" (2 Corinthians 5:7) he certainly made the point that proof, in the sense of demonstration, has no place in the sphere of religious belief. Consequently we live by faith, love and hope, but in a time when all customs, traditions, and authorities have been challenged or overturned, it may be most important to affirm that we live by hope.

In the old legend of Pandora's box, when all the other good things had been lost and all evils had been let loose upon mankind, hope remained. As so often, the legend pictorially expresses profound truth. Man cannot live without hope. If hopelessness descends upon tribes and peoples, they fail to reproduce their kind, die out, and disappear. As we have seen, despondency settled down upon large masses of people in the Roman empire during Paul's time and the decades of the early church. In an age of distress and anxiety men asked whether religion could, on the far side of the grave, offer such happiness as earth denied. For the most part religion returned an ambiguous or disheartening answer. It was the almost universal conviction of the ancient world that this earthly life is the only real life, and that what lies beyond the grave can be no more than a shadow of the reality that exists here. Christianity burst upon this weary world with hope of eternal life through participation in the resurrection of Jesus Christ through whom God had reconciled the world to himself. The confident proclamation that life here was worth living well, because it is a preparation which has its fulfillment in another and eternal world, was the monopoly of the Christians.

The completion to which Chrisitans looked forward, the fulfillment in redemption of the grand panorama of God's loving self-expression through and beyond the created order, is described in the New Testament under a variety of concrete images. It is the "day of Jesus Christ" (Philippians 1:6, 10), the "day of the Lord" (2 Peter 3:10), the "day of judgment" (Romans 2:5-16), the "Day" (1 Corinthians 3:13). It is the coming (Acts 1:11; James 5:7), the return (John 14:3), the arrival (Mark 13:32), the appearance (1 John 3:2), the revelation (1 Corinthians 1:7) of Jesus Christ at "the end" (1 Corinthians 15:24) of world history.

It is difficult to think of a state of completion without associating it in some way with the end of a process or a series of events. But the idea of an "end," projected on such a scale, is not as simple as it might appear. If we think of the end of the world, or of history, or of the universe as a last moment in time, we have a problem. For the notion of something which happens strictly last in time is either self-contradictory or empty. If we think of the last event as happening in time at all, we must go on to think of a time when it will have happened, and therefore of something coming after it. On the other hand, the notion of an unending series of events in time is equally unthinkable, if we try to give the idea any concrete significance. We can try to call "last in time" any event beyond which our minds cannot penetrate. But so long as we think of that event as in time, it remains one among all the other events which have happened since the world began, and there is no reason to think that what is last in time should as such have any special importance. What reason is there to think that any event or age at some point in future time should be regarded, because it comes after the others, as outweighing or making worthwhile all the other ages of impermanence and suffering which went before?

Thus the notion of a "last moment" in universal time is either self-contradictory or insignificant. We should give up the attempt to think of the "end of the world" in simply future terms, in the sense that it is an event which will arrive someday, though the exact date is still unknown. "For in that case the world to come would be thought of simply as another temporal world, and not really as eternal at all." [28] This is one of the many ways in which the essential meaning of Christian faith is evacuated by a well-intentioned but misguided literalism.

The very notion of "end" or "finality" has a temporal quality since it is inseparable from the picture of a last event in a series. But the temporal ingredient is a point of departure for the attempt to think of an ultimate goal which cannot be merely the last of a long series nor the first of a series to come. In discussing the "Day of the Lord," C. H. Dodd writes: "If on one side it is an event—the last term in the series of events—on the other side it is not an event in history at all; for it is described in terms which remove it from the conditions of time and space. . . . It is such that no other event either could follow or need follow upon it, because in it the whole purpose of God is revealed and fulfilled. . . . It is unique and unlike any other event, because it is final. . . . It is such that nothing more *could* happen in history, because the eternal meaning which gives reality to history is now exhausted. To conceive any further event on the plane of history would be like drawing a cheque on a closed account." [29] The significance of the idea of completeness, finality, wholeness could hardly be stated more clearly. Christian faith requires the notion of the "eternal" in order to describe the victory of God, that is, the final overcoming of the tension and inconclusiveness of existence, through the re-creation of the universe so as to make it the perfect expression of the divine goodness.

We are here faced with a dilemma. We know that the meaning we want to pack into the "eternal" cannot be adequately expressed by any temporal language. Yet all our thought is conditioned by the categories of time, space, and matter. So we have no choice but to speak of eternity hesitantly and symbolically. We employ ideas or pictures cast in temporal and spatial imagery to express the inconceivable reality of the eternal purpose. The biblical writers probably understood better than most of their subsequent readers that their pictures of the future life were not literal descriptions so much as metaphors in the language of earth's experience for a completed life beyond the reach of eye and ear. The white robes of the blessed are symbols for cleansing from the sins and stains of earth. Crowns and harps are beautiful symbols for victory and gladness. Life eternal is the great feast for those who have known poverty and want. It is a sabbath rest for those who have borne the burden and heat of the day. For the saintly worshiper it is the vision of God, and for the faithful servant it is the joy of his Lord. And when imagination falls short or gives up, one can hold with Paul that it is "what no eye has seen, nor ear heard, nor the heart of man conceived, what God has prepared for those who love him" (1 Corinthians 2:9).

The deeply personal and subjective character of grace as reconciliation can have little to do with any concept of the "end" which does not possess a quality of wholeness or finality which is supra temporal. When Paul said "God was in Christ reconciling the world to himself," he surely meant to say that such reconciliation should be regarded as an end-point which is complete and satisfying and beyond which there is nothing further to be achieved.

The consistency between the personal flavor of reconciliation and a proper understanding of the "end of the world" can also be established by calling attention to the ambiguity of the word "end" even in ordinary human experience and speech. It can mean "last in time," a termination, the point at which a thing is finished or ceases to be. Or it can mean not simply that which comes after everything else, but that which completes a series or process by bringing its purpose to fulfillment. If the last event in a series is the one which fulfills the purpose which has directed the entire series and served as its immanent goal, it ceases to be merely one event among the others, and acquires a unique importance of its own.

O. C. Quick uses the production of a work of art to illustrate the distinction between termination and fulfillment. "The last or finishing touch given to a work of art does not at all derive its special importance from the fact that it happens to come after all the others, but from the fact that it completes the whole. In this case the purpose is only fulfilled if all the touches from the first to the last make a *simultaneous* contribution in their effects to the whole work which they have produced. . . .

The last event or act, which achieves the purpose, is as much a beginning as it is an end. It does not really achieve the end, unless it *initiates* a fulfillment: that is why it derives its special importance from what is *beyond* the series of events of which it is the last. A work of art destroyed in the moment of completion could hardly be said to fulfill the artist's aim." [30]

Alec Vidler makes the same point in a simpler way. "If I am writing a book, I could mean by the 'end' of my work either the moment at which I concluded my correction of the final proofs by inserting or deleting a comma, or I could mean the whole purpose for which I wrote the book, which was present to my mind and influencing my work throughout, but which could begin to take its complete effect only after the book was ended in the former sense." [31]

We have already observed that Christian faith has little interest in the "end" as "last in time" or terminus. The last event in time, if one could conceive of it without using temporal terms, thus eliminating its "lastness," or without falling into the vacuum of timelessness, thus cancelling out any positive content derived from human experience, would not be of any more positive importance than the period at the end of the last sentence in this book. Christian faith has nothing special to say about what will be last in time, nor has it any special interest in the moment at which human existence will cease on this planet. That would simply be "end" as terminus and it would have no human or personal content. A journey on a plane has a time of arrival, but the "end" of the trip is achieved when the traveler leaves the plane and goes about the business which led him to make the trip. His purpose in getting to his destination is fulfilled even if the plane is a bit early or late, and no matter which of several possible routes he has followed.

Christian faith, then, is not concerned about termination but it does care about fulfilled purpose, the personal content of God's mission of grace. When Paul said that "God was in Christ reconciling the world to himself" (2 Corinthians 5:19), and that the "end" would come "when he delivers the kingdom to God the Father" after putting "all things in subjection under him" that "God may be everything to everyone" (1 Corinthians 15:24-28), he is recording the conviction that the process of history has a purpose which will be, and is being, completed and fulfilled by bringing into existence that state of perfection which the Creator originally designed, a state of unhindered freedom, love, and joy which leaves nothing further to be desired.

Although we cannot form any precise intellectual concepts of eternity, we can make some positive affirmations about it. The fact that these must necessarily be symbolic in form does not mean that they are not genuinely significant. The "end of the world" signifies a truly final completion of all that is partial and inconclusive in human experience. What is now achieved only fitfully and ambiguously will eventually be manifested in its fullness. We do not know how or when the "end" will come but we do know that what is fully revealed at the end will be what has already been disclosed in the life and death of Jesus. During his earthly ministry Jesus revealed God's love and judgment, but only to a limited number of people. Moreover, his ministry in Galilee met with mixed results, since some believed and some did not. After his bodily presence was removed from the sight of men, he continued to be present in the church through the Spirit who made him known to his people. But even the church has known him only incompletely, since as a human community it is sinful and not fully open or obedient to his presence.

Human society in general has been modified by the diffused influence of Christ and his church, but for the most part he has been ignored as the incarnation of God's reconciling love. The presence of Christ at the "end" will not differ in meaning or quality from his presence in Galilee or the church. Only the mode of his future or final presence will be different. The New Testament writers describe it as a coming in "glory" and a revelation of Christ's lordship (Matthew 25:31, Philippians, 2:9-11). There is continuity between history and eternity in that God will not send a new "Christ" nor will he institute a different kind of relationship between himself and his people. It will be the same Christ, embodying the same gracious divine will, who is present in glory. The "end" to which Christian hope looks forward is the universal acknowledgement of Christ's lordship, the completion of his reconciling work. There will be no more ambiguity about the meaning of Christ, no more room for doubt and uncertainty.

The completion of God's work in Christ will mean the completion of the life and destiny of the individual believer. No longer will he be a divided self, partly altruistic and partly egoistic, a saint and a sinner at the same time. But we may suppose that final reconciliation to the source of his being will set man's will unshakably upon God. The will is ever and always the battlefield of human life and the tragedies of earthly existence lie in its inconstancy. To be in undisturbed fellowship with the source of all good is to know freedom from the variability that negates even our best intentions. Dante's Piccarda summed it up in the line: "And his will is our peace." [32] Wholeness of will, transparency of knowledge, perfection of service and love are bestowed by grace upon the one who belongs entirely to Christ and is fully open to the Spirit.

The universal recognition of the lordship of Christ will also mean the completion of the church. It will be seen as it really is in the vision and grace of God, not in its present ambiguous condition, partly under the sovereignty of sin. The undisturbed unity between Christ and his people will make perfect the church's worship, knowledge, and service. The completion of being for both the church and the individual is portrayed by the biblical symbol of "heaven," a pictorial expression of the ultimate blessedness when man is wholly reconciled to God in every aspect of his being and God's people are fully and totally united in love and obedience to him.

As we have said before, it is not our aim to present a full discussion of Christian eschatology, including death, judgment, resurrection, heaven, and hell. Our concern has been to make the point that reconciliation language modifies our perspective on this whole range of topics. Paul repeatedly insists that Christians look forward to a final restoration of all things. There are mysterious hints that even the physical universe is destined not to mere destruction, dissolution, or disappearance, but to transformation (Romans 8:21; Revelation 21:2). But the final restoration of all things *is* reconciliation, the operation of grace to build up wholes out of fragments. The goal of the universe is the end of all estrangement, fulness of reconciliation in Christ (1 Corinthians 3:21-23; Romans 8:18-22, 35-39).

It is obvious that the theme of unification is very strong indeed in Christian thought. As a monotheistic religion, Christianity affirms that God is the one source of all being and value. From this it follows that the Christian vision of reality takes the form of a unifying awareness of the world. The created order in all its rich diversity is a unity, and its unity is grounded in God who is immanent in all things including man himself. In his sermon to the Athenians, Paul said that all things live and move and have their being in God (Acts 17:28). The unifying awareness of reality includes the nature of man whose response to God is ideally a total response of the whole person.

We have noted Paul's emphasis upon completion in the personal and corporate dimensions of reconciliation. This bears out our earlier contention that the root metaphor underlying all of Paul's thought is that of the reintegration of a broken organism. But the theme of unification reaches a supreme level when Paul says that God's reconciling action in Christ comprehends the whole cosmos (Colossians 1:20). It must be observed once again that Paul's interest in completion or unification is not unique. Herbert Farmer writes: "No one can read widely in the literature of religion all down the ages without bearing away the impression that among the most central springs of religion in the human soul is the craving for unificaton." [33] The history of religions shows that men have sought in various ways to satisfy the need for integration. The self may be unified by withdrawing from the complexity of the world, or by emptying consciousness of its differentiated contents. The world may be radically unified in thought and feeling by subordinating its diversity to its unity, or by denying altogether the reality of concrete things and dismissing as illusion the awareness of distinctions.

There is something quite arrogant, even scandalous, about treating in such summary fashion the truly impressive achievements of pantheistic religion, monistic philosophy, and mystical devotion. Some have explicitly identified the notion of the absolute one or ultimate unity with the religious idea of God, and some have not. But our concern is with the status of created reality, including human personality, in the ultimate harmony implied by the idea of reconciliation on a cosmic scale. At this point, the radical personalism of Christian thought, implicit in the very concept of grace, and essential to the imagery of reconciliation, comes to the fore as the guardian and interpreter of a world-view which affirms the reality and value of everyday things and of finite selves, and makes room for a genuine encounter between God and men. Christian faith rejects any concept of unification which consigns to insignificance or illusion the distinction between God and man, the differentiations of thought, feeling, and choice within human nature, and the multiplicity of events and things which comprises the real world. To eliminate such dualities is to see the world as completely impersonal. It is perhaps the least of our problems that a strictly non-dualistic world is rationally unintelligible. Much more important is the fact that no Christian belief makes any sense at all except in a world in which real personal encounters are possible and normative for our conceptions of value and fulfillment.

Consequently it is of the utmost importance that when the New Testament speaks of a unification so all-inclusive that Christ is called the cosmic unifier (Colossians 1:20, Ephesians 1:10), it does so in association with the personal word "reconciliation." This term, like all personal words, asserts that selves are not absorbed, but are "brought together into a harmony with God and with one another summed up under the category of love, . . . a term that in New Testament usage contains no hint of the disappearance of duality but rather presupposes it."[34] Nor are things obliterated. They too are reconciled, brought together into one. The whole picture is one not of identity or fusion, but of community. Whatever the reconciliation of "all things" might mean, and one may be pardoned for being mystified by the meteorological and astronautical implications of the ultimate cosmic harmony, it is fundamental that the God who is apprehended as indwelling and sustaining the universe is the same God who has made himself known as personal in Jesus Christ and who calls men into a relationship of reconciled personal fellowship with himself.

In these pages we have considered the image of reconciliation as a mode of expressing the reality of grace-in-action. To the Christian, the reality of grace goes far beyond all images and analogies drawn from human experience. It is felt not so much as an alien force that works from without, as an indwelling power that recreates from within. It is perpetually available. Its operation is hindered only by an unwillingness to respond. It is illimitable in its power to refashion broken human nature, and in some mysterious way the uncompleted universe as well, after the likeness of the One who is believed to be its source. "For the Christian, grace is always the grace of Jesus Christ, through whom the love of God becomes a reality to man, and by whom, in the fellowship of the Holy Spirit, the new community of the redeemed comes into being."[35]

All that needs to be said about the otherness, the availability, and the power of grace can be said most adequately in the language of reconciliation. This image points to the objectivity of God's gracious being and will and at the same time describes with incomparable power and warmth the experienced content of divine and human love. It cannot be said that the special vocabulary of reconciliation dominates Scripture. Yet the idea of reconciliation as the goal, method, and meaning of the all-embracing divine purpose pervades all of Scripture. As we have seen in Paul's thought, this special image serves as an effective proclamation of the gospel as well as a comprehensive organizing principle of Christian theology. Every Christian doctrine is given a special quality of personal depth and practical outreach through its association with the idea of reconciliation.

Our stress on the centrality of grace may sound like theological totalitarianism, as though only one doctrine were important. Our contention is rather that only from this center can other doctrines be seen clearly. There are other doctrines, for Christian theology, as a distinctive interpretation of reality, must reflect on the whole of man's life in the light of the gospel. A multitude of concepts and symbols are used to organize biblical, historical, liturgical, and ethical materials into a more or less coherent whole. It is of first importance that the concept of grace should shape the design and penetrate the elements of any theological perspective. Only so will the coherence of the testimony reflect the coherence of the experience of God's love in Jesus Christ. One who is secure in the central grace of the gospel is free not only from the anxiety of self-justification but also from the grip of theological systems. Among those who differ in theology, mutual respect and toleration flow not from indifference but from conviction.

9

Reconciliation

as a Theological Approach

Reconciliation as grace-in-action expresses the religious and moral inclusiveness of grace. As such, it is the primary word about God. But reconciliation also has significance for the shape of our thoughts about God and his gracious interaction with men. The term is therefore equally well-suited to demonstrate the intellectual or theological inclusiveness of the concept of grace. It would be strange if the nature of the reality which is being studied and expressed did not affect the method and goal of the act of understanding. Yet reconciliation as a theological attitude or approach has not been dominant in the life of the church. Theology has typically been a forum of debate in which conflicting doctrines become the fighting slogans of theologians and churches. "Love, joy, peace, patience, kindness, . . . gentleness, self-control"—all qualities against which Paul tells us "there is no law" (Galatians 5:22 23) have not flourished in the arena of theological controversy. That embattled sphere has seen much more of precision, firmness, and fidelity, not to mention belligerence, suspicion, and hostility, than of the gentler excellences enumerated by Paul. Many would argue that it must be so, for the qualities listed by Paul are to be understood as moral virtues, not as intellectual dispositions. It may well be that in the pursuit of fact and clarity the mind cannot emulate the liberality appropriate to self-acceptance and fruitful interpersonal relations. Yet we cannot be comfortable

256

with the claim that certain virtues pertain to the mind and others to the will. One recalls Reinhold Niebuhr's well-known complaint that intellectuals tend to regard humility as a moral but not an intellectual virtue.

Dualities, distinctions, and theological disagreements

The suggestion that reconciliation should serve as the goal and motive power of theological work is especially pertinent to the doctrine of grace itself. In its historical formulations and in the currently operating theologies of the several churches, the doctrine of grace is associated with a multitude of technical terms that distinguish between various kinds of grace. These distinctions are not unimportant, yet they have the effect of splitting the doctrine into fragments which at first sight seem to have little to do with one another. Since the concept of grace deals in a comprehensive manner with the relation between God and man, distinctions are necessary in order to give expression to the duality between the creator and the creature. But because the mind of man is small, his memory short, and his desires imperfect, dualities easily become dualisms and distinctions become disjunctions. When this happens, man has divided or separated what God has joined together for it is of the essence of grace that it is a gift which unites giver and receiver. John Burnaby argues that grace as a justifying and regenerating divine influence "implies both subject and object" and that "the great divergences in Christian thought about grace have sprung from the tendency to isolate subject or object, to consider grace *either* in its source *or* in its direction, *either* as a property or activity of God *or* as a gift which he has conferred upon man." [1] Distinctions which are made for the sake of analysis are isolated from the larger frame within which they have their contextual validity.

That Christian thought abounds in dualities, distinctions, and disjunctions is plain to one who reads theological books, although Christian thought is not original in this respect. The Christian apprehension of the duality between creator and creature, without which there would be no religion at all, has given rise to differentiations between natural and supernatural, nature and grace, transcendence and immanence, redemption and creation, faith and reason, subjective and objective, omnipotence and freedom, justice and mercy, law and gospel, judgment and salvation, anthropocentric and cosmic, sacramental and material, particular and universal, sacred and secular, church and world, structure and spontaneity, faith and religion, and so on.

These distinctions point to real differences of one kind or another. Any member of the many pairs of opposites is a short-hand term for the extensive analysis of an enormous body of data. It is standard procedure to hold that these differentiations are not contradictions, but reflections of the actual two-sidedness of Christian experience and thought. But it is all too easy, as we have said, to mistake dualities for dualisms and distinctions for disjunctions. Many Christians have tried to resolve the tension or dualism by concentrating on one or the other of the differentiated elements, with the result that the integrity of Christian thought has been compromised by a variety of extremist positions. It is not suggested that the tendency to go to extremes is the product of perversity. Temperamental differences, educational background, strongly felt needs, perceived dangers, group morale, and other factors contribute to the development of one-sided emphases which become "isms" and thereby distort the organic unity of Christian thought.

The possibility of an exclusive emphasis is implicit in the fact that the essential structure of the Christian faith does have, as we have seen, a two-sidedness about It. Take, for example, the role played by the subjective-objective polarity in our knowledge of God. God is transcendent. We recognize him as a power beyond ourselves who creates and limits us. But we can speak of God only insofar as he comes to us and is known by us in our human situation. To exaggerate the independent reality of God, or our interior personal response to him, would be to fall into objectivism or subjectivism, and thus to falsify the actual relationship with him. Religious truths are of a peculiar kind in which both objective and subjective factors are involved. The polarities of the relation between God and man must be reflected in any theological account of the Christian faith.

Errors and heresies arise in the church whenever a half-truth is taken to be the whole truth. We recall John Burnaby's charge, with respect to the doctrine of grace, that divergences spring from the tendency to isolate subject or object, to consider grace either in its source or in its direction, either as a property or activity of God or as a gift which he has conferred upon man. Perhaps it is the fate of theology to swing to one-sided extremes. Surely the complexities of theology and the imperfections of theologians combine to create a dim prospect for the achievement of organic fullness in Christian thought. But more disturbing is the spirit of exclusiveness which has led some Christians to unchurch and persecute other Christians because of the delusion that they were in sole possession of the truth. Whoever thinks that he is in exclusive possession of the truth in religion has identified his insights, symbols, and doctrines with the reality they are supposed to illumine. It is evident that theology must devise propositional forms for the concepts it employs. It is equally apparent that theology cannot afford to equate the propositions it constructs with the religious truths it seeks to convey. Every doctrine must be recognized as in some degree different from the truth it is intended to represent. To identify a religious concept or symbol with final truth or reality is a kind of idolatry.

It is not surprising that Christians should disagree. Their theological divergences often take the form of helpful testimony which stimulates mutual correction and growth. It is both surprising and scandalous, however, that such disagreements should take the form of harmful exclusiveness which leads to isolation and conflict. Since theological disagreement is here to stay, it is essential that a strong tradition of unitive thinking should have a place within the life of the churches. Such a tradition would have as its preoccupation the inclusiveness of grace. The two-sidedness of Christian faith must be reflected in a set of careful distinctions. But if the grace of God is the single, ultimate context of all that exists, then the inclusiveness of grace should also be reflected in theological statements, in ecclesiastical policies, and in the efforts of persons and groups to live as Christians.

Reconciliation and the unitive theological temper

Is it too much to propose that a clear understanding of the freedom, generosity, and inclusiveness of grace can, or should, translate into a unitive habit of mind? No simple notion of direct transfer between ideas and the general disposition of one's mind will do justice to the largely subterranean character of the elements that enter into mental formation. Joseph Sittler writes: "The dynamics of a disposition, if traced to their roots . . . , are formed in large part by the majesty and gravity, or the banality and superficiality, of one's earliest memory of the Christian story in private and public encounters with it. . . . Every man has a dispositional bent which, when acknowledged, goes a long way toward understanding what one historian has called 'the mystery of the mind's attention.' Why does one person 'attend' to what another does not?" [2]

It is difficult to believe that so powerful and exciting a thought as that of the inclusiveness of grace could be anything but a decisive factor in

the shaping of a disposition. Whatever its source, it is a fact that in contrast to the tendency to sharpen and defend theological distinctions, there
has always operated within the church another tendency which reacts
against the one-sided emphases which have been so productive of dis-
sension and division. There are theologians whose natural approach to
the problems of theology is not from one side or another of the con-
tending factions or schools of thought, but from a detached position in
which they have attempted to pass beyond the partial and sometimes
extravagant statement of doctrines, and the controversial handling of
them, to a more comprehensive solution.

This theological temper reveals itself in an intellectual attitude and
method of approach. It concentrates upon those central beliefs in which
the gospel has been given doctrinal expression, and shows a readiness
to be content with diversity where beliefs of that order are not involved,
and a willingness to engage in a constant reconsideration of the nature
of such diversity. It is an irenic temper which holds that men do not
always differ as much as they think they do. This principle applies to
theologians as well as to the rest of mankind, and it is possible to
overestimate through long tradition both the depth and the significance
of theological disagreements. Nor should it be forgotten that such disagreements are often, to a great extent, the result of a difference in emphasis. That was partly true of the Christological controversies in the
ancient church. In commenting on those disputes, J. K. Mozley writes:
"The stress fell either on the Godhead or on the manhood of Christ.
Each stress was in itself legitimate, for since Christ is both God and man,
no exception can be taken to the theologian who draws out, with particular attention and care, what is the meaning and what is the outcome of
either of these great truths. It was only when the interest of the theologian or of the school was focused on the particular truth in such a way
that the reality of the other, equally necessary, truth was obscured, that
the danger of what might properly be called heresy became real." [3]

When Mozley applies the same reasoning to the conflict which arose
in the sixteenth century between Catholics and Protestants, his point of
view will seem to some to show an excess of the judicious spirit for that
conflict continues to agitate theologians and churches. Yet his argument
is consistent with what Christians have generally accepted with respect
to the Christological dogmas. "The reality of justification by faith and
the reality of sacramental grace stand in no essential antithesis to one
another, but it is natural that one Christian should emphasize the former,

another the latter. So far there is no dispute. But if either doctrine be treated as though the other did not rightfully exist, then it is inevitable that such acute controversy will arise as will lead many to suppose that a choice must be made between the two. Thus, an unreal contrast will be set up, and the doctrines will confront one another as alternatives." [4]

When the irenic temper expresses a preference for the formula "both-and" rather than for the formula "either-or," it is acknowledging that a large amount of truth is conveyed in the saying that men are mostly right in what they affirm and wrong in what they deny. There are, of course, limits to such formulas. For if theology were to be regarded as positive only in its affirmations and not also in its denials, it would be difficult to justify the contrast which Christian theology as such draws between itself and others forms of religious understanding. So, within Christian theology we must not close our eyes to real oppositions which cannot be smoothed out, as though they represented semantic differences, misunderstandings of what the other person or group is really saying, or survivals from an earlier time of thought patterns which stood for genuine differences. Yet, many, if not all, theological disagreements do arise from such circumstances. Thus the unitive temper is not simply naive in hoping to find a synthesis in which justice is done to the apparently contrary positions. Moreover, it is a positive move to attempt to grasp the central idea within a position to which one is opposed, for there is no desire to defeat or to undermine that position but rather to preserve and to vindicate the strength and value of the essential truth which it expresses. This can be done not by condemning or merely fighting against points of view with which one disagrees, but by setting what is true in them within the wider context of the entire Christian faith. The half-truths which become distortions when broken off from the whole are given their due when seen as part of the total Christian faith. John Macquarrie writes: "It is only within the organic fullness of the whole faith that any Christian truths can become really effective in the lives of men and can bring forth the fruits of the Spirit." [5]

Paradox and the two-sidedness of Christian faith

To aim at reconciliation in theology is to reflect in some degree the sense of inclusiveness which is a part of the living experience of grace. The effort to show how particular doctrines cohere within the organic fullness of Christan theology is worth making even though it must always remain incomplete. In addition to the temperamental, political, and logical factors that impede the quest for theological inclusiveness, there is within the enterprise of theology an inherent limitation which warns us against pushing the ideal of systematic unity to an extreme. If the unity of grace validates the impulse to reconcile differences, the equally real two-sidedness of Christian faith prepares us to accept the fact that no theological system, however well thought out, can avoid entirely a certain significant lack of coherence.

It is clear that theology stands under the same criteria as any other form of thought of this general type. It cannot, therefore, tolerate downright inconsistencies in its assertions. But theology does involve us in paradoxes. Since a paradox is a statement which asserts the truth of two contradictory but necessary propositions, its use is clearly compatible with the two-sidedness of Christian faith. But how is a mode of expression which appears to involve self-contradiction related to the inclusiveness of grace and the impulse to reconcile differences?

We cannot do without paradox when thinking or speaking about matters of faith. God's redemptive action in Christ can surely not be described in any straightforward, unilateral, and thoroughly self-consistent way. When a Christian says that the universe is fashioned by God's will out of nothing, or that man's God-given freedom is the source of his sin, or that death illuminates life, he is expressing himself in a paradoxical way. Clearly there is something in our faith which resists tidy, non-paradoxical formulas. Donald Baillie, in his classic work, *God Was in Christ,* has given a most helpful discussion of paradox. He maintains that Christian faith, when thought out, conceptualized, and put into human language, runs into paradox at every vital point. Whenever we introduce God as the ultimate source of anything in our experience, he comes in on the vertical line from the eternal world to touch the horizontal line of space, time, and matter, of human experience and knowledge. The actual strangeness of the intersection between the vertical and the horizontal, the uncreated and the created, the eternal and the temporal, shows up in the doctrine of creation out of nothing, in the doctrine of God's providential rule working through the network of natural causes and effects, in the crucifixion of Christ which we see as the worst thing that ever happened, and supremely in the doctrine of the incarnation which asserts that a completely human life in history is the life of God himself.[6]

Paradox is inevitable in all theology because God cannot be comprehended in any human words. It is impossible to confine divine activity and human existence within the static limits of logical constructions. To think and speak of God in the third person, to objectify God, is to fall into contradictions and to falsify the knowledge of God that comes to us in direct personal relationship. Yet we must have theology even though we can conceptualize the living religious experience only by breaking it up and distorting it. Thus our sense of paradoxical language "presupposes that the object of discourse has a mystery and depth which our ordinary words and propositions cannot totally explicate . . . and we speak about the mystery in paradoxical terms to indicate facets of it that we do understand, but which we cannot put into a comprehended rational unity.[7]

The Christian faith presents us with neither sheer conundrum nor rational system. It brings us into the presence of a mysterious reality called God, who creates, calls, and judges us, and makes us whole in Christ. There are two inadequate ways of dealing with paradox in the Christian faith. They result from a failure to maintain the tension between the duality and the inclusiveness of our experience of God. There is the tendency to assert that paradox is ultimate and final. Some Christians assert contradictions and oppositions at every possible point. This approach is right in protesting against excessive rationalism in theology and in affirming that every statement of Christian truth must have at least a paradoxical edge to it since all objectification of God is at the same time falsification. But it is wrong in obscuring the ultimacy of grace and in transforming religious mystery into theological mystification by casting almost the entire gospel into the mold of paradox. Quite another approach is taken by those who attempt to smooth out contradictions by ignoring one side of the truth which they seek to express and exaggerating the other. The result is an unbalanced picture, even if it takes the form of a readily understandable scheme of thought. This tendency is on the right track in thinking that the paradoxes of faith exist to be overcome, but it is wrong in supposing that theological reason by itself can see through and set aside paradox and deliver to us a faith free of offense.

Fortunately we are not restricted to either of these ways. A sound approach to paradox proceeds by distinguishing between thought and being and by vindicating the paradox. First, paradox should be seen as an intellectual and linguistic phenomenon. There is no reason to think that paradox is a quality of existence. It is rather a property which attaches to statements about existence. As Roger Hazelton puts it: "A paradox is a statement, not a situation.... We have no warrant for saying that existence contradicts itself. . . . That would be to presuppose on our part an intimate . . . knowledge of the real which none of us can possibly possess. So far as knowledge goes at any rate, only selves can be self-contradictory, and it is thought and language which reveal this. Paradox, then, belongs characteristically to our interpretations and expressions of the real and not—at least primarily or certainly—to that reality to which our words and ideas refer." [8]

If we distinguish between thought and being, then we can use paradoxical language about God without thinking or implying that God is self-contradictory in his nature and action. It is one thing to say that the doctrine of the incarnation is paradoxical, another to say that Jesus Christ is paradoxical. God does not contradict himself in creation, providence, atonement, or incarnation, but we cannot think or speak of God without having to contradict ourselves. It would be far better if we did not speak about the contradictions of existence, but about its mystery. For "the only contradictions of which we have sure knowledge are those within our creaturely existence as thinking subjects or selves. But this does not imply that the mystery with which we have to deal and the appalling lack of consistency in our statements concerning it are one and the same." [9]

The mystery to which paradox testifies is, however, actualized and lived in religious experience, that is, in the direct faith-relationship with God. Although our minds are torn with inconsistencies in saying it, our faith must always be that God is one and that his single, undivided will is one of grace. For the sort of mystery encountered in Christian faith is surely more than a mere unknown. In using the word "God" we are calling the ultimate mystery by its right name. Donald Baillie urges that "there should always be a sense of tension between the two opposite sides of our paradoxes, driving us back to their source in our actual religious experience or faith." [10] The classical creeds of the church took it as their essential task to point to and to protect the evangelical mystery of the Christian revelation from attempts to explain it away as something less than a gospel. In order to perform this task, those who composed the creeds found themselves driven against their will to employ to some extent the language of the current philosophy. Although the creeds incorporated the word "homo-ousion," they never intended to set forth a particular philosophic theory of the incarnation. They were concerned to safeguard the gospel of the union of God and man in Christ.

To this end the Athanasian Creed insists that in his person both natures in their completeness are joined without being confused, since confusion could only mean the production of a new and strange creature, irrelevant alike to the grace of God and the sin of man. The fathers of the church saw that the gospel message by its very nature is as theoretically mysterious as it is evangelically simple. But the simplicity lies in the actual experience of reconciling grace. The complexity lies in what we must say to describe both the transcendent being and the manward action of God. Avery Dulles sums up the matter: "At every point the subject matter of theology touches on mystery. And how can mystery be expressed? Unlike historical or abstract truth, mystery cannot be described or positively defined. It can only be evoked. Religious language must contrive to point beyond itself and to summon up, in some fashion, the gracious experience of the mystery with which it deals." [11]

In order to point to the oneness of the gracious mystery and the duality of our human experience, thought, and language, theology speaks in terms of metaphor, image, analogy, and paradox. These linguistic devices deal not with identities but with comparisons. They acknowledge the distinction between thought and being and suggest meanings which lie beyond explicit definition. They tacitly acknowledge their inadequacy to express fully the mystery to which they point by incorporating opposites. But paradox calls attention to its own limitations by the very fact that it is self-contradictory. The bluntness of its form enables paradox to emphasize the mystery and to protect it from being lost through simple understanding.

Although paradox, at first glance, would seem to be an unwelcome stranger in the camp of a reconciling theology, it does have an affinity with the unitive theological temper in that it is a both-and, not an either-or, type of proposition. Roger Hazelton, who writes perceptively on this topic, points out that a paradox "is internally complex rather than simple; its two antithetical sides have equal weight and one must not be permitted to outrank the other. Each, without the other, would be incomplete and false; only when taken together can each side say what needs to be said. . . . Its opposite stresses are integrally related to each other by virtue of the fact that both refer to a common object. So we speak of goodness and power in God, or of freedom and bondage in man. . . . Since there are two stresses in every paradox, each needs and corrects the other. On this living tension between them the validity and effectiveness of any paradox depends." [12]

Hazelton also points out that, contrary to popular opinion, paradox is very much like analogy. Since the word "analogy" means "according to proportion", and since proportion has to do with sameness among different things, therefore analogy is the marking of likeness in diversity or of unity in variety. By recognizing both unlikeness and similarity at the same time, analogical thinking "helps us to avoid extremism and lack of balance. Both over-confident identification and over-anxious separation . . . are held thereby in check. There is paradox in every analogy so long as proportion is maintained; there is also analogy in every paradox so long as tension is preserved." [13]

Once we have distinguished between thought and being and between contradiction and mystery, we are in a position to suggest that most of the acrimonious controversies in the history of theology and within the churches have turned more upon the question of the adequacy of one set of symbols in preference to another rather than upon the truth which such symbols are selected to exhibit. [14] We are also able to see the propriety and relevance of the effort to "vindicate the paradox." A concise explanation of the meaning of this phrase is given by John Macquarrie: "To vindicate a paradox means that the theologian will have to show that both sides of it correspond to genuine elements in that living experience which theology seeks to conceptualize, and further that the two sides are not in flat contradiction to each other but rather constitute a polarity of opposites within a whole." [15]

We have already seen that many pairs of opposites, such as subjectivity and objectivity, transcendence and immanence, nature and grace, redemption and creation, church and world, contain terms that imply one another, and that each needs to be supplemented by the other. It is clear that an emphasis on one or another of these terms is sound and recognizably Christian if it is not pushed beyond a certain limit, that is, if it is not made so absolute as to crowd out its partner. Now we observe that the whole purpose of symbolic representation, including paradox, is to point beyond itself to what it is intended to convey. It does not follow from this that since symbols are not facts, they are matters of indifference and hardly worth serious, even controversial, discussion. For it is not the case that one symbol is as good as another. E. Ashby Johnson contends that the church showed sensitive insight in rejecting "the symbols of sexual generation and of metaphysical emanation as inappropriate symbols in which the relationship between God and the universe may best be described. Likewise, it has rejected illusion as a metaphor to describe the force of evil. Some symbolic representations are more apt than others. The function of theology is not that of freeing itself from the use of symbols but of determining the most adequate mode of expression." [16] Throughout this chapter, we have urged that the idea of reconciliation provides the most adequate and strategic imagery for the communication of the doctrine of grace today.

Grace as the ultimate coherence

But what is the whole, the reality, the mystery, the actual experience to which theological language, with its balanced pairs of opposites, points? Once due respect has been paid to the polarities of Christian thought, what is the ultimate coherence to which the unitive tendency in theology wants to bear witness? Quite clearly, it is the generous, unrestricted, and inclusive grace of God which builds up wholes out of fragments, overcomes separations, and reconciles that which is estranged.

The special theme of John Oman's theology was his insistence that the many contrasts and distinctions within Christian theology could be set forth as "a harmony of opposites." [17] The center or cover under which the differentiated elements come together is the concept of grace. He wrote: "Grace has always a convex side towards God, and a concave side towards man. Taken separately, they are contradictory and opposite, but, united, they are as perfectly one as the convex and concave sides in one line. As acts of grace and acts of will, they are sheer conflicting forces; in the gracious relation to us of the Father of our spirits, their harmony is the essential expression of our fellowship." [18] In discussing divine omnipotence and human freedom, he argued that as long as these are understood in terms of power they will remain irreconcilable "mechanical opposites". But it is "the very business of a doctrine of grace ... to show how grace maintains a relation between God and his children, wherein we remain persons even as he is a person. . . . An account of the way of the working of God's gracious relation to us, therefore, is just an account of these opposites, which, so long as they are opposed mechanically, are irreconcilable contradictions, and of how love overcomes them by a personal dealing which turns them into the perfect harmony of unbroken peace." [19]

The same emphasis upon gracious personal relationship as the solvent of contradictions introduced into theology by the use of such non-personal categories as force and merit, is found in Donald Baillie. The deepest paradox of all, according to Baillie, is "the paradox of Grace. Its essence lies in the conviction which a Christian man possesses, that every good thing in him, every good thing he does, is somehow not wrought by himself but by God. This is a highly paradoxical conviction, for in ascribing all to God it does not abrogate human responsibility." [20] This paradox of grace, experienced in fragmentary form in our own Christian lives, is "a reflection of that perfect union of God and man in the Incarnation . . . that perfect life in which the paradox is complete and absolute, that life of Jesus which, being the perfection of humanity, is also, and even in a deeper and prior sense, the very life of God Himself." [21]

To see in the incarnation itself the very pattern of unifying grace is an inevitable motion of the Christian mind, for in the Incarnate Lord humanity was so perfectly united to God that there could be no division between what was of God and what was of man. In Christ the divine love and the human response are inseparable. That fullness of personal unity can never be equalled in those who belong to Christ, but they may receive of his fullness (John 1:16). Eugene Fairweather says of the Christological dogma of the early church that it provides the perfect, concrete expression of the duality and the unity of the experience of grace. "On the one hand, it insists on the essential diversity of the divine and the human, while on the other hand it points to the possibility of their fruitful union through the loving condescension of the transcendent God." [22]

The incarnation rightly stands as the supreme paradigm of grace. But the early fathers of the church insisted on linking the doctrines of incarnation and creation. They saw the incarnation as a kind of "recapitulation" of creation. It is as if the incarnation focuses in a single point what God has, in a sense, been doing always and everywhere. Christ, in whom God is uniquely present, becomes the essential clue to the interpretation of the whole mission of God to the world. Joseph Sittler recaptures the spaciousness of this perspective when he proposes a relocation of the reality of grace within the Trinitarian plenitude of God's being. For "the God of grace *is* a God of grace in the fullness of his being as Creator, Redeemer, and Sanctifier." Such a relocation does not entail a reduction in the scope or significance of the act of God in Christ. But the gospel of Christ is the "focal point" of the total mercy of God, while the "focal region of God's grace is not less than the whole creation." [23] If it is the case that the conventional theologies have unduly narrowed the scope of grace by relating it almost exclusively to man as sinner, then it is well to be reminded of Paul's affirmation that God was in Christ reconciling "all things" to himself. Under this rubric, the doctrine of grace is capable of indefinite expansion without losing its existential focus in the life, death, and resurrection of Jesus Christ.

But if our understanding of the scope of grace is to be in any way appropriate to the magnitude of God's reconciling mission to all of creation, we must take seriously the lessons to be learned from a consideration of the role of paradox in Christian experience and thought. The presence of paradox and other dramatic and pictorial expressions in Scripture and theology implies that the subject matter of our testimony overflows the forms of our understanding. Thus theology can never be kept within the tight confines of a deductive system. Since theology must use language, it is limited to the meaning which language is able to convey. It is further limited by the changing nature of language. Even though the truths conveyed are of unchanging nature, the theological formulations of one generation cannot serve following generations unless they are modified to take account of new circumstances, expanding knowledge, and fresh questions. We must recognize the partial character and the broad contextual setting of all our Christian assertions. At the same time, we must honor the necessity of grounding these assertions in Scripture, tradition, and sound learning.

We have seen that a paradox contains opposite stresses which are integrally related by virtue of the fact that both refer to a common object. Thus it is the characteristic function of theological language—paradox, analogy, metaphor—to seek to clarify mystery by pointing to unity in diversity. The paradoxical element in experience and interpretation generates a theological rhythm of differentiation and reconciliation. But just as grace is more primordial than sin, and reconciliation more ultimate than estrangement, so the apprehension of unity supersedes and controls the awareness of diversity. The living experience of the grace of God in Christ is fundamental. What we say about that experience is essential, indispensable, and of endless fascination. Yet it is subordinate and reformable. That is why, as Ian Ramsey often said, we can be sure about God, but we must be tentative in theology.[24] If we could not be tentative and exploratory in theology, it would not be possible to enlarge our understanding of grace beyond the deliverances of the past. It is in the ongoing discussion between opposing points of view that we learn the delight of theological discovery. And it is our conviction of the harmony of opposites within the ultimate unity of grace that gives us the assurance that as members of the one Body of Christ we are exploring together "the many-colored wisdom of God" (Ephesians 3:10). The truth of faith moves back and forth between the poles of the mystery of God and the reality of God and we bear witness as best we can to the grace we have received.

Epilog:

Grace and Gratitude

It need hardly be said that grace and gratitude are intimately associated in experience and theology. The Greek word *charis* and the Latin word *gratia* express both "grace" and "thanks" and in so doing point to the inseparable connection between the spring of God's action towards us and the spring of our response to him. We recall that the total behavior of Jesus was shaped by thanksgiving and that Paul finds cause for gratitude in everything that happens. Moreover, the early Christians called the central act of their worship the Eucharist, a word closely related to *charis*. The Eucharist was for them a service of thanksgiving, a grateful celebration of grace.

John Baillie declares that "gratitude is not only the dominant note in Christian piety but equally the dominant motive of Christian action in the world. . . . A true Christian is a man who never for a moment forgets what God has done for him in Christ, and whose whole comportment and whole activity have their root in the sentiment of gratitude."[1] These words are surely true of Paul who was overwhelmed by the thought that the God who had made the world had come to men as a child, had suffered and died for our sins, had risen again and was forever active in the lives of humble believers. When Paul spelled this out in a theology of grace, he made gratitude the basic motive of the moral life. This is especially clear in Romans 12:1-2, where he makes the transition to the ethical section of the epistle on the grounds of gratitude, looking back to his theological exposition of justification or reconciliation by grace: "I appeal to you, therefore, brethren, by the mercies of God, to present your bodies as a living sacrifice." He admonished the Thessalonians: "Give thanks in all circumstances; for this is the will of God in Christ Jesus for you" (1 Thessalonians 5:18). The whole of Christian existence ought to be a eucharistic action, a life of thanksgiving lived in a community of grace. The practice of saying "grace" at the table when we thank God for our food should be understood as a representative act, that is, a symbolic expression within a small span of space and time of the gratitude we owe God in all times and places for all his gifts.

The topic of gratitude has never received the attention it deserves in theology and ethics, despite its close correlation with grace. Perhaps it has seemed too obvious, or too subjective. When a woman, who was said to have been living an immoral life in the town, entered the house of Simon the Pharisee to show her gratitude to Jesus by anointing him with perfume, he said of her: "Her sins, which are many, are forgiven, for she loved much" (Luke 7:47). Jesus told Simon that great love can be the product of great forgiveness. Her love was not the ground of a forgiveness she had come to seek, but a magnificent gesture of gratitude for a pardon already received. Soren Kierkegaard summed it up: "The profound humiliation of man, the boundless love of God, endless striving born of gratitude."

Notes

Introduction

1. *God and Men* (New York: Abingdon-Cokesbury Press, 1947), pp. 23-24.
2. "Theology as Risk," *The Christian Century,* June 2, 1965, p. 707.
3. *Systematic Theology: A Historicist Perspective* (New York: Charles Scribner's Sons, 1968), p. 58.

1. Thinking about God: Experience and Theology

1. *Creeds in the Making* (London: SCM Press, 1935), pp. 14, 16.
2. G. W. H. Lampe, *I Believe* (London: Skeffington, 1960), p. 13.
3. John Macquarrie, "Foreword," in Peter Fransen, S. J., *The New Life of Grace* (London: Geoffrey Chapman, 1971), p. ix.
4. See Fransen, pp. 169, 171, 173.
5. See Alan Richardson, *Christian Apologetics* (New York: Harper and Brothers, 1947), pp. 123-127.
6. *Do You Believe in God?* (New York: Paulist Press, 1969), p. 86.
7. *Ibid.,* pp. 11, 105.
8. "Grace," *Encyclopedia of Religion and Ethics,* ed. by J. Hastings (New York: Charles Scribner's Sons, 1961), Vol. 6, p. 364.
9. H. D. Gray, *The Christian Doctrine of Grace* (London: Independent Press Ltd., 1949), pp. 9-21.
10. *The Doctrine of Grace in the Apostolic Fathers* (Edinburgh: Oliver and Boyd, 1948), pp. 1, 2, 5.
11. Albert Outler, *Who Trusts in God* (New York: Oxford University Press, 1968), p. 57.
12. D. M. Baillie, *Faith in God and Its Christian Consummation* (London: Faber and Faber, 1927), p. 52.
13. Outler, pp. 58-59.

273

14. *The Attributes of God*, p. 164; as quoted by John Baillie, *The Sense of the Presence of God* (New York: Charles Scribner's Sons, 1962), p. 232.
15. *Principles of Christian Theology* (New York: Charles Scribner's Sons, 1966), pp. 70-71.
16. *Maker of Heaven and Earth* (New York: Doubleday & Company, 1959), p. 35.
17. *Religion in Contemporary Debate* (London: SCM Press Ltd., 1966), p. 16.
18. *Essays Philosophical and Theological* (London: SCM Press Ltd., 1955), p. 98.
19. *Faith and Doctrine* (New York: Paulist Press, 1969), pp. 15-16.
20. Large Catechism, in Theodore G. Tappert, editor and translator, *The Book of Concord* (Philadelphia: Muhlenberg Press, 1959), p. 365.
21. *The Reality of God* (New York: Harper and Row, 1963), pp. 33-34.
22. *Ibid.*, pp. 37-38.
23. Gilkey, p. 29.
24. Wolfhart Pannenberg, *The Apostles' Creed* (Philadelphia: The Westminster Press, 1972), pp. 3, 6.
25. *The Responsible Self* (New York: Harper and Row, 1963), pp. 118-119.
26. John E. Smith, *Experience and God* (New York: Oxford University Press, 1968), p. 13.
27. John Shea, "Human Experience and Religious Symbolization," *The Ecumenist*, May-June, 1971, p. 50.
28. Perry D. LeFevre, "Experience as a Datum for Theology," *The Chicago Theological Seminary Register*, February, 1973, p. 36.
29. *Ibid.*, p. 38.
30. "On the Meaning of 'God,'" in *New Theology No. 4*, ed. Martin E. Marty and Dean G. Peerman (New York: The Macmillan Company, 1967), p. 74.
31. E. Ashby Johnson, *The Crucial Task of Theology* (Richmond: John Knox Press, 1958), p. 174.
32. *The Truth of the Gospel* (London: Oxford University Press, 1950), p. 88.
33. *The Opaqueness of God* (Philadelphia: The Westminster Press, 1970), pp. 149-150.
34. *Essays on Nature and Grace* (Philadelphia: Fortress Press, 1972), pp. 2, 101.
35. "Christianity and the Supernatural," in *New Theology No. 1*, ed. Martin E. Marty and Dean G. Peerman (New York: The Macmillan Company, 1964), pp. 237-238.
36. Outler, p. 39.
37. Ian T. Ramsey, *Christian Discourse* (London: Oxford University Press, 1965), p. 88.
38. *How the Church Can Minister to the World Without Losing Itself* (New York: Harper and Row, 1964), p. 101.
39. Outler, p. 118.
40. Sittler, p. 96.
41. John Baillie, *Our Knowledge of God* (New York: Charles Scribner's Sons, 1939), p. 62.
42. Outler, p. 28.
43. *No Faith of My Own* (London: Longmans, Green and Co., 1950), pp. 26-29.

2. Grace in the Christian Tradition

1. "Grace," by F. Baudraz, *Vocabulary of the Bible*, ed. by J.-J. von Allmen (London: Lutterworth Press, 1958), pp. 157-158.
2. Alan Richardson, *An Introduction to the Theology of the New Testament* (London: SCM Press, 1958), p. 282.
3. Torrance, *The Doctrine of Grace in the Apostolic Fathers*, p. 21.
4. "Grace," by C. L. Mitton, *Interpreter's Dictionary of the Bible*, Vol. II, p. 464.
5. *Ibid.*, p. 464.
6. James Moffat, *Grace in the New Testament* (New York: Harper and Brothers, 1932), p. 280.
7. *Ibid.*, pp. 280-281.

8. *Ibid.*, p. 197.
9. Sittler, *Essays on Nature and Grace*, p. 35.
10. A. W. Argyle, *God in the New Testament* (London: Hodder and Stoughton. 1965), p. 87.
11. Torrance, p. 141.
12. John Burnaby, *Christian Words and Christian Meanings* (London: Hodder and Stoughton, 1955), p. 130.
13. *Ibid.*, p. 130.
14. J. F. Bethune-Baker, *An Introduction to the Early History of Christian Doctrine* (London: Methuen and Co., 1903), p. 308.
15. Philip S. Watson, *The Concept of Grace* (London: The Epworth Press, 1959), p. 80.
16. *Ibid.*, p. 85.
17. K. E. Skydsgaard, *One in Christ*, trans. Axel C. Kildegard (Philadelphia: Muhlenberg Press, 1957), pp. 135-137.
18. Fransen, pp. 27, 33, 42, 46, 52, 56, 113; Jean Daujat, *The Theology of Grace* (London: Burns and Oates, 1959), pp. 51, 54-57.
19. Mackintosh, "Grace," in *Encyclopedia of Religion and Ethics*, Vol. 6, p. 367.
20. Oscar Hardman, *The Christian Doctrine of Grace* (New York: The Macmillan Company, 1947), p. 37.
21. Robert M. Brown, *The Spirit of Protestantism* (New York: Oxford University Press, 1961), p. 55.
22. Burnaby, p. 123.
23. *Ibid.*, p. 132.
24. Watson, p. 13.
25. *Ibid.*, p. 13.
26. Hardman, p. 86.
27. Lampe, *I Believe*, pp. 46-47.
28. Gustaf Aulen, *The Faith of the Christian Church*, tr. Eric H. Wahlstrom (Philadelphia: The Muhlenberg Press, 1960), p. 112.
29. F. A. Cockin, *Does Christianity Make Sense?* (London: SCM Press, 1948), p. 71.

3. Grace and Creation

1. Langdon Gilkey, *Maker of Heaven and Earth: A Study of the Christian Doctrine of Creation* (New York: Doubleday and Company, Inc., 1959); Eric C. Rust, *Science and Faith: Towards a Theological Understanding of Nature* (New York: Oxford University Press, 1967); Richard H. Overman, *Evolution and the Christian Doctrine of Creation* (Philadelphia: The Westminster Press, 1967); Ian G. Barbour, *Issues in Science and Religion* (Englewood Cliffs: Prentice-Hall, Inc., 1966); Donald Evans, *The Logic of Self-Involvement* (London: SCM Press Ltd., 1963); Evode Beaucamp, O.F.M., *The Bible and the Universe* (London: Burns and Oates, 1963); John B. Cobb, Jr., *God and the World* (Philadelphia: The Westminster Press, 1969); Peter Schoonenberg, S. J., *God's World in the Making* (Dublin: Gill and Son, 1965).
2. Gordon D. Kaufman, *Systematic Theology: A Historicist Perspective* (New York: Charles Scribner's Sons, 1968); John Macquarrie, *Principles of Christian Theology* (New York: Charles Scribner's Sons, 1966).
3. H. H. Farmer, *The World and God* (London: Nisbet and Co., Ltd., 1935); William Temple, *Nature, Man and God* (London: Macmillan and Co., Ltd., 1949).
4. Gilkey, pp. 18, 33-34.
5. Ian G. Barbour, *Christianity and the Scientist* (New York: Association Press, 1960), p. 69.
6. Gilkey, p. 30.

276 *Notes*

7. *Ibid.,* pp. 85-86.
8. Arthur Michael Ramsey, *Sacred and Secular* (London: Longmans, 1965), p. 28.
9. John Macquarrie, "How Is Theology Possible?," in *New Theology No. 1,* ed. by Martin E. Marty and Dean G. Peerman (New York: The Macmillan Company, 1964), p. 27.
10. Gilkey, p. 210.
11. *Ibid.,* pp. 211-212.
12. *Ibid.,* pp. 15-16, 79.
13. Otto Weber, *Ground Plan of the Bible,* tr. Harold Knight (Philadelphia: The Westminster Press, 1959), p. 33.
14. C. A. Coulson, *Science and Christian Belief* (London: Fontana Books, 1958). pp. 32, 41.
15. G. W. H. Lampe, *I Believe* (London: Skeffington, 1960), p. 73.
16. Lampe, p. 59.
17. *Ibid.,* pp. 60-61.
18. John Burnaby, *The Belief of Christendom* (London: SPCK, 1960), p. 36.
19. H. H. Farmer, *God and Men* (New York: Abingdon-Cokesbury Press, 1947), p. 127.
20. Gilkey, pp. 95, 105.
21. Burnaby, p. 37.
22. Rust, p. 305.
23. *Ibid.,* p. 302.
24. Gilkey, p. 57.
25. *Ibid.,* p. 63.
26. Burnaby, p. 40.
27. Farmer, *The World and God* pp. 73-74.
28. W. Macneile Dixon, *The Human Situation* (London: Edward Arnold and Co., 1937), p. 430.
29. Roland H. Bainton, *Here I Stand* (New York: Abingdon-Cokesbury Press, 1950), pp. 216-217.
30. Farmer, *The World and God,* pp. 278-283.
31. James S. Stewart, *The Life and Teaching of Jesus Christ* (New York: Abingdon Press, no date), p. 93.
32. J. S. Whale, *Christian Doctrine* (New York: The Macmillan Company, 1946), p. 50.
33. F. A. Cockin, *God in Action* (Harmondsworth: Penguin Books Ltd., 1961), p. 101.
34. Hendrikus Berkhof, *The Doctrine of the Holy Spirit* (Richmond: The John Knox Press, 1964), p. 10.
35. Cockin, p. 97.
36. Berkhof, p. 11.
37. Wolfhart Pannenberg, *The Apostles' Creed,* tr. Margaret Kohl (Philadelphia: The Westminster Press, 1972), pp. 130, 133.
38. Berkhof, p. 111.
39. Alan Richardson, *The Gospel and Modern Thought* (London: Oxford University Press, 1950), p. 140.
40. *Ibid.,* p. 141.
41. Berkhof, p. 33.
42. R. C. Johnson, *The Meaning of Christ* (Philadelphia: The Westminster Press, 1957), p. 14.
43. Cockin, p. 95.
44. J. N. D. Kelly, *Early Christian Creeds* (London: Longmans, 1950), p. 267.
45. Cockin, pp. 96-97.
46. Claude Welch, *In This Name: The Doctrine of the Trinity in Contemporary Theology* (New York; Charles Scribner's Sons, 1952), pp. 64-5, 299.

47. George S. Hendry, *The Holy Spirit in Christian Theology* (Philadelphia: The Westminster Press, 1956), p. 36.
48. *Ibid.*, p. 41.
49. Berkhof, p. 23.
50. *Ibid.*, p. 23.
51. *Ibid.*, pp. 17-18.
52. *Ibid.*, pp. 18-19.
53. *Ibid.*, p. 14.
54. *Ibid.*, p. 69.
55. John Macquarrie, *Principles of Christian Theology* (New York: Charles Scribner's Sons, 1966), p. 204.
56. Berkhof, pp. 19, 30, 35, 63.
57. John Macquarrie, *Three Issues in Ethics* (New York: Harper and Row, 1970), pp. 125, 136.
58. Berkhof, pp. 115-116.
59. Burnaby, p. 138.
60. Berkhof, p. 65.
61. *Ibid.*, p. 94.
62. *Ibid.*, pp. 30, 38-39.
63. *Ibid.*, pp. 49-50.
64. Pannenberg, pp. 133-134.
65. Lampe, p. 101.

4. Grace, Personality, and Social Process

1. Augustine, *The City of God, tr.* Marcus Dods (New York: The Modern Library, 1950), pp. 846-847.
2. John Baillie, *Invitation to Pilgrimage* (New York: Charles Scribner's Sons, 1945), pp. 115-116.
3. Robert L. Calhoun, *What Is Man?* (New York: Association Press, 1939), p. 58.
4. Langdon Gilkey, *Maker of Heaven and Earth* (New York: Doubleday and Company, Inc., 1959), p. 233.
5. Richard Dickinson, *Line and Plummet* (Geneva: The World Council of Churches, 1968), pp. 38-39.
6. R. Newton Flew and Rupert E. Davies, editors, *The Catholicity of Protestantism* (London: Lutterworth Press, 1950), pp. 45-46.
7. Albert C. Outler, *Psychotherapy and the Christian Message* (New York: Harper and Brothers, 1954), p. 175.
8. *Ibid.*, p. 102.
9. *Ibid.*, p. 179.
10. Gilkey, p. 168.
11. William F. Lynch, S. J., *Images of Hope* (New York: The New American Library, Inc. 1965), pp. 196-197.
12. Herbert H. Farmer, *Towards Belief in God* (New York: The Macmillan Co., 1943), pp. 67-68.
13. *Ibid.*, pp. 68-69.
14. Blaise Pascal, *Penseés,* trans. W. F. Trotter (London: J. M. Dent and Sons, Ltd., 1931), p. 121.
15. Edward Young, From "Night Thoughts," *Masterpieces of Religious Verse,* ed. by James Dalton Morrison (New York: Harper and Brothers, 1948), p. 273.
16. Daniel Day Williams, *God's Grace and Man's Hope* (New York: Harper and Brothers, 1949), p. 81.

17. Outler, p. 147.
18. Gilkey, pp. 55-56.
19. David E. Roberts, *Psychotherapy and a Christian View of Man* (New York: Charles Scribner's Sons, 1950), p. 93.
20. Lynch, pp. 177-180.
21. Daniel Day Williams, *The Spirit and the Forms of Love* (New York: Harper and Row, Publishers, 1968), pp. 205-206.
22. Roberts, p. 93.
23. *Ibid.,* p. 133.
24. *Ibid.,* p. 93.
25. *Ibid.,* p. 116.
26. Thomas C. Oden, *The Structure of Awareness* (Nashville: Abingdon Press, 1969), p. 81.
27. Lynch, p. 31.
28. Roberts, p. 135.
29. *Ibid.,* p. 93.
30. John Macquarrie, *Three Issues in Ethics* (New York: Harper and Row, Publishers, 1970), p. 126.
31. Outler, p. 260.
32. Macquarrie, p. 122.
33. Roberts, p. 91.
34. Gilkey, p. 226.
35. *Ibid.,* p. 228.
36. Alexander Miller, *The Man in the Mirror* (New York: Doubleday and Company, 1958), pp. 37-38.
37. Williams, *God's Grace and Man's Hope,* p. 78.
38. Claude Welch, *The Reality of the Church* (New York: Charles Scribner's Sons, 1958), p. 50.
39. *Ibid.,* p. 53.
40. Edgar M. Carlson, *The Reinterpretation of Luther* (Philadelphia: The Westminster Press, 1948), pp. 207-208.
41. Emil Brunner, *The Divine Imperative,* trans. by Olive Wyon (New York: The Macmillan Company, 1942), pp. 333-337.
42. G. W. H. Lampe, *I Believe* (London: Skeffington, 1960), pp. 95-98.
43. Alexander Miller, *The Renewal of Man* (New York: Doubleday and Company, 1955), p. 106.
44. John Calvin, *Institutes of the Christian Religion,* Book II, Chap. II, Par. XIII.
45. John C. Bennett, *When Christians Make Political Decisions* (New York: Association Press, 1964), p. 52.
46. Reinhold Niebuhr, *Man's Nature and His Communities* (New York: Charles Scribner's Sons, 1965), p. 125.
47. Carlson, p. 210.
48. Philip S. Watson, *Let God Be God!* (London: The Epworth Press, 1947), pp. 105-6.
49. Carlson, p. 211.
50. Myron B. Bloy, Jr., *The Crisis of Cultural Change* (New York: The Seabury Press, 1965), p. 36.
51. *Ibid.,* p. 39.
52. Gustaf Aulen, *Church, Law and Society* (New York: Charles Scribner's Sons, 1948), pp. 62-63, 72.
53. Hendrikus Berkhof, *The Doctrine of the Holy Spirit* (Richmond: John Knox Press, 1964), p. 51.
54. Roger Shinn, *Tangled World* (New York: Charles Scribner's Sons, 1965), p. 53.

55. Williams, *God's Grace and Man's Hope*, p. 97.
56. Calhoun, p. 12.
57. Shinn, p. 55.
58. John Macquarrie, *God and Secularity* (Philadelphia: The Westminster Press, 1967), p. 135.
59. Colin W. Williams, *The Church* (Philadelphia: The Westminster Press, 1968), p. 29.
60. Quoted in John C. Bennett, *Christians and the State* (New York: Charles Scribner's Sons, 1958), p. 106.
61. Benjamin H. Cardozo, *The Nature of the Judicial Process* (New Haven: Yale University Press, 1921), p. 72.
62. Shinn, pp. 96-97.
63. Bennett, *Christians and the State*, p. 107.
64. *Ibid.*, p. 106.
65. Williams, *God's Grace and Man's Hope*, p. 99.
66. Bennett, *Christians and the State*, p. 35.
67. George F. Thomas, *Christian Ethics and Moral Philosophy* (New York: Charles Scribner's Sons, 1955), p. 265.
68. Bennett, *Christians and the State*, pp. 50, 62.
69. Miller, *The Renewal of Man*, p. 112.
70. Williams, *God's Grace and Man's Hope*, p. 23.
71. Charles W. Forman, *A Faith for the Nations* (Philadelphia: The Westminster Press, 1957), p. 48.
72. Cited in Harold J. Berman, *The Interaction of Law and Religion* (Nashville: Abingdon Press, 1974), p. 155.
73. *Ibid.*, pp. 53-54.
74. H. G. Wood, *Christianity and Civilization* (New York: The Macmillan Company, 1943), p. 13.
75. Berman, pp. 55-61.
76. Berkhof, pp. 101-2.
77. Ronald Gregor Smith, *The New Man* (New York: Harper and Brothers, 1956), p. 38.
78. *Ibid.*, p. 39.
79. *Ibid.*, pp. 40-41.
80. *Ibid.*, pp. 38-39, 41.
81. Charles Davis, *God's Grace in History* (London: Collins, 1966), pp. 60-61.
82. Charles C. West, "Community—Christian and Secular," *Man in Community*, ed. Egbert de Vries (New York: Association Press, 1966), pp. 335, 349-351; Harvey Cox, "The Responsibility of the Christian in the World of Technology," *Economic Growth in World Perspective*, ed. Denys Munby (New York: Association Press, 1966), pp. 174-178.
83. Berkhof, p. 102.
84. Davis, p. 28.
85. *Ibid.*, pp. 29-30.
86. *Ibid.*, pp. 30-31.
87. *Ibid.*, p. 32.
88. *Ibid.*, p. 77.
89. Berkhof, p. 102.
90. Regin Prenter, "Jesus Christ—The Hope of the World," *The Lutheran World*, Spring, 1954, p. 38.
91. Miller, *The Renewal of Man*. pp. 116-117.
92. *Ibid.*, p. 117.
93. _____, *Church and State* (New York: Board of Social Ministry, Lutheran Church in America, 1963), p. 36.

94. Williams, *The Church*, p. 21.
95. *Ibid.*, p. 174.
96. James Sellers, *Theological Ethics* (New York: The Macmillan Company, 1966), p. 95.
97. *Ibid.*
98. Per Lönning, "The Theological Basis of the Geneva Conference," *Christian Century*, March 1, 1967, p. 271.
99. Sellers, pp. 95, 96, 99.
100. Ian Barbour, *Science and Secularity* (New York: Harper and Row, Publishers, 1970), p. 73.
101. Paul L. Lehmann, *Ethics in a Christian Context* (New York: Harper and Row, Publishers, 1963), p. 124.
102. *Ibid.*, p. 101.
103. Richard Shaull, "Revolutionary Change in Theological Perspective," in *Christian Social Ethics in a Changing World*, ed. John C. Bennett (New York: Association Press, 1966), p. 32.
104. *Ibid.*, p. 41.
105. *Ibid.*, p. 35.
106. Barbour, p. 140.
107. Berkhof, p. 103.
108. F. A. Cockin, *God in Action* (Hammondsworth: Penguin Books, 1961), p. 121.
109. J. H. Oldham, *Life Is Commitment* (New York: Association Press, 1959), pp. 114-115.
110. John Macquarrie, *Three Issues in Ethics*, p. 137.

5. The Emergence of the Reconciliation Image in the Nineteenth Century

1. The United Presbyterian Church in the United States of America, "Report of the Special Committee on a Brief Contemporary Statement of Faith," (Philadelphia, Office of the General Assembly, 1965), p. 32.
2. Paul C. Empie and James I. McCord, editors, *Marburg Revisited* (Minneapolis, Augsburg Publishing House, 1966), p. 37.
3. Paul Tillich, *A History of Christian Thought*, ed. Carl E. Braaten (New York: Simon and Schuster, 1967), p. 157.
4. *Ibid.*, p. 136.
5. David W. Lotz, *Ritschl and Luther* (Nashville: Abingdon Press, 1974), p. 35.
6. *Ibid.*, pp. 61-62.
7. John Calvin, *Institutes of the Christian Religion*, ed. John T. McNeill, trans. Ford Lewis Battles (Philadelphia: The Westminster Press, 1960), pp. 503-507.
8. John Leith, editor, *Creeds of the Churches* (Richmond: John Knox Press, 1973), pp. 411-412.
9. Albrecht Ritschl, *A Critical History of the Christian Doctrine of Justification and Reconciliation*, Vol. I, trans. John S. Black (Edinburgh: Edmonston and Douglas, 1872), p. 10.
10. Lotz, p. 31.
11. *Ibid.*, p. 78.
12. Justo L. Gonzalez, *A History of Christian Thought*, Vol. III, (Nashville: Abingdon Press, 1975), pp. 317-318.
13. Quoted in Lotz, p. 30.
14. Albrecht Ritschl, *The Christian Doctrine of Justification and Reconciliation*, Vol. III, English tr., H. R. Mackintosh and A. B. Macauley, editors (Clifton: Reference Book Publishers, Inc., 1966), pp. 141, 113.
15. *Ibid.*, p. 85.

16. *Ibid.*, p. 357.
17. *Ibid.*, p. 78.
18. Lotz, p. 180.
19. *Ibid.*, pp. 162-169.
20. Tillich, p. 411.
21. Alec R. Vidler, *The Church in an Age of Revolution* (Baltimore: Penguin Books, 1961), p. 30.
22. Tillich, p. 420.
23. Robert C. Tucker, *Philosophy and Myth in Karl Marx* (Cambridge: Cambridge University Press, 1969), p. 46.
24. *Ibid.*, p. 49.
25. *Ibid.*, p. 34.
26. *Ibid.*, p. 51.
27. Lotz, p. 177.
28. Tillich, p. 460.
29. Tucker, p. 238.
30. Kenneth Scott Latourette, *Christianity Through the Ages* (New York: Harper and Row, 1965), p. 237.
31. Alexander Miller, "Towards a Doctrine of Vocation," *Christian Faith and Social Action*, ed. John A. Hutchison (New York: Charles Scribner's Sons, 1953), pp. 128-129.
32. Tillich, p. 504.
33. Lotz, pp. 30-31.
34 J K Mozley, *The Doctrine of the Atonement* (London: Duckworth, 1915), p. 133.
35. L. W. Grensted, *A Short History of the Doctrine of the Atonement* (Manchester: The University Press, 1920), p. 328.
36. *Ibid.*, p. 371.

6. Reconciliation in Twentieth Century Theology

1. James Denney, *The Death of Christ* (Cincinnati: Jennings and Pye, 1902) pp. 176-179.
2. James Denney, *The Atonement and the Modern Mind* (New York: A. C. Armstrong and Son, 1903), pp. 119-120.
3. *Ibid.*, pp. 70-71.
4. James Denney, *The Christian Doctrine of Reconciliation* (New York: George H. Doran, 1918), pp. 287, 291.
5. *Ibid.*, p. 6-7.
6. P. T. Forsyth, *Positive Preaching and the Modern Mind* (London: Independent Press, 1949), pp. 144-145. (First published in 1907).
7. P. T. Forsyth, *The Church and the Sacraments* (London: Independent Press, 1947), p. 142. (First published in 1917).
8. J. K. Mozley, *The Doctrine of the Atonement* (London: Duckworth, 1915), pp. 183-184; Robert M. Brown, *P. T. Forsyth: Prophet for Today* (Philadelphia: The Westminster Press, 1952), p. 79.
9. P. T. Forsyth, *The Work of Christ* (London: Independent Press, 1948), pp. 44, 53, 57. (First published in 1910).
10. John Oman, *Grace and Personality* (London: Collins, 1960), p. 128. (First published in 1917).
11. *Ibid.*, p. 112.
12. *Ibid.*, p. 187.
13. *Ibid.*, p. 141.
14. *Ibid.*, p. 110.
15. *Ibid.*, p. 103.

16. *Ibid.,* p. 107.
17. *Ibid.,* p. 111.
18. Donald M. Baillie, *God Was in Christ* (New York: Charles Scribner's Sons, 1948), pp. 197-198.
19. *Ibid.,* pp. 200-201.
20. Karl Barth, *Church Dogmatics,* IV, 1. tr. G. W. Bromiley (New York: Charles Scribner's Sons, 1956), p. 79.
21. *Ibid.,* pp. 22, 89.
22. Emil Brunner, *The Christian Doctrine of Creation and Redemption,* tr. Olive Wyon (Philadelphia: The Westminster Press, 1952), p. 290.
23. *Ibid.,* p. 291.
24. *Ibid.,* p. v.
25. *Ibid.,* p. vi.
26. *Ibid.,* p. 290.
27. *Ibid.,* p. 296; see also, Emil Brunner, *The Mediator,* tr. Olive Wyon (Philadelphia: The Westminster Press, 1947), pp. 519, 522, 524, 527.
28. Rudolf Bultmann, *Theology of the New Testament,* Volume I, tr. Kendrick Grobel (New York: Charles Scribner's Sons, 1951), p. 227.
29. *Ibid.,* p. 232.
30. *Ibid.,* p. 245.
31. *Ibid.,* p. 253.
32. Rudolf Bultmann, *Primitive Christianity,* tr. R. H. Fuller (New York: Meridian Books, 1956), p. 165.
33. Bultmann, *Theology of the New Testament,* Volume I, p. 270.
34. *Ibid.,* pp. 285-286.
35. *Ibid.,* p. 287.
36. Paul Tillich, *Systematic Theology,* Volume I (Chicago: The University of Chicago Press, 1951), p. 285.
37. Paul Tillich, *The Protestant Era,* tr. James Luther Adams (Chicago: The University of Chicago Press, 1948), p. 209.
38. Tillich, *Systematic Theology,* Volume I, p. 204.
39. *Ibid.,* p. 49.
40. Tillich, *Systematic Theology,* Volume II, p. 125.
41. *Ibid.,* p. 57.
42. *Ibid.,* p. 166.
43. *Ibid.,* p. 49.
44. *Ibid.,* p. 79.
45. *Ibid.,* p. 170.
46. Paul Tillich, *The Shaking of the Foundations* (New York: Charles Scribner's Sons, 1952), pp. 161-162.
47. Gustaf Aulen, *The Faith of the Christian Church,* tr. from fifth Swedish edition by Eric H. Wahlstrom (Philadelphia: The Muhlenberg Press, 1960), p. 140.
48. *Ibid.,* p. 197.
49. *Ibid.,* p. 198.
50. *Ibid.,* pp. 201, 202, 204.
51. *Ibid.,* p. 213.
52. John Macquarrie, *Principles of Christian Theology* (New York: Charles Scribner's Sons, 1966), p. 235.
53. *Ibid.,* pp. 246-247.
54. *Ibid.,* p. 283.
55. *Ibid.,* p. 292.
56. *Ibid.,* p. 293.

57. Gordon D. Kaufman, *Systematic Theology: A Historicist Perspective* (New York: Charles Scribner's Sons, 1968), p. 379.
58. *Ibid.*, p. 389.
59. *Ibid.*, p. 409.
60. *Ibid.*, p. 410.
61. Daniel Day Williams, *The Spirit and the Forms of Love* (New York: Harper and Row, 1968), p. vii.
62. *Ibid.*, pp. 2, 5.
63. *Ibid.*, p. 155.
64. *Ibid.*, p. 175.
65. *Ibid.*, pp. 176-177.
66. The United Presbyterian Church in the United States of America, *op. cit.*, pp. 27-28.
67. *Ibid.*, p. 28.
68. Edward A. Dowey, Jr., *A Commentary on the Confession of 1967 and an Introduction to the Book of Confessions* (Philadelphia: The Westminster Press, 1968), p. 14.

7. Paul's Theology of Reconciliation: Its Roots in the First Century

1. F. W. Dillistone, *The Christian Faith* (London: Hodder and Stoughton, 1964), p. 147.
2. "Reconcile," by F. J. Taylor, *A Theological Word Book of the Bible,* ed. by Alan Richardson (New York: The Macmillan Company, 1951), p. 185; "Reconciliation," by M. Bouttier, *Vocabulary of the Bible,* ed. by J. - J. von Allmen (London: Lutterworth Press, 1958), p. 351.
3. Anders Nygren, *Commentary on Romans,* tr. Carl C. Rasmussen (Philadelphia: Muhlenberg Press, 1949), pp. 196-197.
4. C. K. Barrett, *A Commentary on the Epistle to the Romans* (London: Adam and Charles Black, 1957), p. 108.
5. Rudolf Bultmann, *Theology of the New Testament,* Volume I, pp. 285-286.
6. Victor Paul Furnish, *Theology and Ethics in Paul* (Nashville: Abingdon Press, 1968), p. 149.
7. Barrett, pp. 107-108.
8. *Ibid.*, p. 108
9. F. W. Dillistone, *The Significance of the Cross* (Philadelphia: The Westminster Press, 1944), p. 114.
10. *Ibid.*
11. Furnish, pp. 146-152.
12. Amos N. Wilder, "Reconciliation—New Testament Scholarship and Confessional Differences: Part Two," *Interpretation,* July, 1965, pp. 312-313.
13. *Ibid.*, p. 315.
14. *Ibid.*, p. 314.
15. Wolfhart Pannenberg, *The Apostles' Creed* (Philadelphia: The Westminster Press, 1972), p. 160.
16. Dillistone, *The Significance of the Cross,* p. 110.
17. *Ibid.*, p. 111.
18. *Ibid.*, pp. 111-112.
19. Daniel Day Williams, *The Spirit and the Forms of Love* (New York: Harper and Row, 1968), p. 177.
20. Hendrikus Berkhof and Philip Potter, *Key Words of the Gospel* (London: SCM Press Ltd., 1964), pp. 40-41.
21. Clinton Morrison, "God's Reconciling Work," *McCormick Quarterly,* January 1966, p. 85.

22. Berkhof and Potter, p. 43.
23. Marcus Aurelius, *Meditations*, tr. Maxwell Staniforth (Harmondsworth: Penguin Books, 1964), p. 51.
24. *Ibid.*, p. 64.
25. *Ibid.*, p. 99.
26. *Ibid.*, p. 187.
27. *Ibid.*, pp. 93, 160.
28. *Ibid.*, p. 105.
29. *Ibid.*, p. 64.
30. Seneca, *Letters from a Stoic*, tr. Robin Campbell (Harmondsworth: Penguin Books, 1969), p. 96.
31. *Ibid.*, pp. 88-89.
32. *Ibid.*, pp. 127-128.
33. *Ibid.*, pp. 104-105.
34. *Ibid.*, p. 103.
35. *Ibid.*, p. 72.
36. Epictetus, *Moral Discourses*, tr. Elizabeth Carter (London: J. M. Dent and Sons Ltd., 1957), pp. 185-186.
37. *Ibid.*, p. 255.
38. *Ibid.*, p. 185.
39. *Ibid.*, p. 157.
40. *Ibid.*, p. 245.
41. *Ibid.*, p. 191.
42. *Ibid.*, p. 209.
43. *Ibid.*, p. 178.
44. *Ibid.*, p. 210.
45. *Ibid.*, p. 261.
46. *Ibid.*, p. 156.
47. E. R. Dodds, *Pagan and Christian in an Age of Anxiety* (Cambridge: The University Press, 1968), p. 137.
48. James S. Stewart, *A Man in Christ* (New York: Harper and Brothers, 1941), p. 64.
49. A. H. Armstrong, *An Introduction to Ancient Philosophy* (London: Methuen and Co., Ltd., 1947), pp. 145-147.
50. T. R. Glover, *The Conflict of Religions in the Early Roman Empire* (London: Methuen and Co., 1909), p. 196.
51. Michael Grant, *The World of Rome* (New York: The World Publishing Company, 1960), p. 155.
52. Gilbert Murray, *Five Stages of Greek Religion* (New York: Doubleday and Company, Inc., 1955), p. 123.
53. *Ibid.*, p. 119.
54. Armstrong, p. 115.
55. Grant, p. 149.
56. Cyprian, cited in Dodds, p. 12.
57. Dodds, p. 13.
58. Pliny the elder, cited in Grant, p. 150.
59. Murray, p. 139.
60. Grant, p. 157.
61. Dowey, cf. Chap. 6 n.68.
62. Rollo May, *Man's Search for Himself* (New York: Dell Publishing Co., 1953), p. 34.
63. Langdon Gilkey, *Naming the Whirlwind: The Renewal of God-Language* (Indianapolis: The Bobbs-Merrill Company, 1969), pp. 402-403.

8. Paul's Theology of Reconciliation: Its Meaning Today

1. C. H. Dodd, *The Epistle of Paul to the Romans* (New York: Harper and Brothers, 1932), pp. 21-22.
2. James S. Stewart, *A Man in Christ* (New York: Harper and Brothers, 1941), p. 219.
3. Gustaf Aulen, *The Faith of the Christian Church*, pp. 117-121, 203-204, 207-208.
4. Alan Richardson, *An Introduction to the Theology of the New Testament* (London: SCM Press, 1958), p. 217.
5. Stewart, p. 216.
6. G. W. H. Lampe, *I Believe* (London: Skeffington, 1960), p. 123.
7. The most sensitive and adequate treatment of the work of Christ known to me is to be found in two books by G. W. H. Lampe, *Reconciliation in Christ* (London: Longmans, Green and Company, 1955) and *I Believe* (London: Skeffington, 1960). Lampe develops the Pauline concept of Christ as the "Second Adam" and in doing so provides an up-dated version of the *recapitulatio* theory of St. Irenaeus.
8. Lampe, *Reconciliation in Christ*, p. 96.
9. Berkhof and Potter, *Key Words of the Gospel*, pp. 38, 43.
10. Alvin C. Porteous, *The Search for Christian Credibility* (Nashville: Abingdon Press, 1971), p. 74.
11. Soren Kierkegaard, *Repetition*, tr. Walter Lowrie (Princeton: Princeton University Press, 1941), p. 114.
12. Julian N. Hartt, *A Christian Critique of American Culture* (New York: Harper and Row, 1967), p. 81.
13. John S. Whale, *Christian Doctrine* (New York: The Macmillan Company, 1946), pp. 124-125.
14. Eugene C. Bianchi, *Reconciliation: The Function of the Church* (New York: Sheed and Ward, 1969), p. 7.
15. Herbert H. Farmer, *Towards Belief in God* (New York: The Macmillan Company, 1943), p. 83.
16. Lampe, *Reconciliation in Christ*, p. 67.
17. William Glasser, *Reality Therapy* (New York: Harper and Row, 1965), p. 7.
18. *Ibid.*, p. 9.
19. James A. Pike, *Doing the Truth* (New York: The Macmillan Company, 1955), p. 155.
20. Berkhof and Potter, p. 44.
21. Dietrich Bonhoeffer, *Prisoner for God: Letters and Papers from Prison*, ed. Eberhard Bethge, tr. Reginald Fuller (New York: The Macmillan Company, 1954), p. 180.
22. Pannenberg, p. 147.
23. Lampe, *I Believe*, pp. 160-161.
24. Berkhof and Potter, p. 45.
25. Bianchi, p. 40.
26. John Macquarrie, *Three Issues in Ethics* (New York: Harper and Row, 1970), p. 136.
27. Farmer, pp. 97-98.
28. Oliver C. Quick, *Doctrines of the Creed* (London: Nisbet and Co. Ltd., 1938), p. 245-246.
29. C. H. Dodd, *The Apostolic Preaching and Its Developments* (London: Hodder and Stoughton, 1936), pp. 80-81, 83-84.
30. Quick, pp. 246-247.
31. Alec R. Vidler, *Christian Belief* (New York: Charles Scribner's Sons, 1950), pp. 107-108.
32. Dante Alighieri, *The Divine Comedy*, tr. Henry Wadsworth Longfellow (Boston: Houghton, Mifflin and Company, 1895), p. 502.
33. Herbert H. Farmer, *Revelation and Religion* (London: Nisbet and Co. Ltd., 1954), p. 104.

34. *Ibid.*, p. 233.
35. Stephen Neill, *Christian Faith Today* (Harmondsworth: Penguin Books, 1955), p. 95.

9. Reconciliation as a Theological Approach

1. John Burnaby, *Christian Words and Christian Meanings* (London: Hodder and Stoughton, 1960), p. 155.
2. Joseph Sittler, *Essays on Nature and Grace* (Philadelphia: Fortress Press, 1972), p. 21.
3. J. K. Mozley, *Some Recent Tendencies in British Theology* (London: SPCK, 1951), p. 86.
4. *Ibid.*
5. John Macquarrie, *God and Secularity* (Philadelphia: The Westminster Press, 1967), p. 130.
6. Baillie, pp. 110-112.
7. Langdon Gilkey, *Naming the Whirlwind*, p. 176.
8. Roger Hazelton, "The Nature of Christian Paradox," *Theology Today*, October 1949, p. 325.
9. *Ibid.*, p. 330.
10. Baillie, pp. 109-110.
11. Avery Dulles, "Symbol, Myth, and the Biblical Revelation," in *New Theology* No. 4, ed. Martin E. Marty and Dean G. Peerman (New York: The Macmillan Company, 1967), p. 40.
12. Hazelton, p. 332.
13. *Ibid.*, pp. 332-333.
14. E. Ashby Johnson, *The Crucial Task of Theology* (Richmond: John Knox Press, 1958), p. 188.
15. John Macquarrie, *The Scope of Demythologizing* (London: SCM Press Ltd., 1960), p. 28.
16. Johnson, p. 189.
17. John Oman, *Grace and Personality*, p. 221.
18. *Ibid.*, p. 159.
19. *Ibid.*, pp. 161-162.
20. Baillie, p. 114.
21. *Ibid.*, p. 117.
22. Eugene R. Fairweather, "Christianity and the Supernatural," in *New Theology No. 1*, ed. Martin E. Marty and Dean G. Peerman (New York: The Macmillan Company, 1964), pp. 246-247.
23. Sittler, p. 86.
24. Ian T. Ramsey, *On Being Sure in Religion* (London: The Athlone Press, 1963), pp. 23, 27, 47, 88; *Christian Discourse* (London: Oxford University Press, 1965), p. 89.

10. Epilog: Grace and Gratitude

1. John Baillie, *The Sense of the Presence of God* (New York: Charles Scribner's Sons, 1962), pp. 236-237.

Index of Subjects

Index of Names

Index

of Biblical References